PRAISE FOR JAMES BRADY

Why Marines Fight

"Brady's book succeeds in delivering honest, front-row accounts of war—the gritty details and the hard realities—and provides a veritable smorgasbord of answers to the question of why Marines fight." —*Chattanooga Times Free Press*

"These inspirational tales cover as many Marine experiences as Brady can pack in." —*Kirkus Reviews*

The Scariest Place in the World

"James Brady has done it again. A riveting and illuminating insight into a dark corner of the world." —Tim Russert

"Graceful, even elegant, and always eloquent tribute to men at arms in a war that, in a way, never ended." —*Kirkus Reviews*

The Coldest War

"His story reads like a novel, but it is war reporting at its best—a graphic depiction, in all its horrors, of the war we've almost forgotten." —Walter Cronkite

"A marvelous memoir. A sensitive and superbly written narrative that eventually explodes off the pages like a grenade in the gut . . . taut, tight, and telling." —Dan Rather

The Marine

"In *The Marine*, James Brady again gives us a novel in which history is a leading character, sharing the stage in this case with a man as surely born to be a gallant warrior as any knight in sixth-century Camelot." —Kurt Vonnegut

The Marines of Autumn

"Mr. Brady knows war, the smell and the feel of it." —*The New York Times*

WHY MARINES FIGHT

James Brady

THOMAS DUNNE BOOKS
ST. MARTIN'S GRIFFIN ≋ NEW YORK

THOMAS DUNNE BOOKS.
An imprint of St. Martin's Press.

WHY MARINES FIGHT. Copyright © 2007 by James Brady. All rights reserved. Printed in the United States of America. For information, address St. Martin's Press, 175 Fifth Avenue, New York, N.Y. 10010.

www.thomasdunnebooks.com
www.stmartins.com

Library of Congress Cataloging-in-Publication Data

Brady, James.
    Why Marines fight / James Brady.—1st St. Martin's Griffin ed.
        p. cm.
    ISBN-13: 978-0-312-38484-5
    ISBN-10: 0-312-38484-X
    1. United States. Marine Corps—History. I. Title.

VE23.B63 2007
359.9'60973—dc22

2007031463

First St. Martin's Griffin Edition: November 2008

10 9 8 7 6 5 4 3 2 1

This story is for my daughters, Fiona and Susan, and for my grandchildren, Sarah, Joe, Nick, and Matthew.

But it is dedicated to all the Marines in all the wars.
Those who fought and came home,
and those who fought and didn't.

CONTENTS

PREFACE

THIS IS THE STORY, RAW AND OFTEN ELOQUENT, LARGELY IN THEIR own words, of the United States Marines who fight America's wars, where they came from and who they were, where and how they fought and too often died, what they later became.

It tries to tell why a man runs toward the guns when every rational instinct would send him away, eluding the guns and their lethal fire. And why Marines do these things not only in so-called "good" wars such as World Wars I and II but in lousy wars like Vietnam and second Iraq.

The Marines in this book have all heard those guns, have fought wars, been ordered into combat by a sheaf of papers directing them to "duty beyond the seas," a lovely and unexpected little poetry lurking in an otherwise banal, bureaucratic boilerplate. It is paperwork like this that over the years has sent men routinely to their deaths, in the France of 1918, to Tarawa and Iwo, to Korea, to Vietnam and Iraq.

Beyond the official blather, with its surprising poetry, is the life-and-death reality of battle, a cruel truth of which Marines are ever being reminded in peaceful places, liberty towns like San Francisco. Where in a classy bar atop the Mark Hopkins Hotel from which you can see the Pacific, and at night watch the riding lights of ships heading toward Asia, there is a small bronze plaque, recalling those thousands of Marines who left this glorious city and its port, shipping out to the Fleet Marine Force Pacific, known in Marine jargon as FMF PAC. Reminding us of men bound for islands under the Southern Cross, for the mysterious East, more recently for the Persian Gulf, Afghanistan, and the Horn of Africa, men pledging in boozy solemnity to their women and fellow Marines, to meet again back here at Top of the Mark after the war.

Which is why the simple little plaque pledges that even in the busiest of happy hours, one bar stool will always be set aside and left empty, held for one of us, for a Marine who had not yet returned, nor probably ever would.

It may be unnecessary to remind anyone, but for two centuries American Marines have been among the most admired of warriors. Fighting as cutlass-swinging boarding parties and as snipers in the rigging and mast heads of frigates in the Revolution and the War of 1812, through the Civil War (on that occasion fighting for both sides!), and in two world wars. More recently in northeast and southeast Asia, in today's Middle East and Central Asia. The Corps' famous battles are bone and sinew of American lore, from the Barbary Coast to Montezuma's Halls and the Boxer Rebellion, from the Great War's Château Thierry to the murderous little banana wars of Central America, to World War II's Guadalcanal and the black volcanic sands of Iwo Jima, to Korea's deadly seawall at Inchon and that epic fight in the snow against the Chinese army at the Chosin Reservoir; still later on the Perfume River at Hue and in the steaming jungles and highlands of Vietnam; and now in the Afghan hills, the Khyber Pass, and snowy crags, and in the deserts, lethal roadsides, and sinister back alleyways of Baghdad, the Persian Gulf, and the Horn of Africa.

Marine uniform trousers are decorated with a vertical crimson stripe symbolic of Marine blood shed by officers and NCOs in the

Mexican War. Officers' caps are still marked with an embroidered cross, signaling to Marine snipers high above the hand-to-hand melee of a ship's deck just who was friend and not foe. It was in October 1859 that a detachment of eighty-six Marines, under Colonel Robert E. Lee and Captain Jeb Stuart, stormed the arsenal at Harpers Ferry to capture abolitionist John Brown and his men, ominously foreshadowing by nearly two years the outbreak of Civil War hostilities at Fort Sumter.

But why do Marines do these things? Why do we fight? And just why fight so well? Are we simply mercenaries, fifteenth-century Italian condottieri five hundred years out of sync? At a time when people are fed up with war, you may ask if anyone really cares why soldiers answer the call? It's not as if we were important, the skeptic remarks, not as if we were the serious men who run hedge funds.

I've confronted such questions for a long time, from the first firefight I was ever in, up in the mountains of North Korea in 1951, and been pondering the answers since. A couple of years ago, following a reporting assignment's return to North Korea, out on a promotional book tour about my trip, I was doing the talk shows, visiting Marine bases, delivering lectures, all this as Afghanistan smoldered and Iraq lapsed from quagmire into religious war. I was asked, and I asked myself and other Marines, why we went to war, when so many other Americans, and understandably so, were turning against even the notion of another war, one not begun out of necessity but of choice, almost out of feckless whim.

It was then that I determined to begin work on this book. In its pages, in their own spoken or written words, emotional or chill, inspiring, often brutal, half a hundred fighting Marines talk about their own wars, good and bad. About how they came to be Marines, about their own combat, delineating the small details that flesh out every man's adventure, how each of us felt and fought, and trying to explain why a sane man would risk his life in an unpopular war that sensible people at home had turned against or half-forgotten. What makes a good soldier go in harm's way not in the national interest or for the country's very existence, but for some cobbled-up, second-rate cause?

Maybe, like Tom Wolfe's astronauts, we just had the right stuff. But whence it came, how sustained and directed, those questions hang there. Colonel John W. Thomason Jr. tried following World War I to define the Marines of 1918, of his time, "They were the old breed of American regular, regarding the service as home, and war as an occupation."

The men in this book are in varying degree heroic figures, many of them anonymous grunts, others celebrated, a few household names. But they have this one thing in common: They all fought this country's enemies as United States Marines in American wars. And are uniquely qualified to answer my impertinent question, Why do Marines fight?

I fought in 1951–52 as a Marine officer in Korea. At first as a skinny, baby-faced, and untested replacement rifle platoon leader, later promoted to first lieutenant and rifle company executive officer, then to battalion intelligence officer, serving the entire tour with Marine riflemen, perhaps the greatest infantrymen in the world, some of the finest foot soldiers ever.

Veterans of actual combat, and not just stateside garrison troops, are famously believed reluctant to tell their war stories. I don't believe that. I've interviewed plenty of them, over beers, a cup of coffee, or more formally and have written books about Marines at war. Try to get some of them to shut up. They love to talk. They're proud of what they did, and are fascinated, often honestly baffled, by what they found themselves capable of doing under hostile fire and how professionally they did it, and they are more than willing to tell you about it. In this book I speak with Chinaside Marines serving before World War II, men now in their nineties, and to veterans of today's Iraq and Afghanistan, still in their twenties, asking questions and getting answers in their own voices, unique and powerful, answers that ranged from thrilling to the laconic, "I was a kid. They told me to go and I went. What the hell did I know?"

And although American law prohibits sending women into certain combat roles, the changing nature of insurgency wars, with their roadside bombings, ambushes, their unscripted violence, have inevitably drawn women into the fight. I've sought out and attempted to speak with women Marines about their experiences under fire, their reactions, their unique stories. To date, one woman Marine, a captain of combat engineers, has been willing to go on the record. As did a navy nurse who landed four times at Iwo Jima under fire to bring out wounded Marines.

From the start I purposely took a different tack from the group-journalism methodology that worked so well in Tom Brokaw's superb and bestselling *Greatest Generation.* To be blunt about it, I lacked Tom's resources, no NBC News staffers, producers, researchers, editorial aides, or interns. Instead, as a seasoned writer and working reporter, I sought no editorial or research assistance, used no freelancers, tracked down sources, did my own legwork. I conducted all the interviews, of men I actually knew and of strangers reached through Colonel Walt Ford's *Leatherneck,* the monthly magazine of Marines, the Historical Branch of Marine Headquarters, and via USMC Web sites peppering the Internet. I called on such Marine "alumni" organizations as the Marine Corps Association, the Marine Corps League, the First Marine Division Association, and the Marine Heritage Foundation. Some questions I choked on, found difficult to ask. Almost no one told me such questions were none of my damned business.

I asked about motivations, what drew a man to the Corps, where and when he joined up, what rank he attained and in which outfits he served, what fights he was in, how war shaped and changed him, and after the guns fell mute, what he'd done with his life.

Once word of this book got out, through an article in the pages of *Leatherneck* and my own supplications, responses came in, the handwritten letters, the phone calls and e-mails, the photographs and poems, the confidences exchanged over drinks, the suggestion by one man of the name of another; here came Marines wanting each in his own style to be a part of what I was trying to do. Attempting in a modest, parochial way to achieve here what the great Sir John Keegan's *Face of Battle* did magisterially in dealing with other wars, from Henry V at Agincourt to the Iron Duke at Waterloo and to 1916 and the Somme, where an English generation died, to answer the question of why one man fights so well, while others don't. On what inner resources does a man draw that make him a good soldier, a canny fighter, a successful killer? Are such warriors born or trained? What fears and hesitations does a combat Marine confront and how does he overcome them?

Do we fight for a cause, for our comrades in arms, because of some undefinable esprit de corps, for glory and promotion, or simply to save our very lives?

Unlike Sir John, that brilliant writer, historian, and analyst, who admitted in the early pages of *Face* that he had never fought, never saw a battle, never even walked a battleground once the guns cooled and went silent, I had done those things. *A New York Times* review of my *Marines of Autumn* put it this way: "Mr. Brady knows war, the sound and the feel of it."

At the heart of the story are the Marines themselves, with their terse, evocative first-person responses, ruthlessly honest accounts of men at war, one combat veteran speaking with another, men talking out their war stories, the absurdities, the ironies, the stupidities, and even the beauty of battle. There are Marines who remember combat, in some perverse way, as one of the good times, and admit, yes, they miss it.

Few of "my" Marines discriminated between fighting in "good" wars or "bad." Are we too easily led? Or were we just being good Marines?

I've tried to make this an authentically American account of our country at war as seen through the eyes of its warriors, not gushing or flag-waving, but honestly, candidly reporting on men's doubts as well as exulting in their triumphant battle cries, a book of some weight and heft that I hope may resonate in the national consciousness and that Marines and other Americans will read, and not swiftly forget.

ACKNOWLEDGMENTS

I'M GRATEFUL TO THE MARINES IN THIS BOOK WHO TOLD ME OF their wars, and of their lives. This book belongs to them. And in a special way to Colonel Walt Ford of *Leatherneck* magazine, who provided me the map coordinates.

I

France, 1918. "Come on, you sons of bitches!"

Hear them, listen to the voices: These are the Marines, the hard men who fight our wars, unscripted and always honest.

Except, of course, when we lie.

Half a dozen wars ago, in France, on June 2 of 1918, Marine gunnery sergeant Dan Daly stepped out in front of the 4th Brigade of Marines, mustered for another bloody frontal assault on the massed machine guns of the Germans that had been murderously sweeping the wheat fields at Belleau Wood. Death awaited. And the men, understandably, seemed reluctant to resume the attack. But old gunnies like Daly aren't notable for coddling the troops, for issuing polite invitations, and Dan was having none of it. Nor was he much for inflated oratory or patriotic flourish. Instead, in what some remember as a profane, contemptuous snarl, and loudly, Gunnery Sergeant Daly demanded of his hesitant Marines: "Come on, you sons of bitches! Do you want to live forever?"

Is that why we fight? Because we're cussed at and shamed into it? Was that what motivated the men of the 4th Brigade in 1918 who went into

the deadly wheat field? Do today's Marines who take out combat patrols in Anbar Province and hunt the Taliban somewhere west of the
Khyber have the same motivations as Dan Daly's men? Or the Marines
who once waded the bloody lagoon for General Howland M. "Howlin'
Mad" Smith at Tarawa, scaled Mount Suribachi, defied the Japanese at
Wake Island, fought the Chinese in the snows of North Korea, and
fought and died on the Perfume River at Hue and in a thousand other
bloody places?

The Marines in this book answer those questions; each in his own
way attempts to say why we are drawn to the guns.

Dan Daly had his methods: Curse the sons of bitches and lead them
into the field. The men were impressed, by the man if not by his shouting, knowing Daly as a legend, with two Medals of Honor already. But
was Daly's leadership and their own training all it took for Marines to
get up and run at the machine guns of Belleau Wood? It became a question I kept asking.

General Jim Jones, tall and tough, a former commandant and more
recently NATO commander, has a mantra: "Sergeants run the Marine
Corps," he told me once on a rainswept drive from Quantico to the
Pentagon. Jones wasn't just blowing smoke, keeping up noncom morale
when he said that. He was attempting to tell me what he believed dif-
ferentiates the Marine Corps from other military arms. Without its
seemingly inexhaustible supply of good, tough sergeants, the Marine
Corps would be nothing more than a smaller version of the army.
Most Marines, officers or enlisted, would agree. They've had their own
Dan Dalys. We all have.

I found mine, thirty-three years after Daly, in a North Korean winter on a snowy ridgeline, the senior NCOs of Dog Company, a couple
of blue-collar Marine lifers, hard men from the South Pacific and up
through the ranks, one hard-earned noncommissioned stripe after another, who tutored me about war, not off their college diplomas but
out of their own vast experience of service and combat, and incidentally about life, women, and other fascinating matters. These were the
professionals; I was the amateur learning from them, not in any classroom but in a quite deadly field.

Stoneking, the platoon sergeant, was a big, rawboned Oklahoman maybe twenty-eight or twenty-nine, who drove a bootlegger's truck back home and was married to an attractive brunette WAVE who sent him erotic photos of herself. He had been a Marine eight or nine years, had fought the Japanese, and was in the bad Korea fighting. The men knew that if it came to that, he would (against the rules) strip his blouse and fight another enlisted man who was giving him angst. Stoneking was a cold, distant man with little regard for me or for most people (I don't believe he really gave a shit about anyone), although for forty-six consecutive nights that winter he and I slept head to toe in our sleeping bags in a stinking, six-by-eight-foot bunker with a log-and-sandbagged roof so low it had to be crawled into and out of. That miserable hole was where we lived like animals and where from Stoneking I began to learn what it was to be and to lead Marines. Once when I'd been in a shooting and crawled back late that night into our bunker to tell about it, Stoneking wasn't much impressed. "So you got yourself into a firefight," he remarked, and rolled against the dirt wall to get back to sleep. "Yeah," I said deflated, and got into my own sleeping bag. A pivotal event in my young life meant nothing to a hard case like Stoney.

The right guide, our platoon's ranking number three, was the more affable Sergeant Wooten.

We weren't supposed to keep diaries (in case we were captured or the damned things were found on our bodies) but I wanted one day to work on newspapers and write about people and things, so, to keep a record and get around the diary rule, I wrote long letters home to family and girlfriends for them to save. The mail back then wasn't censored. Wooten might occasionally have composed a postcard, and little more, but he enjoyed watching me scribble away, marveled at my industry. "You are a cack-ter, suh." Cack-ter being his pronunciation of "character," in Wooten's mind a compliment. He was leagues less surly than Stoney, so I occasionally lured him into deep, Socratic conversation.

"It ain't much of a war, Lieutenant," Wooten would concede, having listened to me blather on, and then patiently explaining his own philosophy to a young replacement officer, "but it's the only war we got." He had other, maturely and placidly thought out commentaries on life and the fates, remarking with sly, rural witticisms on the nightly firefights and their bloody casualty rolls, "Sometimes you eat the bear / sometimes the bear eats you." Or declaring as an unexpected salvo of enemy shells slammed into the ridgeline, scattering the men in dusty, ear-splitting, and too-often lethal chaos, sending us diving into holes amid incongruous laughter, "There ain't been such excitement since the pigs ate my little brother."

You rarely heard a line like that back in Brooklyn.

I ended up loving these men, as chill, as caustic, or as odd as they may first have seemed when I got to the war, an innocent who had never heard the bullets sing, had never fought, who yet, by the fluke of education and rank, was now anointed the commanding officer of hardened veterans of such eminence and stature. Maybe I could better explain about such men and why Marines fight and generally fight so well if only I were able to tell you fully and precisely about combat as my old-timers knew it, and how it really was. And how I would have to learn it.

It's difficult unless you've been there.

War is a strange country, violent and often beautiful at the same time, with its own folklore and recorded history, its heroes and villains. It is as well a profession, strange and sad, poorly paid but highly spe-cialized. Cruel, too. War is very cruel. And surprising, in that it can be incredibly thrilling and rewarding, though not for everyone. There is a sort of complicated ritual to it, a freemasonry, a violent priesthood. Only fighting men are qualified to exchange the secret fraternal hand-shake, the mythic nod and wink of understanding.

Not all men are meant to fight in wars and fewer still do it well. Others, revolted by its horrors, its sorrows and pity, yet hold dear its memories, the camaraderie, its occasional joys. I have even heard men admit, without shame and rather proudly, "I love this shit," speaking candidly about war and their strange passion for it. There are such Marines, plenty of them, men hooked on combat. They love it the way men love a woman in a relationship they suspect will end badly. Others are honest enough to admit they hate and fear it but go anyway. Their reasons may be strangely inspiring, or murky, puzzling.

A few Marines can't or won't go to the battle, and they don't last long, not in the infantry, not in the line outfits. They are transferred out to someplace less. They may still be fine men but they are no longer Marines.

I never knew better, truer men than in the rifle company ranks in which I served, bold and resourceful Americans, beautiful men in a violent life. What each of them was and did later at home and at peace, having let slip the leash of discipline, I can't always say. But in combat such men, even the rogues and rare scoundrels, were magnificent, hard men living in risky places. In this book, I write about some of them. Forget my commentary; hear the Marines, listen to their voices.

The third platoon's right guide, Sergeant Wooten, that salty career man, was a crafty rifleman who knew a little about demolitions. He once volunteered in North Korea to blow a Fox Company Marine's body out of the ice of a frozen mountain stream; using too heavy a charge, he got the guy out, but in two pieces. When he came back to us at Dog Company he looked terrible, like a man after an all-night drunk. "You okay, Wooten?" "No, sir, I ain't. After I got that boy out that way, I threw up on the spot." A three-striper who had fought the damned Japanese for three years, all across the Pacific, Wooten took a drink. He'd been up and down the noncommissioned ranks, as high as gunnery sergeant and then broken back to buck sergeant, a lean, leathery, drawling rustic maybe fifteen years older than I was and lots wiser. Sometimes Wooten lost patience with those who were critical of the Korean War we were then fighting. He was pretty much enjoying himself and thought those people ought to shut the hell up and cut the bitching. As, giving me that flat-mouthed grin of his, Wooten declared with professional regret: "It's the only war we got."

Of course there were plenty of cynical Marines, wise guys aggrieved and irreverent, who never gave you a straight answer. If asked why they enlisted, you got the sarcasm. If they spoke of the Corps, it was as in "I just love this effing Crotch." Then there were the jokers. A fire-team leader and born comedian who could have done stand-up, Corporal Fred Frankville cracked during perilous outpost duty in Korea, "If it wasn't for the pay, I'd quit." Others declared flatly, "It sure wasn't for the dough." Of course for Depression-era kids off the dust bowl farms, or city boys coming off the unemployment lines, it truly was the wages. That and a suit of clothes, some well-soled shoes, and three squares. Did that make us mercenaries, nothing but hired guns, men who don't discriminate between noble or evil causes, do precious little soul-searching, but say our prayers and move out?

One famous Marine certainly thought so, a gallant, flamboyant but disenchanted Marine general gloriously named Smedley Darlington Butler, furious at having been passed over for commandant in 1920 by a rival World War I hero named John A. Lejeune. In retirement, and appointed police commissioner of Philadelphia, Smedley regularly blackguarded his once-beloved Corps for renting itself out to the thuggish ambitions and corporate greed of Wall Street, National City Bank, United Fruit, and Brown Brothers Harriman. His hostile citation of the Harriman family banking interests suggests there was a little of Butch and Sundance in Butler. But remember, ol' Smedley didn't start bitching until he lost the top job.

There are such men. And then there are others, truly in love with the Corps and their roles in it. Hear their more innocent voices.

No irreverence out of gung-ho Marine Chuck Curley of Olean in upstate New York, a machine gunner in Dog Company who never cussed out "the Crotch" or gave a smart-ass answer in his life. We met in 1951 in the Taebaek Mountains of North Korea when I joined Dog Company as a replacement. When I asked Curley years later why he thought Marines fought so well, why we fought at all, Curley didn't hesitate, still addressing me as "Lieutenant."

"Why I joined the Marine Corps, Lieutenant, and why I believe Marines are better fighters than other outfits? Discipline, discipline, discipline, drummed into us at boot camp. If you can survive boot camp, you can survive combat. Maybe they brainwashed me in boot camp but I still believe in my fellow Marines. Because of boot camp and combat. Discipline. It's simple, Lieutenant." And to Chuck Curley, who invariably capitalized the words "Boot Camp," it *was* simple.

John C. Chapin of Manchester, Vermont, recruited off the campus at Yale by a Marine officer, said he joined up because "everyone I knew had enlisted." Chapin ended up in a first-wave landing craft at Roi-Namur in the Pacific, a Yalie lieutenant with his dead platoon sergeant's brains sprayed across his face. And this was his first landing on a hostile beach!

Doug Bradlee, a big redheaded Bostonian from an old Pinckney Street family, prepped at Saint Mark, played tackle for Harvard, was a first cousin to Ben Bradlee of *Washington Post* and Watergate fame, and had worked out a crude but highly personal theory that, through war, he hoped to "find and know God."

Machine gunner Walter Kuhle of New Port Richey, Florida, who fought under the legendary Lewis "Chesty" Puller, to this day recalls the insane joy of battle and half a century after he last fired a Browning machine gun, habitually signs off his letters with a cheerful, "Happiness is a belt-fed weapon."

The former all-star second baseman for the New York Yankees, Jerry Coleman, who retired from the Marine reserve as a lieutenant colonel and at eighty-one is still broadcasting San Diego Padres games, flew Marine dive bombers in World War II against the Japanese and in Korea flew Corsairs against the Commies, and is believed to be the only major-league baseball player to have seen combat in two wars. "Why do Marines fight?" Jerry parroted me. "They fight for the guy next to them. They don't fight to be heroes or anything else."

George Peto of Columbus, Ohio, a sergeant and forward observer for the 81-mm mortars of the 1st Marines, lost a best friend on Okinawa after three and a half years of war together. He says that from there on to the end, "The road to glory was over, I fought for revenge. Out of hatred. Even the old photo of a Japanese soldier today can bring back the hatred."

Baker Company of the 7th Marines in Korea had its "Doc" Teppel, a fierce fellow in a firefight who didn't "hate" anyone, not even the enemy. They were fighting the Chinese up there at the Chosin Reservoir when Doc found himself in sole possession of a Chinese prisoner and decided to keep him around. Since even young "leftenants" of the British Royal Marine Commandos, fighting at our side in Korea, each had his own enlisted servant, his "batman," why couldn't our lieutenants? Doc nominated his prisoner as a personal batman and got away with it until the company commander ruled Teppel out of order and the POW was sent back to wherever it was POWs went. The Chinese trooper is said to have left Teppel with considerable reluctance.

Lance Corporal James Webb of McLean, Virginia, a rifleman in a

Marine weapons company fighting at Ar-Ramadi in Iraq in 2007, decided to enlist in the Marine Corps in the second year of the Iraq war while a student at Penn State. Jimmy Webb realized he was watching Americans fight at Fallujah on television but was himself doing nothing about it. A grandfather had fought on Iwo, his dad in Vietnam, and going to war ran through the family tradition. When twenty-four-year-old Webb and I communicated by e-mail he was in the second half of his one-year combat tour in "the worst place in Iraq."

Lieutenant Pierce Power, of Flushing, New York, was wounded in the horrific and costly September 1951 frontal assault by two Marine regiments on North Korean Hill 749. There 90 Marines died and 800 were wounded, including, on his birthday, Power. As his platoon reached the crest of 749 he and a sergeant, both wounded, found a corpsman, and Power turned over the sergeant for treatment. "Why didn't you turn yourself in?" I asked. "It might have been that million-dollar wound. Might have meant a trip home." Never occurred to him, said Pierce. "I wasn't that smart."

George Krug, a corporal with Fox Company of the 5th Marines, now living and still working in the building trades in Buffalo Grove, Illinois, was only one of many Marine draftees fighting the Chinese in 1952 in Korea. "Why did these men fight? The answer to this question is simple. We were ordinary people, molded into Marines. We came from different backgrounds; however, we became a team, moving and fighting as if we had known each other all of our lives. Not one of us was bitter."

"Taffy" Sceva, who as an enlisted man fought and was wounded by the Japanese under Chesty Puller, was by 1951 a married man called back to a second war, in Korea. But when the now First Lieutenant Sceva was posted at Quantico to train younger officers, he appealed to his former boss, General Puller, to get him into the fighting in Korea. "The old man'll arrange it," Taffy assured us. "Your wife know you wrote Puller?" Sceva was asked. He made a face. "Hell, no. I'm scared to tell her." In the end he got to Korea, fought through the war with Fox Company of the 7th Marines, survived to come home, and to skipper oceangoing yachts out of Hawaii as commodore of the big trans-Pacific yacht races.

Another police commissioner, decidedly not Smedley, Ray Kelly of

New York, admitted he never really had a choice about joining the Corps or fighting a war. His three older brothers were all Marines who raised the child on 782 gear and compulsory lessons from the *Guidebook for Marines*. Kelly ended up fighting in Vietnam as an artillery forward observer, up with the rifle companies. "What options had I?" Ray Kelly asked rhetorically as we sat chatting over coffee in his headquarters office atop One Police Plaza, near where the Twin Towers once stood.

The aforementioned Gunnery Sergeant Daniel Joseph Daly, awarded a first Congressional Medal of Honor in 1900 on the wall at Peking fighting the Boxers, and a second Medal in 1916 fighting the Cacos in Haiti (who roasted and ate the hearts of Marines they captured in order to take on their courage), was a man who got directly to the point. As at Belleau Wood, where Daly got off his legendary line. In that fight the brigade would lose 112 officers and 4,598 enlisted casualties, 1,000 of them killed, more dead than the Corps had lost in its entire 143-year history to then. But Dan Daly survived Belleau Wood and lived until 1937, narrowly missing the onset of World War II, a lively affair the old gunny would surely have enjoyed enormously.

Another Marine gunnery sergeant still on active duty in 2007, seventy years after Daly's death, Keith Milks had his own motivations for battle. Gunny Milks served in both Afghanistan and Iraq. But to him, Afghanistan had been more important. It was, he told me, "personal. A personal war. Because on September 11 of 2001, I was stationed at the Pentagon. I was in the building when the plane hit. That made Afghanistan something personal."

Keith Robbins, member of a Marine family dating back to 1815 (an ancestor was personally commissioned by President James Madison), was born at Parris Island Recruit Depot, fought as an enlisted man and was shot by the Chinese in North Korea, returned to the States to take a job on the *Romper Room* television show, "lived in Paradise [Tahiti]" for a time, and ended up in the hotel business. Family "tradition" was his excuse for "going Marine."

Then there was First Lieutenant Chew een Lee of Baker Company, 7th Marines, a Chinese American who evolved a sort of crude philosophy about why men went to war. Calling on ancestors honored by him but unknown to the rest of us, Lee was celebrated for announcing at the slightest urging, "I hope to die in battle." Not very cheerful, or quite as pithy as Dan Daly, but it had a certain ring. During the battle at the Chosin Reservoir, gallant Lieutenant Lee very nearly had his prayers answered, but survived his wounds, was awarded a Navy Cross, served twenty years in the Corps, retired as a major. Fellow Baker Company first lieutenant Joe Owen of upstate Skaneateles, New York, also badly wounded in the same fight, drily recalls Lee, with his death wish, as a Marine professional, "but hardly a congenial companion."

George Bartlett of Towson, Maryland, who began as an enlisted Marine, was in three wars and ended a brigadier general, had a swift response to my question about why Marines rush toward the guns, "Was it training, discipline, esprit, peer pressure, what?" "Training" snapped Bartlett, leaving little wiggle room for contrary opinions. "It's training. It begins at boot camp and continues the whole time you're in the Corps. Training does it." When we spoke, George, well into his eighties, was off with his wife Donna to ski for six weeks at Beaver Creek.

Lemuel C. Shepherd Jr., a Virginian (and VMI grad) I knew at the Basic School in Quantico, was the brother of several Marine career officers and son of a general (the future commandant), and used to entertain us all with a little barracks humor, his impersonation of a dove, his whining, drawling plaint, "Ma old man and ma brothers couldn't wait for another war to come along, just to get ma ass in the damned Marine Corps." But when the trumpet sounded, young Lem went to the war with the rest of us poor civilians, and did just fine.

Marines maintain a certain standard when it comes to judging battles. Shamus P. Cullen was a lance corporal in a rifle company of the 7th Marines during Desert Storm in the first Iraq War, and today runs a New York security agency. And despite the charms of that bestselling book *Jarhead,* Cullen didn't seem all that impressed by his own war. "We went in before the ground war started, went in across the mine fields," Shamus said. When I asked him what the fighting was like, Cullen, a cool man difficult to please, said dismissively, "What can I tell you? It was a hundred-hour war."

Dr. Gonzalo Garza, Ph.D., Texas-born veteran of two wars, a man whose grandpa campaigned with Pancho Villa, rather neatly defined what inspired some Marines to fight: "Two reels of *Iwo Jima* with John Wayne and a couple of Marine Reserve meetings."

Following Pearl Harbor and at age nineteen, future governor, navy secretary, and senator John Chafee of Rhode Island resigned from his sophomore year at Yale to join the Marines because he worried the United States would defeat the Japanese too swiftly, before his ROTC unit could be called up, and he didn't want to miss the war.

Bestselling author Martin Russ, who lives now in the wine country out in California, at Oakville, fought in Korea on the same ground I had a year earlier. He was a well-educated and quite literary young enlisted man, who got a rather wonderful memoir out of the experience, *The Last Parallel,* which astonishingly was the cover story selection of the book reviews of both *The New York Times* and the *Herald Tribune* in the same week. It also drew a personal letter of enthusiastic notice from reclusive J. D. Salinger and earned Marty a screenplay-writing gig from Stanley Kubrick. That job began as adapting his own book to film and ended with Russ working with Vladimir Nabokov on the script for *Lolita.* Marty confesses without urging that he enjoyed himself immensely during his time on the firing line, suggesting the war could have been specifically arranged for his entertainment.

I must admit I never went as far as Marty Russ in my enthusiasm for battle.

One of my rifle platoon squad leaders, a big tough blond kid from Michigan named John Fitzgerald, joined the Marine Corps because he wanted to play football and didn't have the grades for college. Fitz was wounded several times in Korea, fought again in Vietnam, and then later on was shot while a cop in Flint, Michigan. Fitz went into a dark cellar after a bad guy with a gun, took a shotgun shell in the belly that carried pieces of his cartridge belt into his innards, but he killed the other guy as he went down. He is married to a schoolteacher named Theresa (he calls her "Sam," which makes as much sense as going into cellars after gunmen), who wrote a splendid book about how to get kids hooked on math, and Fitz sails his own trawler on Lake Superior and still splits and chops firewood for their house.

James "Wild Hoss" Callan, the twenty-five-year-old straw-haired son of a Texas family that dated back to when Texas was itself a republic, was a lieutenant saving his Marine Corps combat pay in Korea to help his old dad keep from losing the family ranch to the drought in New Mexico where they'd moved. The Chinese killed Wild Hoss on June 14, 1951, a month after he flew out of San Francisco to join the 1st Marine Division as a replacement rifle platoon leader. I don't know if his father lost the ranch.

Walter Anderson, chairman and CEO of *Parade* magazine, was a tough kid who dropped out of school in Westchester County (a blue-collar neighborhood, not the blue blood) and joined the Marines to escape an abusive father he feared he might eventually kill. He got himself shipped out to Vietnam while still only seventeen, and just as abruptly was sent back to the States until he turned eighteen. At which time, still gung ho, Walt promptly returned to combat, ending up a sergeant. But until recently (early 2007) when his play, *Johnny's War,* was readying an out-of-town first production, Anderson had never written about Vietnam.

Speaking with such men convinced me this book was worth writing when yet another lousy little war was killing Marines and other U.S. troops, draining the country's treasury, and bitterly dividing Americans. There was Vietnam; now we're bogged down in Iraq and Afghanistan, where, instead of sending good mountain troops, airbornes, and a Marine division into the Tora Bora hills to stay there all winter until we nailed Osama bin Laden, we relied on "smart" bombing from 35,000 feet. Which is impressively high-tech but effectively bullshit. So we sort of lost interest and decided instead to beat up on the Iraqis, and we know how brilliantly that strategy succeeded.

As I write, we are edging into Somalia and swapping insults with a blustering Iran, which had resumed taking hostages. While surly North Koreans rattled nuclear cages and test-fired rockets. Pakistan seethed. As usual, Lebanon trembled on the verge. Even Latin America fussed. There seemed trouble everywhere.

"Another fine mess you've gotten us into," as Oliver Hardy used to tell Laurel. Weren't things supposed to be better once the cold war ended and the Soviet Union collapsed? Or was it man's fate always to be fighting somewhere? Far too old to fight again, my three grandsons too young, while halfway around the world, young soldiers and Marines were saddling up again.

But I could interview Marines about battle and still write about it. Here are those stories, theirs and mine, theirs throbbing, thrilling, my own less so, the sometimes wild, unexpected answers to the essentially very simple question that half a century later I am still trying to answer for myself: Why do we fight?

2

Born fighting, Senator James Webb and his Lance Corporal son, Jim

IF THERE IS A WARRIOR-POET IN THIS STORY OR OUT THERE IN TO-day's America, it must be Senator James Webb of Virginia. Even Randall Wallace, author of *Braveheart*, thinks so. In a review of *Born Fighting*, a Webb book about "how the Scots-Irish shaped America," Wallace, a descendant of the difficult fellow, the Scotsman who long ago made all that trouble for the English (and for his sins was drawn and quartered and later portrayed in a movie by Mel Gibson), wrote, "James Webb is a Warrior-Poet and has written an extraordinary book."

Jim wrote an earlier book, a bestselling novel called *Fields of Fire*, set in Vietnam and featuring a protagonist named Robert E. Lee Hodges Jr., who sounds a lot like the young Marine platoon leader Webb in what he does and the anger inside. The Webb biographer Robert Timberg recalls a scene where Hodges and his men are ordered into the rice paddies by cozened and comfortable rear echelon brass. Under fire, "Hodges," or Webb, reacts bitterly:

"Fuck 'em. Just fuck 'em. Fuck everybody who doesn't come out here and do this."

The fictional Lieutenant Hodges may have been speaking not only for Webb but for plenty of Americans in plenty of wars. The odd thing being that it varied from war to war. We hated what we were doing in the North Korean winter but we didn't personalize it. We were just there and had to fight in that shit. If we were sore at anyone, it was the cold and the enemy.

James Webb, born in Saint Joe, Missouri, and educated in a dozen places around this country and in England, is the son of a career air force man who flew B-17 and B-29 bombers in World War II, and later in the Berlin Airlift of the cold war era. Jim himself is a "trade school man" who graduated from the Naval Academy, then taught literature there, fought as a Marine officer in Vietnam, writes bestselling novels (two of them nominated for Pulitzers) and serious nonfiction, worked in Hollywood as a screenwriter and producer, won an Emmy Award as a PBS television journalist in Beirut, speaks Vietnamese, was a secretary of the navy in the Reagan cabinet who resigned on a point of honor (he wanted a 600-ship navy, the administration of the time was mothballing warships), writes for magazines, and as a newly elected United States senator was barely in the job when he was already jousting, on a White House receiving line, with the president of the United States, and a month later delivering an eloquent Democratic response to Mr. Bush's State of the Union address.

Oh, yes, and since it is never dull chez Webb, two months later one of Jim's staff, a former Marine, was arrested by the Capitol police for carrying a sidearm and two clips into the building. Inadvertent, they said. Payback? others wondered.

Senator Webb also has a son in the Marines who at this writing was fighting in Iraq and more of that to come. But in the meanwhile, let me tell you a bit more about Webb père whose suggestion it was that I interview both Webbs together. And a splendid idea at that!

Following a cameo appearance at the University of Southern California (1963–64) Webb received an appointment to Annapolis, where his classmates included Oliver North (the two met in a closely contested championship boxing match still spoken of with considerable awe by boxing buffs at the academy; Ollie won). Author Timberg, also a Marine (severely wounded in Vietnam), wrote about Webb, North, John McCain, and others in a wonderful book called *The Nightingale's*

Song. Following graduation from the Academy in 1968 and the usual Basic School course for newly commissioned Marine lieutenants at Quantico (Jim Webb was first in his class of 243 men), it was off to Vietnam. During his tour there as a rifle platoon leader in Delta Company of the 5th Marines, later a company commander, Webb was wounded twice. He was awarded a Silver Star, two Bronze Stars, and a Navy Cross, which as navy and Marine decorations go, rates just second to the Congressional Medal of Honor. Regarding Webb in combat, Timberg wrote respectfully of Jim as, "the Natural."

His citation for the Navy Cross makes lively, if bureaucratically stilted reading: "For extraordinary heroism in combat operations against the enemy in the Republic of South Vietnam on 10 July 1969 while participating in a company-sized search & destroy operation deep in hostile territory, 1st Lieutenant Webb's platoon discovered a well-camouflaged bunker which appeared to be unoccupied. Deploying his men into defensive positions, Webb was advancing toward the first bunker when three enemy soldiers armed with hand grenades jumped out. Reacting instantly, he grabbed the closest man and, brandishing his .45 at the others, apprehended all three. Accompanied by one of his men he then approached the second bunker and called for the enemy to surrender. When the hostile soldiers failed to answer him and threw a grenade which detonated dangerously close to him, Webb detonated a Claymore mine in the bunker aperture, accounting for two enemy casualties and disclosing the entrance to a tunnel. Despite the smoke and debris from the explosion and the possibility of enemy soldiers being in the tunnel, Webb then conducted a thorough search which yielded several items of equipment and numerous documents containing valuable intelligence data. Continuing the assault, he approached a third bunker and was preparing to fire into it when the enemy threw another grenade. Observing the grenade land dangerously close to his companion, Webb simultaneously fired first at the enemy, pushed the Marine away from the grenade, and shielded him from the explosion with his own body. Although sustaining painful fragmentation wounds . . . he managed to throw a grenade into the aperture and completely destroy the remaining bunker. By his courage, aggressive leadership, and selfless devotion, he . . ." etc.

I don't recall anyone's "brandishing" a sidearm in my time, but that's what they said. Back home, and after being patched up by the naval hospitals, Jim enrolled at Georgetown Law School (1972–75), where he somehow found time to write his first book *Micronesia and U.S. Pacific Strategy*. By '77 he was on the staff of a House Committee on Veterans Affairs and representing veterans on his own time, pro bono. You sort of get the idea Webb wasn't a guy to sit around the house rearranging his sock drawer. The Reagan administration, always on the prowl for a promising young man, made him assistant secretary of defense for reserve affairs in 1984, a post in which he busied himself as well on Marine Corps problems in the post-Vietnam years, drug use, racial infighting, low morale, and a couple of whacking good scandals, the Clayton Lonetree espionage case and Ollie North's woes during Iran-Contra. In '87 Webb was promoted to secretary of the navy but resigned the following year in protest over shrinking the navy. Remember when officials used to do that, submit a "resignation of honor," on a matter of conscience? Webb did.

His Emmy was earned for a seven-minute report for *The Mac-Neil/Lehrer NewsHour* covering the aftermath of that bloody, tragic bombing in 1983 of the Marine barracks at Beirut. Timberg recalls Webb's conversations with young Marines dug in around Beirut airport, capturing their "odd blend of confusion, machismo, commitment, hope, and youthful sweetness." Of such "kids" Webb confessed, on air, that in a way, he felt "deeply protective of these men." For many of us, Jim himself was the Renaissance man of contemporary Marines, a guy we mostly liked and all admired.

I'd known Webb because we had both been Marines and both wrote for *Parade* magazine, and I wanted his story for this book. But when his electoral campaign against George Allen for a seat in the United Sates Senate began to heat up (Jim was a dismal long shot at the start) I decided to leave him alone until the race was over, quite sure he would have plenty of leisure time after Mr. Allen won. Instead, Jim was elected, I was forced to wait. After he'd taken his Senate seat and publicly sparred with the president, I wrote the new senator, and he called back from his Senate office early in March 2007.

I posed the usual questions, some of my queries based on Timberg's writing about Webb, the young lieutenant whose rifle platoon in six weeks lost sixty-five men killed and wounded, counting plenty of replacements to the original forty-man unit. Taking up the crucial matter of motivation, Timberg wrote, "The antiwar movement was of little interest for Webb in those days. He did not recognize the strength and depth of it. As a platoon leader in the bush, he did not have much time for reflection or intellectual musings."

Now I was to do the musing. Why did Webb join up? Did the Naval Academy sell him on the Corps? No. "I wanted to be a Marine long before Annapolis. In high school I talked my way into the NROTC. I was fascinated by the infantry, seeing World War II war movies and watching TV programs like *Victory at Sea*. The army didn't have a scholarship program then but the navy did."

We were barely into the interview when Webb seemed to be elsewhere. I was asking, "Why do we fight so well? Is it training, discipline, esprit, the guy next to us, glory, sheer bad temper?"

He didn't say anything. It was unlike Jim. He seemed strangely reluctant. I tried to slide past his reluctance. I was trying to write a damned book, not make friends and influence people, so I pressed on, looking for keys to his character and personality in stuff he'd written. Asking, "In your book about the Scots-Irish you have a chapter about your people titled, 'Fight. Sing, Drink, Pray." Why in that order, Jim? Is the order important for us to understand?" Did his people fight first and pray last? Was that significant? That's what I wanted to ask but didn't want to irritate the man. I got some of my query out.

"Well," he said, "it pretty much defines the culture."

I was rapidly taking notes when he stopped me. "Look," he said, "I don't want this to be about me." That grudging line was it; he was sloughing off my questions. Had the old Marine suddenly become "grand" as a senator? Instead, his voice deepened, lowered. "Can we include my son? He was comfortable at Penn State but now he's a lance corporal, a Marine overseas. I think we could split this story with my son. He's with the infantry, a lance corporal, 0311 [an infantry military occupation number]."

Suddenly I understood. Webb hadn't changed at all. He was the same guy.

"Sure," I said, brightening up. It was a great idea, and I should have thought of it. It would make the story even better. His reference to 0311 grabbed me. It didn't make a good deal of sense but I said, "I remember the day I was promoted from 0301 to 0302 in Korea. To 'experienced infantry leader.' One of the great moments of my life."

"Mine, too," said Webb senior, sharing with me the pride of an 0302, and shortly after, ended with a promise to contact his son through e-mail and try to set up a three-way conversation. His idea that we involve his son was inspired. I thanked Jim and hung up, sort of hugging myself that he wasn't just cooperating, he was going to give me a more complex, more powerful yarn.

It took a little time to reach the boy. He was, after all, a Marine infantryman fighting a war. Much as his dad had done forty years earlier. All I really knew yet about young Webb was that in the summer of 2004, as a civilian photographer, he'd accompanied his father on a *Parade* magazine assignment in Afghanistan and while there had visited Marine bases and smaller, riskier outposts, and while shooting pictures to illustrate his father's story, had actually gone out with a Marine squad "on a combat patrol up into the steep mountains," as Webb senior's article put it.

Another e-mail from the senator hinted that my blunt interviewing methods might be somewhat challenged. It read, in part, "they have computers they are allowed to use when they are in the base camp area. They are not personal computers. Can't receive attachments. I would suggest putting your questions into the body of an e-mail. For obvious reasons (he is NOT permitted to discuss operational matters) and for less obvious reasons (I have never once heard my son 'count coup' as the Native Americans put it), he will be reluctant to discuss firefights, etc."

Which was, of course, precisely what I wanted Lance Corporal Jim Webb 0311 to talk about. Firefights. Fighting.

While waiting to make connections, I read up on young Webb in a battalion newspaper article from Ar-Ramadi, Iraq, by Corporal Paul Robbins Jr., forwarded by Senator Webb. Lance Corporal Webb, twenty-four, was from Falls Church, Virginia, and was serving as a rifleman in a weapons company, and was quoted as saying, "For me not to respond to the country's call, I'd be letting myself and the history of the family down." Not only was his dad a combat veteran from Vietnam, the young man's grandfather had fought on Iwo Jima. He said, despite this background, the military life was "never pushed" at home, while admitting that "growing up in a family of accomplished Marines gave him a unique outlook on life in the armed forces." Many of his childhood memories were of members of his father's old platoon or "discussing battlefield terrains or history with his dad."

Said young Jim, "I had a cupboard full of role models growing up and they were all Marines. I was raised to be a warrior." It was that which first led him to the Virginia Military Institute ("I wanted to follow in the footsteps of my father and my family history"), but he later transferred to Penn State. It was there he became distracted. "Watching the battle of Al-Fallujah on television from the campus," he concluded he was seeing too much of the war "from the safety of the United States" and decided in December 2005 to leave college.

"The coverage of fighting in Fallujah showed me that I needed to be out there." He enlisted and on graduation from Parris Island boot camp and the ensuing School of Infantry advanced training, Jim was invited to try out for Recon. He passed the tough indoctrination and was sent to Camp Lejeune to the 2nd Recon Battalion, where he fell ill. They promised to keep a seat warm for Webb but on learning the recon boys weren't scheduled to leave for the Middle East, he separated from the battalion and joined "the first deploying unit available." In January '06 Jim Webb became a rifleman with the 1st Battalion, 6th Marine Regiment, and was off to Ar-Ramadi later that year. He was by now about halfway through his deployment to the war zone, amidst the kind of action he had seen on TV at home. "Webb has become the latest piece of his family's rich military tradition," the newspaper concludes.

All the senator is quoted as saying is, "To me he didn't have to live up to anything. I have a great deal of respect for him as a Marine and as my son."

I rattled off a direct e-mail, and on March 19, Lance Corporal Webb replied. "Sir, Time has been a little tight over here as of late, I ask that you give me a couple days to formulate a coherent response."

The man was fighting a war, so of course I said sure. But as a cautionary note I reminded him of a Hollywood tale his father probably recalled from his screenwriting days, about the movie mogul who told the screenwriter, "I don't want it good, Manny. I want it Tuesday." In my case, being on deadline I told young Webb, "I want it both good and Tuesday," The "couple of days" became a couple of weeks and then on the Saturday before Palm Sunday at East Hampton I received an e-mail detailing his first combat in Iraq with this brief preface: "Sir, I can supply you with additional info once I determine whether or not I've been nailed by the powers that be. But in the meantime if you want you can get my exact location from my dad. I'd like that included because it's a big point of pride with me, being that it's the worst place in Iraq."

His narrative follows:

"Mr. Brady, I'm cutting it close but here it is. My access to computers and the internet in particular has been extremely limited, so please pardon my late entry.

"The first time I was engaged [in combat] was not by small arms nor did the enemy have a body, a face, or anything at all I could respond to. However, it did and will forever leave a lasting impression on me and on those who shared the experience with me. It was a sunny September afternoon and my platoon had been called out for a routine occurrence in our area of operations. Some knucklehead had decided to place an IED [improvised explosive device] in an intersection we had just passed through, so as we returned to base, we immediately turned around and went back out with EOD [explosive ordanance detail] to clear the IED. Everything went according to plan, the OED blew the IED in place after checking it out, and we were returning back to the base. My humvee always fell in last in line in the platoon and as we headed down Route Michigan to base we were all still giddy about the explosion as it was still a relatively new experience for all, due to it being the end of the first week we had been in theater. A large IED had hit the lead vehicle of my section earlier in the week, blowing the engine block almost clear off, knocking the driver's head off the com mount, and rendering the vehicle immobile. Other than the driver being knocked goofy, no one was hurt.

"Due to this we were all a little edgy when leaving the wire, and even routine missions in the city left us a little worried about who might be next. Our vehicle wheeled around a traffic circle, sped up and caught the rest of the convoy, and we were about one minute into our five-minute trip back to base over a fairly secure route, when for a split instant, time seemed to slow down, the dust seemed to hover off the inside of the truck for a split second, and I saw a white flash in my window.

"Then there was the explosion. My vision blurred for a second, and I was being plunked in the head and face by something. I knew instantly what had happened. The white flash, the explosion, and now the crap raining down on my face. What I didn't expect was that the shit that had pelted me was Cheetos, being popped out of the cardboard and plastic can due to the concussion. We all looked at one another, realizing we were OK, and immediately began to laugh. We were all OK. Shrapnel had shredded the AC unit in the back, taken off the Comm. antennae, and blown out two of the tires. Other than that and some cool pockmarks on the vehicle, we were all right."

Welcome to the war, Lance Corporal. I liked that part about "cool" pockmarks. Now Webb went on about his introduction to combat:

"Why do I select this first incident instead of a firefight? Because this is a unique instance in Iraq. IEDs are the most common form of enemy activity, and on average the deadliest. Most of the time the other guy doesn't know what he's doing with his weapons system. My platoon had plenty of run-ins with RPGs (rocket-propelled grenades) and idiots attempting to employ small arms and light machine guns; however, those engagements turn out to be one-sided in our favor and eventually become routine. Well, almost. Even the most seasoned Marine will feel a shimmer up his spine when the telltale 'pop' of an RPG is heard. However nothing seems to put you on edge like an unexpected explosion.

"To put this in context in a weapons company, you spend a lot of time clearing IEDs; however, the guys doing the clearing give you a heads-up that they are about to blow something in place. But when something goes 'boom' in the night and you're not expecting it, that usually means only bad things have just occurred. Being hit is violent, confusing, disorienting and completely unexpected.

"At least when someone shoots at you, they have the courtesy (or unfortunate occurrence) of being spotted first, at least giving you a sporting chance to respond in some manner. When an IED goes off, you're either screwed or completely and totally lucky. There isn't really an in-between and it's over before you even know what's happened."

Marine Webb now turned to one of my core questions.

"Why do I think Marines fight this fight (and so well)? Mainly because we have faith in our traditionally good leadership. You put the decision-making in someone else's hands and trust them that they will put you at the minimal risk necessary to perform your assigned task. Essentially you have faith that they will not get you killed for a dumb reason or a mistake that they have made. Added into that is that when you get to square off against an enemy that hits you continually from the shadows, you almost want to prove a point. It's saying, without words, 'You S.O.B. can blow my ass up, good . . . awesome . . . great for you . . . but now you're playing my game.'

"That, coupled with the images of my own father trudging through the paddies and swamps of Vietnam and my grandfather pinned on the beaches of Iwo, make my ride in a heavily armed and pleasantly air-conditioned humvee rather 'skate' by contrast."

Some of Jim Webb's acronyms elude me, passage of time and all that, but I assume "skate" means "posh" or "cushy" or something like that. And I liked it a lot when he spoke of a firefight against an enemy with a "face" being an actual relief from battling IEDs and an enemy in "the shadows." It was a sour and probably stupid little war he was fighting, but there was nothing sour or cynical about Lance Corporal Webb. When he gets home I must ask him about "skate."

I finally heard again from Senator Webb. I had three core questions.

I asked him how he as a young officer back then (1969 Vietnam) maintained motivation in an unpopular war and and kept going.

"Combat was the most apolitical environment I've ever been in. I didn't need to have strong political feelings to be motivated to lead my Marines. The war wasn't going to go away, no matter what I thought about it. My greatest motivations were the traditions of the Marine

Corps and my feelings of accountability to the Marines I led. I have a vivid memory of when this crystallized, during a very bad time for our rifle company when my platoon had taken dozens of casualties. We left one position before dawn, moving by foot on a company-sized patrol toward a different section of the Arizona Valley. We were moving east, through knee-deep rice paddies. I was exhausted, frustrated and disillusioned. The sun began to rise. As dawn lifted I saw before me the timeless majesty of a hundred Marines slogging almost effortlessly through the muck, fifty meters between each man, burdened with flak jackets, helmets, packs, bandoliers of ammunition, canteens, grenades, and weapons carried as casually as a businessman might carry a briefcase. It was, oddly, a beautiful sight. It also reminded me, for some reason, that I was joining a long line, and that if I survived this ordeal I would be accountable to those who had been in such places as Iwo Jima and the Frozen Chosin. I knew that they would judge me. And I wanted to be worthy of their respect, just as much as I wanted to be worthy of the respect of the Marines in my rifle platoon who then walked with me."

My second question concerned his attitude toward the current Iraq war. Had he considered trying to dissuade Jim from joining up and going over? Jim's own words, I said, showed it was his personal decision deriving from being at Penn State and watching the war on TV and knowing he had to be a part of it. What was the senator's feeling when his son told him he was going to get into the war?

"My son and I share a unique bond that preceded his enlistment. We've spent literally thousands of hours talking about strategy, tactics, leadership, and military battles throughout history. We've done terrain walks over countless battlefields: the Revolutionary War, the Civil War, World War One, World War Two. I took him with me to Afghanistan as my photographer when I covered that war for *Parade* magazine. After we left Afghanistan, we went together to the area in Vietnam where I had fought as a Marine, which was one of the most moving father-son experiences I've ever had. Jim has an amazing tactical mind, and our family shares a military tradition that goes back to the Battle of King's Mountain in the Revolutionary War. Consequently, it did not surprise me when he decided to enlist. He is smarter about Iraq than most of the people I now serve with in the Senate, and he shared no illusions about the strategy or conduct of the war. But he decided to honor family tradition and join a long line of service, and I both respect and admire that."

My third and last question was: Barring a permanently disabling wound (or obviously death) do you believe young Americans who go to shooting wars gain something tangible from the experience that helps shape and focus the rest of their lives?

"Fighting in a war—and particularly the drawn-out service in wars of attrition such as Vietnam and Iraq—carries with it a heavy cost that affects you for the rest of your life. Consequently, I don't particularly recommend the experience as a prerequisite for getting one's life in order. There are many things that happened to me in Vietnam that I will never fully shake. On the other hand, certain periods of that experience pushed me farther than any other human experience possibly could have. I learned to make decisions under enormous pressure. I had to deal every day with moral dilemmas regarding the life and death of Marines, enemy soldiers, and civilians. And I came out of this a different person. When you've pulled the trigger as you stared into the eyes of a man who's trying his best to kill you, it kind of puts the day-to-day frustrations of normal life into a different perspective."

In late May 2007 I received this e-mail from Senator Webb. "Subject: Marine back inside the wire. I'm pleased to report that young Jim returned from Iraq on 19 May (OK, it was Ho Chi Minh's birthday, but so what). I was very happy to be there when the buses rolled in at Camp Lejeune. 1/6 had a tough deployment, a lot of fighting and a two-month extension courtesy of the 'surge.' They have a lot to be proud of, I'm certainly proud of them.

"And especially of my son, of course. Interesting debrief. He's a tough dude and his tactical acumen is as good as or better than anyone's that I've listened to over the past several years. Few senior officers have been exposed to actual events on the ground, and few lance corporals have the years of thought and preparation that preceded his enlistment. Jim Webb."

3

A college boy dodges the draft but ends up going to war.

LATE IN THE WINTER OF 1947–48, AS SOPHOMORES AT MANHATTAN College, a small Catholic men's school in Riverdale, New York, several of us—Pierce Power, Dick Brew, and I—went down to the New York financial district to join the Marine Corps. (A classmate, Gene Martin, son of a city fireman, had enlisted earlier.) I can't speak for the others but I thought I knew my own, and perhaps sole, motivation. It was not especially gallant or admirable. I was intent on dodging the draft.

The cold war was well and truly on less than three years after the Nazis and the Japanese had surrendered. The monstrous Josef Stalin ruled in the Kremlin, had the largest army in the world and his own atomic bomb, was developing an H-bomb, and was calling the shots for a Soviet Union growing more powerful every day and with global ambitions. His Red Army had taken over half of Europe, states such as Poland, Hungary, Romania, Czechoslovakia, Austria, Hungary, Bulgaria, plus the Baltic republics, and most significantly, the eastern two-thirds of defeated Germany, while a docile Finland remained free but accepted Russian "guidance and advice." Stalin's sometime puppet Tito ran the old Yugoslavia, civil war raged in Greece, and Communist

parties in France and Italy were winning elections. On the other side of
the world Stalin's Chinese sidekick Mao was fighting a civil war
against our guy (and Henry Luce's favorite generalissimo), the corrupt
and egomaniacal Chiang Kai-shek, and would soon kick him off the
mainland, send him packing to Taiwan. When World War II ended,
America had broken up and sent home an army, navy, and air force
that at its peak had totaled 14 million fighting men. (The Marine
Corps of six divisions was reduced to 74,000 Marines on active duty.)
The tide of history was running in Stalin's direction; the future really
did seem to belong to the Commies. And here we were talking about
the next war, perhaps even World War III. President Truman and the
Congress thought this might be a sensible time to rebuild our armed
forces and reinstitute military conscription.

In 1946, like millions of other Americans, on their eighteenth birthday, I went down to where the local draft board sat, to Sheepshead Bay
Road, four or five self-important local men of no particular distinction,
filled out forms, answered a few questions, and registered for the draft.
Having no interest in spending two years peeling potatoes at Fort Dix
or some other army base, I scouted for options. I wasn't alone, of
course, and the various services offered promising young men attractive
alternatives. The Marine Corps came up with its program, the Platoon
Leaders Class. Physically fit college boys could apply to the PLCs and
spend two summers training at Marine Corps Schools, Quantico, Virginia. If they survived the boot camp rigors (very few flunked out,
though our pal Dick Brew, not the most disciplined of men, was not invited back for a second summer), on graduation from college, along
with a degree, they received a second lieutenant's commission in the
Marine Corps Reserve.

Which in peacetime meant a few weeks of annual summer camp and
one night a week drilling in an armory somewhere. But you wouldn't be
drafted into the army. Sounded fine to me.

The scheme worked perfectly in theory; only my timing was lousy.
I graduated from college with a bachelor's degree and my commission
in early June 1950; I had not been drafted, and I had gotten my BA.
Two weeks later, June 25, the North Koreans invaded South Korea, the
war was on, and the Marine Corps began to call up the Reserves,

including newly minted lieutenants like me. It was, to say the least, something of a shock to realize that while I'd dodged the draft, I might actually have to go to war.

I was a skinny, immature kid with an Adam's apple and a crew cut, bright enough but unsure of myself, wondering if I belonged, whether I had the stuff to fight, much less the capability of leading Marines in combat. My motivation for joining up had been derisory. There was no family martial tradition but for an uncle Matthew Brady, killed fighting with the 4th Infantry Division in Normandy. The family whispered he'd joined up to avoid trouble of some sort. I had rarely won a boyhood fistfight or wrestling match, never owned a firearm (not even a Daisy BB gun). The only dead people I had ever seen were rouged and painted, elderly aunts or neighborhood corpses laid out during Irish wakes in Healy's, the local funeral home. And now I was going to the wars, heading for combat. With no notion of why the Gods of War had chosen me to go, how well or badly I would do.

At Quantico, Virginia, the Basic School where young second lieutenants after commissioning were actually trained for war, we were all expected to be "hard chargers," and plenty of us were. I pretended to be, but wasn't. Every week or so they were asking us our first three duty preferences. The expected reply: "Rifle platoon leader, 1st Mar Div." In other words, please send me to Korea so I can shoot people and maybe get killed. From self-consciousness bordering on shame, I always put that down as my first choice. Followed up immediately by what I really wanted to do after leaving Quantico, just about anything to keep me out of harm's way. You know, embassy guard, Paris. Or Mountain Warfare School, Aspen. If they had had a dirigible training billet available, I would have chosen it as an option. I was frankly embarrassed by all this, though there were guys who cheerfully and shamelessly admitted to an unrequited love for "logistics & supply" or "mess hall and PX management."

Most of my closest pals, men like Bradlee, Dick Brennan, and Mack Allen of VMI, embarrassed me by always writing "Rifle platoon leader, 1st Mar Div," three times. And meaning it.

As it was, it didn't seem to matter what we wrote down. All of us got "Rifle platoon leader, 1st Mar Div," right away. Even the fellows lusting after a career in mess hall management. The casualty lists were growing lengthier and the Marine Corps needed new rifle platoon leaders as replacements. Fresh meat, the more cynical among us had it.

Here's what going to war is like. It is November, Thanksgiving week, and already cold with some snow. We fly in from Japan and from some staging area at division the replacements are sorted out and sent north, the infantry replacements trucked up to the lines, not feeling all that jolly about it. They issue us M-1 rifles and one clip—just in case there's trouble along the road—and the crappy looking six-by-six trucks are open to the cold and the snow, their canvas furled in case of enemy air. It is not considered good form to be surprised by enemy air, and I keep craning my neck looking for Migs to shoot down.

There are maybe twenty Marines in our truck, several coming back from Japan or the hospital ships, but most of us are new. The wounded men are understandably not enthusiastic. And the rest of us are uneasy. The little convoy of maybe half a dozen trucks grinds noisily and slowly up the grade in low gear.

The hills aren't much yet, but higher than before, with the real mountains still ahead and coming. Off to the right occasionally you can see the gray, cold-looking Sea of Japan through a fishing village or two at the head of a little cove, see the wooden masts of moored fishing boats. In the half-light of the coming winter everything is gray and muted, indistinct, a vague landscape like some offbeat school of oil painting that doesn't believe in chiaroscuro. And soon in the trucks you begin to hear the guns.

The artillery, of both sides, is always the first early-warning sound of war. Two mornings later we will be up on the main line of resistance, within small-arms range, and where firing isn't just sound but something that kills.

The stunning surprise, to me as to those who knew me, was my immediate reaction to hostile fire, a sense almost of exhilaration. Not quavering fear, no shock of nerve, no urge to flee. All of which I'd expected. Instead, sheer, manic excitement and an odd sense of happiness that I was here, a Marine. I was one of the guys. I was, to my astonishment, actually in the war.

Under fire, small arms or incoming artillery, I ducked, of course.

Everyone did. I dived into foxholes or trenches, but got up again and was swiftly upright, running around and shouting at people, not making much sense but certainly functioning, rather than coiling into fetal, whimpering postures. Ready, even eager to fire back, to make those other bastards dive into their damned holes. If only I had a target . . .

But why was this? It was very odd. I didn't understand, and still can't explain, why I wasn't afraid. At the Basic School, during infantry training at Pendleton, I was sure that I'd be scared. But from that very first day up on the MLR, the main line of resistance, atop Hill 749 in North Korea, with its gunfire and shelling, artillery slam-banging in, mortar rounds dropping from the sky, there was only a sort of mingled thrill and serenity of mission, of realizing all this shit was going on and I was still standing among what I assumed were more hardened, stronger, braver men, and I was actually doing the same bloody work they did.

Within days I was leading small patrols in the North Korean mountains, directing ambushes and firefights; months later I would be sprinting up sandstone hills against entrenched Chinese regulars hurling grenades at us while I fired away, yelling like hell and going for the barbed wire. Insane, maybe, but not scared. Not in daylight. Daylight was fine. The night was different. Anticipation of action was different as well; I always felt fine when the shooting began. It was waiting for it that was bad. How many of us felt that way? I wondered.

I never did get completely over a morbid fear of mines, of losing not one but both legs, or my anticipatory dread of night fighting. Whenever I knew I was ticketed to go out that night through the wire, I tensed up, gloomily watching the sun's slow descent toward dusk and the western horizon. I guess we all have our particular funks, and that was mine, fighting in the disorienting dark. Except for that, I did okay.

Why? How? What changes had battle and the Marine Corps wrought in a decidedly uncertain warrior? Those are among the questions I was asking as I worked on this book, and still hoped to answer. Maybe one day . . .

Other Marines seemed less uncertain; others like the Jim Webbs seemed born to fight.

4

Yale student John Chafee frets we will defeat Japan before he gets there.

THERE IS IN THIS BOOK ANOTHER, EARLIER-GENERATION UNITED States senator, a Yale man and gallant Marine officer. His story begins in New Haven on December 7, 1941. I will tell you about him shortly. When Pearl Harbor was attacked on that Sunday, the nation found itself standing at attention and ready to volunteer. For something, for anything.

In Sheepshead Bay, Brooklyn, as a thirteen-year-old eighth-grader, I organized a few kids the following morning, a Catholic school holiday honoring the Immaculate Conception, to collect newspapers (for some reason I thought this might assist the suddenly significant "war effort"). We bundled up some papers, piled them in a red wagon, and took them over to Saint Mark's Catholic rectory, to me the local symbol of authority, to ask that they be shipped off to President Roosevelt or some other official in Washington. Or anywhere a stack of old newspapers would somehow help defeat "the Japs." Father Bradley, a young priest who would later, as a military chaplain, be killed in a plane crash on New Guinea, shooed us away. I can't recall what happened to our trove of bundled newsprint. Just threw it away, most likely.

John Chafee did more meaningful (and sensible) things when World War II began. He was a Providence boy who had spent a year at school in Switzerland, attended Providence Country Day and then classy Deerfield Academy, where he played football and wrestled, and at nineteen was a sophomore at Yale, a varsity athlete, scion of a prominent Rhode Island family that boasted two governors of the state, a great-uncle in the U.S. Senate, and other distinguished folk. There was a little money as well ("My family was involved in manufacturing," he would say simply). They actually owned an iron foundry and later a company that made measuring instruments, and had plenty of the sort of connections old-line families of means customarily have. With his connections alone, but surely as a Yale man, and an athlete, Chafee probably would have qualified for some sort of officer candidate program, but instead he enlisted in the Marine Corps as a private and was shipped off to boot training at Parris Island. What drove that decision? Why did he join the Marines?

This is how Chafee recalled it years later:

"I'd never given the Marine Corps much thought prior to the US entering World War II. I'd just had my 19th birthday, was on the wrestling team and a member of the Yale ROTC. In not my most accurate prediction, I was concerned the US would win the war before our ROTC unit ever got into it, so I thought I'd better hurry up and join up. What drew me to the Marines? I'm not sure, but do clearly remember a poster of a Marine, charging up the beach, holding an '03 rifle over his head, wearing a World War I helmet, and the bold-lettered message: 'Join the Marines—First to Fight.'

"That's for me! I thought, and went to my hometown—Providence, Rhode Island—recruiting station to join up. I still have my notice from the recruiter. It says, 'Recruiting Station, Providence, 27 January, 1942. Chafee—report to this office on 3 February 1942 at 7:30 AM for transfer to Boston for final check, and if OK, enlistment in the U.S. Marine Corps. Be sure to bring the things I mentioned. Staff sergeant Stanley H. Rose.'"

As a proper Yalie, Chafee kept a diary. "Monday, Feb. 2, resigned from college. Tuesday Feb. 3 at recruit office 7:30. Ride in cold station wagon to Boston with 6 others. Have temperature taken and wait and wait. Told at 1:30 Boston quota filled, and we've got to wait a week or two. Station wagon back to Providence. What a mess." Eleven days later the diary picks up: "Feb. 14. Took trolley downtown to recruit office at 7:30. Station wagon to Boston. Brief physical—only took temperature. Waited and waited in hall—signed papers, took oath—went to cafeteria for lunch—government gave us 30 cents."

So far it all sounds like today's Corps, especially the waiting, though the thirty cents lunch money may have gone up.

"And off we went to Parris Island by train—changed trains at Yemassee, South Carolina, to ancient coaches of Charlestown and Western Carolina RR—go to Port Royal, and then trucks to Parris Island."

So began John Chafee's service to the United States, as a Marine in two wars, as a state legislator, as governor of his state, as secretary of the navy, as a four-term United States senator.

Those early months of World War II were, for America, a mournful time, a debacle, one military disaster after another, an uninterrupted series of defeats. The Japanese seemed unbeatable, winning everywhere, our battleship fleet sunk at Pearl, Manila captured, the Bataan survivors sent off on their "death march," Guam and Wake Island fallen. Our Allies were doing just as badly. The British lost Malaya, including Singapore; thousands of British Tommies marched off at the point of Japanese bayonets to build that bridge on the River Kwai; Hong Kong surrendered. The Dutch East Indies held out gallantly but briefly; Burma was invaded, India threatened, and Japanese planes were bombing Australia's northern coast. MacArthur was smuggled out to safety just before Corregidor surrendered. An impertinent Japanese sub surfaced by night off Long Beach to shell the California oil refineries. Our navy won a few, at Midway and the Coral Sea, but on land, Americans lost everywhere. Which was why Guadalcanal was important.

The Canal, as Marines would christen it, was a large island in the Solomons, chill mountains and malarial swamps, with big sharks cruising offshore, cannibals in the impenetrable interior, and manned by a strong Japanese garrison that had just built an airstrip from which enemy fighters and bombers could threaten U.S. sea-lanes and bomb American targets. The newly formed 1st Marine Division of about 15,000 men, few of them ever having seen combat, was given the job of launching the country's first offensive land action, tasked with invading, seizing, and holding Guadalcanal for use as a forward base from which we could finally counterattack the everywhere victorious Japanese. On August 7, 1942, exactly eight months after the attack on Pearl, the first wave of American Marines landed unopposed on Guadalcanal's beaches.

Marine private John Hubbard Chafee, late of Yale, was among them.

The peaceful arrival was deceptive. The division was soon engaged in combat against determined, even ferocious Japanese opposition. The fighting raged at sea as well, with three American and one Australian cruiser being sunk in a single night's action against the Imperial Navy. Conditions were dreadful, supplies short; fever hit most of the men. In what some hoped might be a campaign of weeks, Chafee's unit (the 11th Marines, artillery) was still there, still fighting, four months later, before being pulled out on December 15 to be shipped to Australia for rest and refit. Chafee spent nine months Down Under and returned to the States in November 1943. Someone had noticed they had a pretty good Marine with a year-plus of college on their hands, and the young corporal (by now) was sent to an officer candidates detachment at Camp Elliott, San Diego, then to Quantico, where in June 1944 he was commissioned a second lieutenant and sent to combat intelligence school. There were a couple of other stateside postings, and in March he sailed back to the Pacific. Back to the fighting. This time, on May 16, John landed on Okinawa and fought there as an intelligence officer of the 6th Marine Division until July 8. When the war ended in August, Chafee and the Marine Corps were preparing for the final landings, the assault on the Japanese home islands, where the casualties were expected to be staggering. Instead, peace.

Though not quite yet for a few Marines, like Chafee and the 6th Division, who were shipped off to Tsingtao in North China in October to accept surrender of the last Japanese troops and to cool things in a bandit-ridden, outlaw, and chaotic country where Chiang and his Nationalists were already shaping up to fight Mao and his Chinese Communist army.

Back in San Francisco in November '45, Chafee was discharged, returned to sophomore year at Yale, and to the wrestling team. Here was a combat veteran of nearly four years in the Pacific, and he was still a college soph, and once more a tournament-winning varsity wrestler. He was tapped for Skull and Bones, the junior secret honor society, got his degree in '47, and immediately entered Harvard Law; he graduated in 1950 and was admitted to the state bar in Rhode Island. He met Virginia Coates skiing in Vermont, they married, he began practicing law in Providence, and on June 25, 1950, the Korean War began. Chafee, a Reserve captain, was recalled to active duty in March of 1951.

I later asked him why, with a pregnant wife and plenty of combat behind him, Chafee didn't look for some way out, some easy stateside duty. "Well, I was bored practicing law and wasn't making all that much money and thought, maybe we'll be stationed in California for a year or so, and Ginnie and I thought that sounded pretty good." Instead, he was shipped out to Korea in August and ended up in the bloody fighting for North Korean ridgelines in September. There in one firefight lasting four days, 90 Marines were killed and more than 800 wounded. He was commanding Dog Company, 2nd Battalion, 7th Marines, when I arrived as a replacement second lieutenant and reported in to "the Skipper," as his men called him.

He was then twenty-seven or twenty-eight years old (I thought of him as middle-aged), tall and trim, having lost weight, as most Marines had in the autumn fighting, sported a luxuriant dark brown mustache (the 'stache would not survive the war) and a high color. I knew his name, his rank, that he was my commanding officer, and that the men considered him the beau ideal of young officers, as approximately God. I remember mostly how cool and apparently unflappable he was, especially during night alarms when I reached him by sound-power phone from my bunker to tell him, excitedly, what was going on at our stretch of the MLR. I was a hyper kid and unsure; he was a mature leader, calming me down, suggesting what next to do, assuring me that if I felt the need, he would make his way along the line and be there to help. Traveling by night along that mountainous line, icy and snow-covered, with North Korean troops on the same ridge, was a risky proposition, but it was a trek Chafee often made in the dark.

I can see him still by day, loping easily as athletes do, along the ridgelines or down the trenches with a sort of alpenstock in one fist, ducking into this bunker or that, chatting with the men and checking on them, joshing or concerned, no fire-eater or charm boy as you sometimes find among officers, but just a good professional at his tasks, formed by years of combat, looking to his men and their readiness. I knew nothing of his background, thought in fact that he was a French Canadian. I knew nothing of Yale or Harvard or family or of his experience in the big war, not even that he'd fought on the Canal, which by now had passed into Marine legend. I only knew that whatever the hour of night, Chafee was at the other end of the sound-power phone hookup by which we platoon leaders could contact him if we were unsure or confused or confronted with a situation we didn't understand or couldn't cope with.

Long after Korea, on first reading Keegan's *Face of Battle*, I was reminded of the Chafee we knew when Keegan quoted from an essay by Donald Hankey, killed on the Somme in 1916, entitled "The Beloved Captain." Hankey wrote: "He came in the early days . . . tall, erect, smiling. For a few days he just watched, then he started work. Picked out the awkward ones. . . . marched them away by themselves. His confidence was infectious . . . his simplicity . . . very soon the awkward squad found themselves awkward no longer. The fact was he had won his way into our hearts . . . if anyone had a sore foot he knelt and looked at it. If a blister had to be lanced, he very likely would lance it himself. There was something almost religious about it . . . something of the Christ about it."

I might well have been one of Chafee's "awkward squad." I was his youngest, and greenest (in so many ways) lieutenant. Bob Simonis and Mack Allen had been Marines before and had fought the Japanese; Red Phillips and Tex Lissman were both older than Chafee himself; and he took time to continue my training, to counsel me, to nod approval or to chew me out. When an idiotic order came down from division that after any firefight, the men would retrieve the brass, the shell casings, and cartridge detritus left on the snow or the frozen earth, to be recycled back in the States, I ignored it as absurd. Chafee called me on it. "I didn't take it as a serious order," I told him. "All orders are to be taken seriously by Marine officers," he said coldly. I later learned he, too, thought the order was ridiculous (it was soon rescinded), but it wasn't the type of issue worth fighting over. You said, "Aye, aye," and did the damned thing. Whatever it was. Chafee taught me that.

The fighting along the main line of resistance at that time occurred mostly at night, patrolling and ambushes at night, raids by one side or the other at night, mean, nasty little brawls by small units, the North Koreans still hanging on to a piece of the ridgeline, at some places only forty or fifty yards distant. It was trench warfare that men in Flanders fields of the first great war would have recognized; Lee's men and Grant's would have recalled it from the Wilderness campaign. The artillery on both sides was too good for much fighting in daylight. It would just murder you. So we sniped at each other, raided each other's trench lines, hated the mines, damn them! and fought through the cold and suffered under the wind out of Siberia.

The first or second day I was on line atop Hill 749 (its height in meters) a random mortar shot landed atop a Dog Company bunker where four Marines, enjoying a rare balmy day in the North Korean winter, lazed in the sun. It killed three of them and took the legs of the fourth. I ran to the place along with others, not knowing why, but just to be there. I remember the wounded man's moans. He was a cousin to one of the dead men, a Massachusetts boy, and he was thinking about the family.

"How do I tell his ma?" How he could tell the family their boy was dead? Almost as if it had been his fault, and not the North Koreans' mortar. I didn't know the dead men; Chafee did. I watched his face. Sad, resigned, anguished, all at the same time.

But this company had taken plenty of casualties during September. They were accustomed to death. Just not having it come like this, not on the jump under hostile fire but unexpectedly on a sunny day. Well, Chafee said, try getting Marines not to enjoy the sunshine. Just try. I'll write their people, he said, half to himself. How many letters like that had he written already? In another few days maybe this platoon would be my responsibility, this or one of the other rifle platoons. Letters would be mine to write, a kid, a year out of college, still feeling like an imposter.

They carted off the dead. Korean laborers, who backpacked supplies out of the valley and up to the ridgelines each morning, would lug the stiffs (and that was a word we all used, trying to make death less personal) back down to battalion and eventually the morgue, collecting the bodies the way big cities picked up the trash each morning. Except these were healthy, shouting, laughing young American boys. Suddenly dead.

A night later the North Koreans hit us with three or four hundred mortars, and behind the incoming, their infantry came through the snow toward the Marine lines. The machine guns caught them as they worked through the barbed wire, all except one who got to the roof of a bunker, meaning to shove a grenade down the stovepipe. I saw him up there, thought he was a Marine, wondered why the damned fool was standing up like that in a firefight, and then another Marine snapped off a shot past me to kill him. The Marine rifleman looked at me contemptuously.

I should have killed the Korean myself. Before he killed me. That's how dumb I still was. When day broke, there were five bodies in the wire, North Koreans. Marines picked through their pockets, as they were taught to do, looking for intelligence; they came up with some paper currency, sodden with drying blood. One of them held the wad out to me, laughing.

"Here, Lieutenant, a souvenir for the kiddies."

Thanks, I said. What else should I have said, and I pocketed the dead man's money. Still have it today in a lockerbox. Dumb, huh?

Red Phillips, the executive officer, and a half dozen of us tracked the surviving North Koreans that morning down the forward slope toward the valley of the Soyang-gang, following their tracks in the snow, and the bloodstains the wounded left behind. Chafee sent us after them. "Take prisoners if you can, Red. If you can't, kill them." Matter of fact about it, he was. One of the wounded kept stopping to take a shit. He had worms, you could see them writhing in the stool, and he was gut shot, too. Plenty of blood in the snow and in the shit. One Marine, a big guy with a Browning automatic rifle and a grease gun as well, bounded downhill, hot after them. But we ran out of real estate and never did catch up. I was kind of glad, remembering that poor bastard wormy with the runs and shot at the same time. I had to learn about things like that. You saved emotion for our side. Let the other bastards mourn their own.

Chafee gave me the third platoon eventually when Ed Flynn was rotated home. He'd been with the platoon when they assaulted Hill 749 and the men trusted Ed. They weren't sure about me.

After a time it was Chafee's turn to be rotated, first to a staff job someplace, and then out of Korea entirely and home. Charlie Logan took over the company, and I was promoted to executive officer when Red Phillips left. I didn't see Chafee after that for a long time.

I became a journalist, covered Washington, then was sent to London and Paris. Chafee's name turned up in *Time* magazine, one of the Republican comers, a governor with presidential prospects. Then he was elected to the Senate. In 1990, when they published a book of mine about Korea and I did the talk shows in D.C., Chafee invited the other senators who'd fought in Korea—Rudman, Glenn, John Warner—and we got together in his Senate office. Spending his own dough, he had bought copies of the book and I signed them. A reporter from the *Providence Journal* was there taking notes and offhandedly asked Chafee where he had been when the Korean war began.

"I didn't even know about it," Chafee said. "I was on a yacht sailing in the Newport to Bermuda race and my girl [soon to be his wife, Ginnie] was in Bermuda waiting for me at the dock, and that's all I was thinking about."

Chafee spoke often of war, privately or on the Senate floor, frequently in speeches. Not about his own heroics, but about other men, mainly Marines, and their performance. He'd seen so much combat and in so many disparate places, he'd become something of a connoisseur of war, appreciating and even savoring its nuances and subtleties, its vintage moments and masters of the craft.

In a talk at the Marine Corps War Memorial in Arlington in 1994, the senator briefly recalled Guadalcanal, an almost antique battle by then. "We landed on Guadalcanal armed with the Springfield '03 rifle, designed in 1903, a bolt-action single-shot weapon—fire a shot, pull back the bolt, ejecting the spent cartridge, push the bolt forward, and fire another shot. It had a clip of five rounds, nothing automatic about

it. Our landing craft were wooden Higgins boats: no ramps, we clam-
bered over the side and dropped into the water. Bazookas didn't exist.
Flame throwers were experimental; the operator had to be careful not
to incinerate himself. Radar was in its infancy. The Japanese controlled
the seas and control of the air was touch and go."

Speaking of why Marines fight so effectively, he recalled the
bloody lagoon of Tarawa. "What goes into taking a young man fresh
from high school and nine months later putting him into four feet of
water off Tarawa where he has to wade 500 yards ashore against machine gun fire from entrenched Japanese defenders?" In Chafee's judgment, there were five basic principles in the making of Marines:
"Rigorous training. Strict discipline. The installation of pride, in himself and pride in the Corps. A sense of responsibility toward each
other, officer for enlisted man, enlisted man for officer. Finally, deter-
mination to prevail, and not to let down our country, our Corps, or our
fellow Marines."

Chafee would have political wars to fight as well.

He was a Republican elected over and over in a Democratic state.
Not that it was ever easy. His moderate ways got him into trouble with
the right wing and at one point he was demoted from his position as
Senate whip. During one primary in the 1990s the NRA helped finance
and back a Republican opponent who assailed Chafee as "soft on
guns." John Chafee soft on guns? The guy who dropped out of Yale
to go to war, who fought on the Canal and Okinawa and in North
Korea? Who the hell were these bastards with their patriotism on their
sleeves, an American flag in every lapel, and a Vietnam draft deferment
in every pocket? My own outrage was apparently shared by his voters
back home, and they nominated and then reelected Chafee once more.

We corresponded, talked by phone; we visited back and forth when
he got to Manhattan for an Audubon Society dinner, and several times
on my trips to D.C. or Rhode Island. I followed his career in the *Times*.
He wasn't a wisecracking comic, too serious for that, but Don Imus
liked him, put him on the morning radio show. When I asked what he
might do with his life after the Senate, John had a ready answer. "If my
health permits, start a boys' wrestling club in the inner city. I still have
a few holds I could show them and there's a lot of anger you can work

off, wrestling." Other rich and famous men retired to golf and Palm Beach. Chafee would coach kids to wrestle. Then some years ago I was in Washington doing a story for *Parade* and called John. Could he and Ginnie have dinner on me at the Jockey Club? Sure. He had a cranky back, he said, and was impatient with the current mood and tone of the Senate, the "contentious" spirit of the place he had so long loved and considered a second home. We had a cocktail, ordered dinner and a bottle of wine, and the three of us talked about our children, mostly. Then he asked what I was writing these days.

"Well, I have a new novel. *The Marines of Autumn.* And to be honest, I stole you for the protagonist, changing the name of course."

In writing celebrity interviews and profiles for *Parade* I'd grown accustomed to hearing, "Now, wait a minute. Did you clear this with my PR people? Have you talked to the lawyers?"

None of that crap with Senator Chafee.

Instead, "Well, Jim, that's the damndest thing!" He turned to his wife. "Ginnie, have I ever been in a novel?"

"I don't think so, Johnny."

He toasted the book happily, and I promised to send him an early copy as soon as I got the galley proofs.

Later that week he felt poorly and Ginnie called the doctor. He died over the weekend at Bethesda Naval Hospital.

My daughter Fiona and I drove up to Providence for the funeral. The Clintons came, the Marine commandant, half the Senate, John McCain and the others, flying up in a single government plane, every pol in Rhode Island, and lots of family. "What a man! What a life!" one of his sons, Zechariah, cried out in eulogy. And the mournful church filled with joy and elation at having known him. Those like me who, as a scared kid, remembered the young Chafee of the Korean ridgelines, lean and brown and loping along, alpenstock in hand, seeing to his Marines.

If only the old soldier who'd fought the Japanese, the North Koreans, and the Communist Chinese had lived another few years to get those inner-city kids of his together somewhere and start them wrestling. His death was their loss. And ours.

5

Ron Christmas outwits the Corps and stays on duty despite his wounds.

VIETNAM ALWAYS GOT MORE INK THAN THE SO-CALLED FORGOTten war of Korea. Not always good ink, either.

Vietnam wasn't a bigger war than Korea, but longer and more bitterly divisive here at home, hated by millions of Americans, grinding on for ten bloody years instead of Korea's three. We lost 37,000 American dead in Korea's thirty-seven months, a thousand a month, month after month for three years. Vietnam took 54,000 U.S. lives, and those over a decade. Here at home, Vietnam was much more controversial than Korea, and had angry Americans marching in protest, or fleeing to Canada or Sweden to avoid the draft, college boys chanting, "Hell no, we won't go," other college boys being shot down at Kent State by kids the same age in National Guard uniforms, and customarily polite civilians in the street spitting at returning veterans of deadly, very tough fighting. Yet Marines and other Americans were still going to Vietnam. And dying there.

Many of today's most famous politicians ducked the Vietnam draft or service over there, Bill Clinton, George W. Bush, Dick Cheney. Chuck Hagel and Jim Webb and John McCain and Bob Kerrey went to Vietnam, and so did John Kerry, and some of his enemies never forgave candidate Kerry for later denouncing the war in congressional testimony.

George R. (for Ron) Christmas, an Ivy Leaguer himself (University of Pennsylvania, class of 1962, BA, with a major in history), wasn't a protestor or a draft dodger. He not only went to Vietnam and fought, but very nearly lost a leg in battle and was awarded the Marine Corps' second highest decoration, the Navy Cross. In 2006 I first met Ron Christmas, spent a pleasantly informative day in Virginia with the man, and being shrewd in my expenditures, rather crassly permitted him to buy lunch at a Marine hangout run by an old major, Richard T. "Rick" Spooner, his joint called the Globe & Laurel, located at the crossroads of I-95 and Triangle, Virginia, just outside the main gate of the Quantico base. I could tell you stories about Triangle and the local girls who lived there, just beyond the main gate but within reach of not only of brutal and licentious soldiery, but far worse, of randy young Marine officers seeking debutantes and Southern belles. Or failing that, just plain pretty, backwoods, up-country Virginia girls.

Instead, let Ron Christmas tell you how the young Ron became a Marine and something about his war. About why he fought.

A native Philadelphian, born in 1940, Ron joined the NROTC during college and on graduation was commissioned a second lieutenant in the USMCR. He went on active duty, took the Basic School class given all new Marine lieutenants at Quantico, served in the usual stateside posts, was promoted to first lieutenant, and went regular (as they say). Christmas must have been seen as having potential, being stationed for a time at 8th and I, the prestigious and politically well connected Marine Barracks in Washington, where they stage the famed invitation-only Sunset Parade, so beloved of visiting senators and congressmen from nearby Capitol Hill, and by their influential constituents, and where he was promoted to captain and company commander. In July 1967, after five years as a Marine, Ron Christmas finally went to war.

At first, he had a service company in Vietnam (what old salts call "rear echelon pogue duty"), but by the start of 1968 Christmas was into the real stuff, in command of Hotel Company, a rifle outfit in the 2nd Battalion of the 5th Marine Regiment. Ron takes it from there.

"By that time we had been lulled into complacency. Giap and Ho [the senior North Vietnam and Viet Cong leaders] said, we must bring in the main North Vietnam Army and the Viet Cong and our underground people, and by January 30, they were ready. They picked the holiday [Tet] stand-down period and some of their units attacked on the 30th and the rest on January 31. They infiltrated and overran Hue City. The 2nd Battalion 5th Marines [Ron's outfit] was down on the Troi River. Hue was seized by two regiments of the North Vietnam Army, except for two pockets we held. The Citadel on the Perfume River was held by the ARVN, Army of Vietnam [our allies], and another stronghold held out. The 1st Battalion 1st Marines and the 2nd Battalion 5th Marines were sent into the city to regain it. Later the 1st Battalion 5th Marines and other units came in.

"I was Hotel Company commander and we were already in a big firefight down on the Troi River. I had a platoon on two bridges and we tried to support them in the middle of the night. Those kids called down artillery fire on themselves [something an infantry unit only does in extremis]. But 'Big Ernie' [Cheatham, the battalion commander] told me, 'You've got 'em on the run. Attack!' Our battalion had them [the enemy] boxed in when a cease-fire was called. I was pissed. Hotel [Company] was ordered to move back and Fox [Company] went in. They took fire and the next morning, the very next day, I got a call. 'Go in,' they told me."

So began what would for Captain Ron Washington be his longest day, the start of his longest years.

"We formed a convoy to fight our way back into the city. We came up in trucks, in daylight, and two blocks later, we got ambushed. Our kids returned fire and we fought our way into the MACV compound [I asked and I think Ron said the acronym stood for Military Assistance Command, Vietnam, something like that]. It was like the old 'Beau Geste' days, and today that place is a five-star hotel. I've been back there to see it. Next day, 'Big Ernie' comes in. He says we hold the southern side of town, the old French colonial part of Hue, the good hotels and the restaurants and cafes, the bars, and in a block by block fight, we took the provincial capitol building. Resistance began to wane. And elements of the 1st Battalion 5th Marines came in. It was Friday the 13th of February [the battle had now been going on for two full weeks, what they called at Quantico "combat in built-up areas"], and I got wounded that day."

It was a Vietnamese B-40 rocket that hit Captain Christmas.

"It took the nerves out of my left leg. That Navy Cross they gave me really belongs to my Marines and to the Navy corpsman who saved me. I had a high fever and was evacuated to Da Nang. There were so many casualties and so much chaos I ended up on the Air Force side of the base instead of the Navy side. The first thing I remember seeing was an Air Force nurse all in white. They wore white back here but our nurses didn't and when I saw this woman in white approaching me I thought, well, so this is it, this is what it's like. When they realized I wasn't Air Force they sent me on to Cam Ranh Bay but the Navy lost my records and for two and a half months I was lost in the system. We had two kids and I'd never even seen one of them and all my wife [the former Sherrill J. Lownds] knew was that I wasn't dead but they didn't know how bad I was hurt or where I was or when she would hear from me. I had a lot of surgeries and then they sent me to Philadelphia Naval Hospital [where Mrs. Christmas would finally see her wounded husband]."

From what Ron said, it wasn't his wounds or physical condition that most concerned him, but his fear that the Marine Corps would kick him out, as no longer physically up to active service. During continuing medical care and physical rehab, and being a good people person, Ron called on pals and charmed old NCOs and navy petty officers into a benign sort of bureaucratic conspiracy intended to keep young Captain Christmas, not quite thirty, on active duty in the Marines.

One cleverly doctored optimistic fitness report followed another, each seeming to promise that Ron was very nearly back in top form, an aggressive young officer impatient to get back into the fight, if only just one more brief period of limited service could be arranged. It was all a con job, of course, an absolute swindle. As General Christmas admits now, "They hid me at the Basic School for a while. I was getting stronger and they sent me to armored warfare school." Apparently another good safe house in which to hide. Next came a gig as instructor at the American army's JFK Institute for Military Assistance at Fort Bragg, North Carolina. It began to look as if young Captain Christmas was doing a national tour of American military bases, Bob Hope and the USO without the chorus girls. "In all," the future general told me, "I had about three years of limited duty, and then I went back to work."

Christmas had played the military rules and red tape like a violin and eventually was able to circumvent the very real possibility he'd be thrown out of the Corps on physical grounds and, in the end, returned to full, robust, active duty. He ticked off for me and in order, starting in 1971, a list of his postings. In '71 he reported in to Marine headquarters as an aide to the deputy commandant and a year later was promoted to major. He did another tour at the Basic School in Quantico, served in Okinawa with the 4th Marines, then commanded Marine Barracks at Annapolis, was promoted to light colonel, had a training command at Parris Island, was selected to attend the Army War College in Carlisle, Pennsylvania, where the military sends its best. You sort of get the idea this guy was a very promising young gentleman, destined to wear stars, maybe even become commandant. While there at Carlisle, a man who never rests, Colonel Christmas found the time to go back to college, taking a master's degree in public administration at Shippensburg University.

Shortly after I met and spoke with the general, and without his knowledge, I received a letter from former Marine PFC Charles B. Wilson Jr. of Lexington, Kentucky, who now lives in Jerome, Idaho. In the letter, Wilson writes mostly about his own war, Vietnam and the bloody fighting at Hue, but then this one reference grabbed me.

"On the evening of the day I was shot [February 1968] and then blown up by a mortar round," Wilson wrote, "my tour of duty as a warrior came to an end. My commanding officer, Captain Christmas, had just saved my life by hand-carrying me city blocks to an aid station. I was in a state of nonconcern because of the amount of morphine the medics had given me. This did not seem to affect my will to survive. . . ." Charlie Wilson, as he now signs himself, went on in considerable detail about his treatment and evacuation and recovery but it was that casual mention of Ron Christmas under fire and his devotion to one of his men, and sheer endurance in carrying a wounded Marine "city blocks" to safety, that stayed with me.

I wonder if Charlie Wilson knew that his Captain Christmas eventually made lieutenant general, three stars. In the Marine Corps, which doesn't throw rank around casually, that's a very big deal. A Marine was wearing stars who once feared the Corps was about to truncate a promising career and throw him out, just because a North Vietnamese rocket took out a big chunk of his left leg.

When he and I met at Quantico in September 2006, now Lieutenant General Christmas (Retired), had been out of the Marine Corps for about ten years, was looking more "Father Christmas" with that white hair than "General Christmas," but he was hardly inactive or ready for the shelf, gimping slightly but striding along on the rough ground of what was really still a construction site. He was by then president of the Marine Corps Heritage Foundation, a private nonprofit which, among other things, was partnering with the Marine Corps itself to create a smashing new National Museum of the Marine Corps that was to open that November 10, birthday of the Corps, with a dedication by the president as commander in chief.

Just over six feet tall, solid but not beefy, Ron walked with only a limp on the left side, and trotted me around the hilly, 135-acre site like a much younger man. Not quite the young Captain Christmas of Hotel Company of the 5th Marines fighting block to block through Hue with Big Ernie urging him on, but you get the idea. When we sat together on a kind of stone bench talking about the new museum and his hopes for it, I got him to tell me the story of his fight at Hue. And of his own lengthy and painful rehabilitation. Which got him talking about those hospital months and of other, more seriously wounded Marines.

"I used to hobble down the hall visiting them in their wards, paraplegics and quadriplegics, men so much more worse off, that I forgot my own problems. In those days, men wounded like that knew their careers were over, that they were finished. You could see the depression in their faces. These new prostheses they have now are wonderful. These kids have hope now; they have a chance. And the Marine Corps has gotten smart, too. They aren't automatically kicked out for their wounds. Many of them can stay. They're not always finished." He liked those changes in the Corps.

At the end of our talk on the stone bench, Ron Christmas got up, shook my hand, and apologized, "I wish I could have been more articulate."

"No," I said. "You weren't articulate, General, you were eloquent."

6

Sergeant John Fitzgerald: "I killed an awful lot of people in two days."

Such matters are always subjective judgments, never precise, but as a rifle platoon leader I thought Sergeant John Fitzgerald of Michigan was the most natural warrior I ever knew. More authoritative, and most impressive, was what Captain Chafee, who had himself seen so much more fighting, thought of Fitz, and how as a senator years later he remembered him in a speech.

Fitz was a big, blond, twenty-year-old kid with the good looks but none of the soft edges of a Hollywood juvenile of the school of Tab Hunter or Richard Jaeckel. He was tougher, a harder man, and, when he needed to be, meaner, a stone killer. In one firefight on Hill 749 in North Korea, they said Fitz killed nineteen. He himself was unsure of the stats, but he admitted in conversation with me, "I killed an awful lot of people in two days, Lieutenant."

I phoned Fitz in November 2006 out in Byron, Michigan, where he now lives with his wife, Theresa, who teaches the fourth grade in nearby Linden, telling him that, for a new book I was working on, I had some questions. "It's cold as hell and pissing rain," he informed me. "Jack and I are just sitting around, so go ahead." Jack was his dog, who now promptly barked, as if on cue. "There must be a deer around," said my old sergeant. "A beer?" I asked incredulous, "Does the dog drink beer?"

"Lieutenant," Fitz said patiently, "I said he must have smelled a deer. With a 'd.' But, yes, of an afternoon, Jack and I will sit around and have a beer."

He sounded happy, and when the dog barked again, he seemed content as well, so I concluded everything was quite normal chez Fitzgerald and launched into my usual catechism. "Why did you join the Marine Corps?"

"I ask myself that still," he said with a rough laugh. Yes, wanting to play football and not having the grades for college had something to do with it. But there was a more serious, tragic motivation.

"I was born in Minnesota, but there wasn't much work there and my father came down to Michigan a couple of times to find work and finally he got a job in the [auto industry] shops and so they moved here to stay. I was born in '31, so I grew up in the middle of the Second World War. The reason I joined up was a guy named Gordon, who was killed at Peleliu. Gordon Walker. I didn't know anything about the Marine Corps, didn't care about it. But Gordon came home on leave once from the Pacific and I saw him. No dress blues or anything, just in his khakis, but I remember how he looked. I was a thirteen- or fourteen-year-old kid, and I remembered. And then word came that he was killed. So when I graduated from high school in 1948 I joined the Marine Corps right out of school."

Following boot camp Fitzgerald pulled guard duty at Key West "and was there until Korea started [June 1950]. A couple of officers tried to get me into an ROTC program. So I took a test. But Korea was now on and rather than wait for the test results, I went to this pear-shaped little captain who had a Congressional Medal. He looked like the last guy you'd ever think would be charging up hills at the Chosin Reservoir but he did. I made my pitch, told him, 'Sir, if I don't get into this war, I may never get into a war.' So they put aside all that ROTC stuff and my tests and I was assigned to a replacement draft." The only thing bothering Fitz at this point was that "I'd never been an infantryman. Just guard duty. They ran me through some infantry training at Pendleton but that was all."

In Korea he was sent up to Dog Company of the 7th Marines as a replacement. He must have done okay because by September 1951, when the 7th and 1st Marine Regiments would be mounting their frontal assault on the North Korean ridgelines in the Taebaek Mountains of eastern North Korea, Fitz had been promoted to fire-team leader. A Marine fire team of that time consisted of a leader, usually a corporal, armed with an M-1 rifle, a BAR man with his Browning automatic rifle, and two more infantrymen with rifles. That was where Fitz made his bones, the attack on what we later called Hill 749 and which to me Fitz said was called Bunker Hill, or simply, "that big hill."

Whatever you called it, the height of ground along the Kanmubong Ridge was part of one wall of an extinct volcano rearing itself skyward out of the flat, circular piece of ground called the Punchbowl. And it was where John Fitzgerald was turned into something of a local legend in Dog Company. Other stretches of the ridge had more romantic labels, Heartbreak Ridge and Bloody Ridge, but 749, a lousy hill that didn't rate a real name, but only its height in meters, was as lethal as any of them. Nearly a thousand Marine casualties in one four-day firefight for a no-name piece of high ground. Later on, of course, lots of other Marines died in holding the hill against enemy counterattacks. But that was later and in my time.

John Fitzgerald was one of those September casualties. But not before experiencing considerable thrills and a few excitements in getting up that damned hill. I interviewed him about it twice and also sent along for clarification an old photo of what our platoon looked like after 749, because some parts of his story are confused, erratic. Which, when you read the account, and realize how shot up he was, is pretty understandable.

I appreciated why Fitz and his men called it Bunker Hill because the south-facing forward slope of the entire Kanmubong Ridge was simply honeycombed with North Korean bunkers, many of which we would later use ourselves, living in them over the late fall and winter. What I couldn't grasp was how Marines and American soldiers ever made it up that hill under fire and at that degree of slope. I'd first climbed it myself in November as a replacement for officers hit or killed in September, and found it a steep climb without anyone shooting at me, though in a foot of early snow. I asked Fitz to tell me again what he remembered of the attack on Hill 749.

"I was a fire-team leader [in Dog Company] and we were tied in with Fox Company. You notice in that picture there's almost no one from the first squad. We pretty much got wiped out. So was my fire team. There was a bright moon and McClellan was shot through the mouth and Mr. Flynn [Lieutenant Ed Flynn, their platoon leader and the guy I would eventually replace] was hit and suddenly I found myself alone with Luke [for Luke the Gook, meaning the enemy] for company and I saw two more Lukes standing there and I got them with my M-1 and I threw a grenade into one of the bunkers. We were on the reverse slope. We got over the ridgeline and were heading downhill and there were three more bunkers. A couple of us were sheltering in the shadow of a bush against the moonlight. You know how moonlight throws a shadow, and [on] the other side of the bush was another Luke. I jumped out and gave him six rounds to the gut and he went down and was lying there gurgling and I got out my knife to cut his throat, but then suddenly they were all around us and firing. And I'm standing there looking stupid with a knife in my hand.

"Godsey, the machine gunner, got hit, Bobby Knight told me. Bobby's still alive, lives in Grand Blanc, Michigan. I'll ask him for you, Lieutenant. But that was when Hollywood was killed, the assistant machine gunner attached to us. I don't know why we called him Hollywood. I took over the machine gun. There were two Banzai attacks. They say I killed nineteen. I dunno about that, but I killed an awful lot of people in two days. They wrote me up big time, but the company commander had something on me, I mouthed off or something, and I ended up with the Bronze Star with combat V."

These are Fitz's words, but there is confusion here. I've since met Bobby Knight of Grand Blanc and he tells me he was the one they called Hollywood. And he assured me he hadn't been killed. Chuck Curley, another machine gunner in the fight, backs up Knight as the only Hollywood in the company and says he definitely is alive and well.

Fitz picked up the account. "King was the only one left and we were on the wrong side of the hill. And a grenade hit me above the ankle and my knee went out. I slid down the hill but my leg got wrapped in com wire and I look up and there's this gook with a burp gun. I don't know how I did it, but I used my M-1 rifle on him like a pistol. But his burp gun got me." After that Fitzgerald was taken off Hill 749 and processed through the medical mill, ending up on the hospital ship *Haven*. "At some point an officer asked me how I was and I said, 'Sir, we haven't had a bite to eat for two days. And now it's the third day, I think.' So I got some food but also a six-hour operation. You know how grenade fragments feel when they hit you? The metal that comes off a grenade is white hot, as if guys were holding lighted cigarettes against my legs."

At that stage of the Korean fighting only the terribly wounded, chest and head mostly, or those who'd lost limbs or had been blinded or were otherwise disabled, were shipped home to the States. The rest were patched up on the hospital ships or in Japan and then sent back to their outfits, back to combat. So by the time I arrived at Dog Company back up on Hill 749, Fitzgerald, now a buck sergeant with a medal, was back in harness. And would shortly become one of my three squad leaders in the platoon I took over from Ed Flynn. I asked Fitz when it was that other Marines began to look up to him and when Captain Chafee first singled him out for praise. Was it the medal? Was it his killing role on 749? Or was it something else?

To jog Fitz's memory I read him a few lines from speech Senator Chafee gave a Marine group on February 28, 1998, half a century after the fighting.

"In Korea we were sending out a small patrol from my rifle company into the steep valley that separated us from the North Koreans. The leader was to be a young sergeant named Fitzgerald—he had that special quality called 'leadership.' As the patrol made its preparations, a lance corporal named Burns sought me out. He hadn't been a particularly helpful individual. But he said he'd learned Fitz was going to take that patrol, and he wanted to go with him. That impressed me and even though I had some reservations, I said OK. Later, Fitzgerald told me Burns did an excellent job, and I thereafter looked at him in a different light."

"I don't think so," Fitz said in rebuttal and surprisingly. "You know how that winter they had us set up ambushes at night and we were ordered just to stay in one spot and not move around because we'd make noise. Well, we just lay out there in the snow shivering and not doing anything. It was so cold we came in early; they had to let us come in. I had the idea it would be better if they let us go out there and move around. Stay warm and alert that way. So I suggested that. The captain [Chafee] walks up to me and he says, 'You take it easy. They know about you back at regiment. They're saying, 'Watch out for Fitz and his crazy Irishmen.'

"I still had a fire team and by now I knew everyone and knew my way around so I had a fire team with three BARs, not just one. And when a new replacement draft came in, I had first pick of men. And I picked men with Irish names. So we wandered around all over out there on patrol trying to get into trouble."

As one of my three squad leaders, and until his tour ended, Fitz was always the guy I called for in a tough spot. I also got him wounded one more time, taking out his squad on January 13, 1952, on a sunny day in deep snow, a patrol I decided for some damn-fool reason to lead myself, and I tripped a mine under the snow, blew myself into the air, and sent shrapnel through Sergeant Fitzgerald's wrist. I can still see the look Chafee gave me when he realized I'd damned near killed myself and, more importantly, had wounded his favorite NCO. Nor was Fitz too happy with me. Understandably.

When he was ordered to a rotation draft to go home, I asked Fitz what he was going to do, urged him to try college. He didn't think he could handle the books, he said, and thought he might take on an armed-guard job at the auto plants. "I kind of got used to wearing a uniform, carrying a weapon."

Home in the States but still a Marine on active duty, he was stationed at Great Lakes Naval Training, "running down deserters, sort of a police job, and went all around the country bringing them back." It occurs to me now I wouldn't want to be a deserter with Sergeant Fitzgerald on my trail. He wound up his tour of duty and took his discharge. "I got out but couldn't settle anyplace," he said. "So I went to college to play football. Alma College up in Michigan, and reported to the team for training, but after a couple of weeks they realized I hadn't filled out my GI Bill forms or even applied to the college. And that was that." (Paperwork was his problem, never the enemy or the football coach.)

"I went to welding school, then got a plant protection job at Chevrolet, but in 1957 I went back to the Marine Corps." Why? I asked. "Fish out of water, I guess. I had been a part of something and been successful at it, so why not?"

He returned to active duty as a buck sergeant and was sent to weapons school, where he qualified on everything but the H-bomb. "I got to be able to hit a tank in a field with an 81-mm mortar. Trouble was, when they gave me a written exam and asked how many 81s are in a battalion, I didn't know. Then I was a drill instructor in San Diego [Marine boot camp] and then went to Okinawa for eighteen months." Vietnam was in its very beginnings then, with the first American advisers in country, training the South Vietnamese. Fitzgerald's comments on the American army echo the usual Marine regular's contempt.

"The U.S. Army didn't want the Marine Corps there. They [the army] had a racket going and even the PFCs were making good money and a captain making plenty, and they didn't want to spoil it. The army was even hiring armed guards so they didn't have to pull guard duty themselves. They was training the Viets and I never did find an outfit anywhere in the world trained by the U.S. Army that was worth a shit."

But did Fitz himself eventually get to Vietnam? He did, in what in his account sounds like recon or ranging duty, deep-penetration patrols and raids, and in those early stages of the war, possibly extralegal and slimly publicized if at all. "We were in Vietnam three or four times. In and out. You can't write this, Lieutenant [I made no promises], but there was these little villages where the Cong up there on the border [Cambodian or Laotian he didn't say] would come in and rape the women, kill the papa-sans [the village elders or chiefs]. They would just hang up the papa-san and beat the shit out of him. And we were in a position outside the village in the boondocks to see this stuff. At one village we heard the Cong was coming. So I got a sniper rifle and waited for the Cong. You never try to kill everyone in that situation;

you wait until the officer comes along leading them, and you kill him first, then you take down the others. I got six in all that time."

Back in the States the Marine Corps concluded once again that here was an asset they could use in training other, inexperienced Marines. Fitz became a series gunnery sergeant drill instructor at the Marine Recruit Depot of San Diego. "I came into it cold, but a platoon had trouble; a kid broke his leg running in the bleachers but his mother got into it and complained the drill instructors broke his leg. I asked the kid myself in the hospital, who did it, and he said he fell in the bleachers. But the mother kept complaining and saw a bird colonel. So they sent that platoon into 'seclusion' until someone talked. That's what they did to a platoon if they were trying to get them to talk. I took them aside and told them, 'Just tell the truth,' but after a few days someone broke and said, yeah, a drill instructor did it. I was up on charges before a court-martial but it never got past the prosecution witnesses, and they dismissed all charges. But when a staff NCO gets something like that on his record, he knows he's never going to make master sergeant or sergeant major, so I got out again in 1964.

"I sent a letter to the police department in Flint, Michigan, and they hired me right away. I got shot in '65 [going into a local cellar after a shotgun-wielding gunman that he killed in a shootout; the shotgun blast Fitz took carrying half his gunbelt, metal and leather both, into his innards], but I healed up and stayed in until I retired in '81." He and Theresa had a daughter, Amanda, their only child, a phenomenal high school softball player about whom Fitz regularly sent me clips from the Michigan papers. Impressive stuff; the kid was a fast pitcher and star batter, too.

But proud daddy Fitzgerald hadn't quite yet strapped on his last gunbelt and holster. In his mid-sixties, Greyhound went on strike and advertised for armed guards to ride shotgun on buses going through picket lines or being sabotaged on the road. The dough was apparently pretty good, and there was Fitz one more time, in uniform and "packing." I spoke with him on the phone, tried to talk him out of it, but he laughed me off, said it was no strain, and he'd be careful. I guess he was and the strike ended and, to my knowledge, no one was hurt or got shot. On either side.

Which may have been a first for Fitz.

Then on Easter weekend a few years back his daughter, Amanda, that great softball star now in college on a scholarship, and their only kid, was killed in a car crash. Fitz called East Hampton to tell me about it. Only time in half a century and two shooting wars that this extraordinary man, and warrior, ever for a moment sounded beaten.

After that, Theresa and John did what they could to pull their lives together. Theresa wrote a successful book for youngsters on the charms of higher math, and Fitz, who had always sailed and done those good outdoorsy, *Field & Stream* magazine sort of things we city boys only fantasize about, bought an old trawler so they could spend their summers cruising on the Great Lakes. "We're trying Lake Superior next year after the ice breaks," was a typical Fitz report from "the front." When I spoke with him last fall about this book, I asked after the trawler.

"I'm trying to sell it. I think we're going to get ourselves a mobile home and get out and really see the country. First time for me since I was chasing deserters and bringing them back."

At Christmas Theresa sent along a note with their card. It's a rather strange and wonderful thing that the wives of old Marines try to keep their husbands' old lieutenants up to date on how "our" men are doing. "John's adjusting to life with hip troubles again. But overall he's doing well. He stays busy around the house and with the boat. He's cutting and splitting our own wood for the wood burner, taking care of the yard, taking care of the boat. He just does it at a slower pace and with a bit more discomfort.

"We've decided to sell the boat," she confirmed. "We've enjoyed our trips up to the North Channel so very much, it's hard to say good-bye. But it's time . . . with so many happy memories, there are few regrets. Once it sells, we're looking into a mobile home or RV so we can do some land traveling. When Amanda was in softball we got to see such a wide variety of country, a grand opportunity for all of us, and such a blessing for our family life. But now we'd like to take the time and make some stops at the national parks we only got a taste of the first time through. The possibilities are there, and time and events will lead us where we're supposed to go. And of course there's Jack, the

Airedale. Ginger our Siamese cat is his house friend and antagonizes him as much as he does her. Both love the other to chase them. Neither of us would go without them at this stage of the game, so there we are."

Simple things, simple pleasures, cutting and splitting wood, a love of the country they wanted to see more of, memories of softball fields and a girl named Amanda. There are such women as Theresa "Sam" Fitzgerald who love their men. Are content with their lives together.

Fitz had ended his last chat with me like this: "This time next summer look out for us. We may be pulling up that big mobile home of ours onto your front lawn out there in East Hampton."

I assured Sergeant Fitzgerald it would be East Hampton's pleasure.

7

George Howe, one of the last of the Chinaside Marines

He was by now ninety years old and living with his wife, Zora, in a two-bedroom apartment in Fredericksburg, Virginia, at the time (spring of 2006) when I sent a note to let Howe know I was writing a book and wanted his help. Within days I got his letter back, cogent and very much to the point. As brisk and businesslike as you might expect an old Marine sergeant major to be in correspondence. Or in battle.

"The question is put," wrote George Howe. "Why do Marines fight? The short answer, To accomplish the mission. But what is the motivator?

"I was born in Boston during World War I. Since that time life has taken me to two major battles during World War II, and later the Korean War placed me at the battle of the Chosin Reservoir. I was a U.S. Marine a total of twenty years on active duty that included three years in North China."

That was how the old man began the first and longest, at thirty-three pages, of several letters that Captain Howe would send, neatly printed on lined paper, some white and some yellow, entirely legible.

At an age when George deserved to have others fussing over and caring for him, he had become instead, according to him, "a 24/7 caregiver to my darling, senile dementia wife."

It was, he told me, a joy and something of a release to have a literary purpose of sorts, beyond the usual domestic chores of cleaning and feeding and cleaning up after her, and he promised to send along more information as it occurred to him. I called to say thanks but instead got his granddaughter, Diana M. Almy, DDS, an orthodontist with her own practice who said Captain Howe was now too deaf to talk at any length by phone but that he wanted to say hello.

So as a couple of aging gyrenes do, George and I shouted at each other with enthusiasm and merrily for a bit and I thanked him, and Diana got on the line again. Could Captain Howe give me a bit more? Or would that be an imposition? She understood what I was after and liked the notion and said that given the time, she would try to type some of her grandfather's offerings for him to send along. The assignment, clearly, meant something to Howe, and she thanked me for getting the old gentleman involved.

In his letters, some typed, others not, Howe sketched out a typical American background of the time.

"I went through the public school system of the city where I was reared, Quincy, Massachusetts, next to Boston, and graduated in 1934. Our class was exposed to much of the history of our great nation that included battles in the nearby towns of Concord and Lexington and in Boston a place called Bunker Hill. Our schoolteachers emphasized the significance of the battles, their meaning for our land— in a word—freedom. There became embedded in my character the quest to be helpful to others in all kinds of situations. To be helpful required diligence, honesty, and truthfulness. As a Marine I intended to do my best at all times, to volunteer when asked, to watch out for the man on my left and the man on my right, to support the accomplishment of any and all missions with honor, courage, and commitment.

"The Great Depression was on and I joined the Civilian Conservation Corps and was sent to Vermont. Returning home I saw a USMC recruiting poster. I was hooked. And with orders in hand, I was on my way to Parris Island."

At this point he broke off briefly from his written account only to return with a "Hooray! The apartment is quiet, including my wife, and I can answer your questions.

"I was in North China from December 12, 1936, to August 1939," and as far as Howe was concerned, "World War II hadn't begun in September of '39 when the Germans invaded Poland, and England and France declared war, but several years earlier. Like many other Marines then stationed in North China, I believed that World War II had begun when the Japanese Imperial Army invaded China in 1937 at a place called the Marco Polo Bridge, a few miles distant from Peking [now Beijing], and that WWII ended in 1945."

Detailing his duty Chinaside Howe said, "I served in Company B, American Embassy Guard, Peking, Marine Barracks Company C, Tientsin, and temporary duty at the rifle range, Chingwantao (where the Great Wall meets the sea), for about five months. No, never in the 4th Marines [who, having been warned, embarked the week before Pearl Harbor from Shanghai to safety in Manila, where ironically they were all killed or rounded up by the Japanese early in 1942, and sent on the Bataan Death March]."

Early in the war Howe, by now first sergeant of a hundred-man Marine detachment, spent fourteen months on Little Goat Island off Jamaica, British West Indies. "At Little Goat the U.S. Navy had activated a facility for anti-German submarine patrol duty. We were there to give protection to the naval facility, on duty twenty-four hours a day for ten days, then off with two days liberty, usually in Kingston. The climate was hot, with sometimes a cooling breeze."

So far, George Howe's Marine career sounded pretty cushy. But let him tell it.

"To get to Little Goat I boarded a Navy ammunition ship at Norfolk, the (deliciously named) USS *Nitro*. On its journey south the *Nitro* was escorted by two U.S. destroyers. There were about fifty Marines aboard as passengers bound for Guantánamo Bay, Puerto Rico, or as in my case to Kingston, Jamaica. We Marines stayed topside all the way except for chow and head call. Marines topside acted as [U-boat] spotters, too, although most of the time we joked and laughed until we heard a commanding voice from the bridge, 'You goddamned boy scouts, SHUT UP!' We knew the captain was nervous, and rightly so. All of us topside saw it, a torpedo crossing our bow. The German missed on that one but he tried again and the second torpedo crossed our stern. The two destroyers were already in action, doing fast-turn maneuvering, dropping many depth charges. Someone said the sub had been badly hit.

"Scuttlebutt was that [because of the risk] crew members were changed on ammunition ships after every trip. That kind of life would make anyone, even a navy captain, nervous."

Howe's next post was the antiaircraft artillery of the 16th Defense Battalion on Johnston Island in the Pacific. He'd given the Nazis a crack at him aboard USS *Nitro* and now it would be the Japanese. Not that Johnston Island was all that perilous. Listen to George:

"The enlisted men of that Defense Battalion had already established their way of life, especially the sergeants and staff NCOs. The staff NCOs were cribbage players. They played every time they weren't eating or sleeping, and betting hundreds of dollars on the game. They had coffee breaks in the mess hall in the morning and midafternoon, and worked an 8 to 4 day. They hardly knew there was a war on."

I've actually been to Johnston Island (southwest of Honolulu) on a refueling stop flying out to Korea in November 1951, and I began to understand about the cribbage, there not being very much to see or do on Johnston. But George Howe had more serious gripes about this bunch, very especially including its commanding officer.

"The C.O. or the executive officer never did offer to take me around to the guns and the crews or to meet the other officers. The battalion had 90-mm, 40-mm, and 20-mm guns, also .50-caliber machine guns. Gun crews and officers were armed with .45s." As the senior NCO, George was assigned to run the office. Early on, the commanding officer gave Howe a draft letter to be typed for his signature. Howe gave the assignment to a staff sergeant, only to be informed, "It's almost four and our day ends at four." Said the aggrieved Howe, "I didn't expect him to type it but to give it to a corporal or clerk or someone, but to get it done. But when he told me that, I took the paper back and said, 'Sergeant, you are fired. Get the hell out of my office. I never want to see you again.' He left his space and I never did see him again [until Okinawa, it turned out]. And by that action, I set the tone for my clerks."

Now this wasn't precisely storming a hostile beach, but it stamped Howe as a Marine NCO who believed in direct action, and expected results. George also volunteered to tend bar at the staff NCO club and to act as a control on the drinking (beer only, but a variety of brands). Life in that outfit wasn't too rough, it seems.

Unless you happened to die there. Howe recalls:

"On Johnston a Marine pilot crashed (and was killed) and someone stole the pictures from his effects and had copies made of very personal nude and semi-nude photos and passed them around. A staff NCO in the 16th gave me a complete set, and after the war I saw one of those photos of the Marine officer's wife in *Look* magazine. And I wrote to the editor to tell him how those photographs came to be."

Howe's low opinion of the Defense Battalion boys (now renamed the 16th Anti-Aircraft Artillery or AAA Battalion) survived a training tour of duty on Maui, and what he called, "the tail end of the battle of Tinian when Seabees were already very active and had 'the right of way' on getting the air fields ready for the big B-29 bombers [to use en route to their saturation bombing of the Japanese home islands]." But late in the war, on Okinawa, Howe, now a sergeant major, which is a very senior job in the Marine Corps, realized the outfit still hadn't shaped up and, in actuality, wasn't improved at all. "The staff sergeant I fired on Johnston Island turned up as chief clerk. Our AAA Battalion was set up around Yontsii airfield with our big searchlights scanning the night. Six Japanese bombers got through our ack-ack fire safely and landed. About 100 Jap soldiers jumped out and destroyed more than a few American planes on the ground. Aircrew men and ordnance Marines and mechanics killed them all. Not the 16th," he emphasized sourly.

"At daybreak I went over to the airfield and I saw some Marines pulling gold teeth out of the Jap mouths with pliers. [The 16th, it seems, wasn't very good with their guns but okay with pliers.] Only one member of our battalion was KIA [killed in action] in the war. Only one. The battalion barber. He had asked permission to go to the searchlight battery to cut hair. It was fired on by the Japs and the barber was killed." All these years later Howe is still indignant about the 16th's pathetic war.

In the Marines, as anywhere else, the body rots from the top. This is how George Howe remembers this crummy outfit.

"From the time I joined the 16th the commanding officer spoke to me only twice, first, when I was introduced to him in his office by the S-1 [adjutant] and second, when we were on Yellow Beach 3 on Okinawa. He handed me an overlay of the island and directed me to establish the battalion command post, which I did with no problem. A week later the executive officer [second in command to the CO] came to me and said, 'Sergeant Major, the CO wants to know what is wrong with this battalion?' I said, 'Sir, the commanding officer [the CO] is what is wrong with this battalion." The XO took this in, said nothing, turned and left."

The CO was A. F. Penzold Jr., and Howe says he spoke with a Norfolk, Virginia, accent, whatever that is, and later George encountered the executive officer again, by this time a lieutenant colonel, who confirmed to George, 'You know, you were right about the CO, Sergeant Major."

All things considered, after his time with the antiaircraft artillery bunch, and not having much use for them, George concluded late in the war, "I would rather be an infantryman any day."

Five years and one war later, in Korea, Howe would get his wish. By now, after fourteen years in the Corps, he would wryly admit to me, "all that time and I was never yet in a real firefight." He would soon get all he wanted.

The Korean War began Sunday, June 25, 1950. Following VJ Day and the Japanese surrender that officially ended World War II, Howe had been posted at the Boston Navy Yard, Parris Island, and other stations, and in mid-1950 was at Camp Lejeune, North Carolina, a very senior master sergeant (peacetime and a smaller Corps had reduced him from sergeant major) assigned to the 6th Marines, an infantry regiment, second only to his pal Mike Knott.

Said Howe, "A big change was about to take place in the lives of all U.S. Marines. Word flashed through the regiment that General Douglas MacArthur had made an urgent request to President Truman for a division of Marines to be sent to South Korea ASAP. The situation was critical. A brigade was quickly assembled (no full division then existing) under Brigadier General Edward Craig to hold the line in South Korea while MacArthur and his staff planned for the 1st Marine Division to land at a place called Inchon, Major General Oliver P. Smith to be commanding general.

"Elements of the 6th Marines were rushed across country to Camp Pendleton (Oceanside, California). Mike and I felt we were just along for the ride, not yet having been given assignments. While we waited, the sergeant major of the newly designated 7th Marines fell ill and Mike got the job while I was left adrift."

But not for long.

When two of the three Marine regiments hit the beaches and swarmed over the seawall at Inchon, the 7th, in reserve under Colonel Homer Litzenberg following a day or two later, was ordered to hold Uijongbu as a blocking force. There was, in George's words, "an initial chaos." The regiment was made up 38 percent of reservists, and on their first days ashore Litzenberg realized men were discarding their heavy packs by the roadside, and officers and senior NCOs were left to pick up the discards and toss them into passing trucks. Litz halted the entire bunch "in its tracks," and called all the officers and men together. Howe remembers, "He gave everybody a hard kick in the ass and chewed us out as only a tough commander can do."

Out of that chewing out, good things came. George was assigned to work directly under the S-1 and help out the regimental sergeant major. After the bloody battle for Seoul, the entire division was shipped around to the east coast at Wonsan, and then, after a mine-clearing delay, the 1st Marine Division headed north on foot toward the Chosin Reservoir as a jumping-off place for the Chinese border at the Yalu River. "The 7th Marines leading," said Howe, the division set off along the main supply route (MSR), the only northbound road through steep mountains and narrow, easily ambushed passes, with the first snows already falling.

"The 7th," George Howe wrote, "suffered some brutal casualties in the early stage of the advance against North Korean soldiers, such as seven Marines killed in their sleeping bags. The division objective was a small village on the west bank of Chosin Reservoir. The 5th Marines under Colonel Ray Murray followed, with the 1st Marines, commanded by Chesty Puller, as the reserve element ordered to take the village of Koto-ri, just above Funchilin Pass. The 7th Army [Infantry] Division was also headed north along the east side of the reservoir.

"So this was the picture," George Howe continued, as his battle story neared its climax in the snowy Korean mountains, "Marines fighting North Koreans all the way along the MSR from Koto-ri to Hagaru-ri, thence to Yudam-ni, with elements of the 7th Army Division strung out from Hagaru-ri east of the reservoir to the Yalu River, the north side of which was Manchuria [China].

"On or about November 28, 1950, Lt. Col. Frederick Dowsett, XO of the 7th Marines headed north of Yudam-ni with a small party, his radio operator, two fire teams (four men each), and me. Suddenly two shots landed in front of the XO and he turned to face me, 'This is where we will establish the regimental C.P. [command post],' he said.

"What happened next was a hellish, scary surprise. The Chinese army, at about sunset, with 100,000 troops attacked all Marine and U.S. Army units in the Chosin area. It was really no surprise to Captain Donald R. France the 7th Marines S-2 [intelligence officer, a job I held for the 2nd Battalion of the 7th Marines the following year]. Captain France had intelligence that the same Chinese soldiers had engaged elements of the 7th Marines near a place called Sudong-ni as we fought our way north along the MSR. He forwarded his information up the chain of command to Major General Willoughby, who was MacArthur's G-2, Willoughby didn't believe it. He said something to the effect that 'U.N. forces will never be fighting the Chinese in this war.'

"By December 1, General Willoughby became a believer. The Eighth Army (U.N., mostly U.S.) on the west coast fell back from thousands more Chinese in their area. It turned into a rout. And we [Marines] began 'attacking in a new direction,' heading for Hamnung and Hungnam and the sea." And an embarkation aboard ships to safety.

It is the old gentleman's perspective more than half a century later that makes his account so remarkable, recounting the dreary garrison slog, the exotic Chinaside posting, the South Pacific backwaters of rear echelon roster keeping and paper shuffling, the second-rate "superior" officers and "shifty-eyed" enlisted men playing cribbage, goofing off, and stealing from the dead, all this leading up to the dramatic clash of arms at the Chosin Reservoir, which would become the pivot of his Marine career, a fight he recalls as precisely as plump, bespectacled, terrified Pierre Bezukhov remembered the battlefield of Borodino in *War and Peace*.

Here is Howe's telling of that rearguard action at the reservoir.

"During all my time in Korea I was in only one ferocious firefight. On December 6, 7th Marine headquarters staff elements in their jeeps were headed out of Hagaru-ri in column near nightfall on the MSR. Mike Knott and I were walking behind a tank leading the way, Mike to my left. The tankers' hatch was open with a gunner at the ready with a .50-caliber machine gun. Following was the S-1 jeep, PFC Snedeker the driver, Captain Grove to his right in the passenger seat. The rear held two passengers, Second Lieutenant Balzer and PFC Rubio, both cowering behind the jeep windbreaker. The S-2 jeep followed with Captain France and his assistant First Lieutenant Clarence McGuinness, then the S-3 (ops) jeep, the S-4 jeep, then the HQ & Staff jeep with the First Sergeant, McCoy, and Staff Sergeant Cotton with his .30-caliber machine gun, a few clerks and Chaplain Cornelius 'Connie' Griffin with his driver and assistant, Sergeant Matthew Caputo."

The mind boggles at this ninety-year-old man's memory for names, ranks, and even place in line during what must have been a shambling, desperate, and chaotic forced march through hostile mountains as the frigid night closed in, and with thousands of Chinese infantrymen on their tail and swarming all about them. Consider George Howe's terse, cool account of the firefight about to erupt.

"Suddenly," Howe continued, "from our left flank a fusillade of rifle and machine-gun fire from the Chinese caught the headquarters staff in an ambush that came close to total disaster. Mike Knott immediately began returning fire with his carbine [a fairly useless light weapon, I might remark—JB] and in a moment he was wounded, knocked out of action. My carbine in hand, I heard PFC Richard Austin call to me, 'Sergeant, I'm hit.' He'd been hit in the back when he turned to reload his rifle, he told me. Laying my carbine down next to the tank I called out to Corporal Sandowsky to give me a hand. He

replied, 'Sarge, we will never make it. Too much machine-gun fire.' "
Howe wasn't buying it. "Fuck you," he said. "Get over here."

"With me on one side and Sandowsky on the other we lifted and
half dragged Austin to an ambulance forward of our position, maybe
50 yards ahead. The corporal and I returned to our ditch positions on
the run, and resumed firing. Captain Grove attended to Mike Knott
and neither Snedeker or the other passenger were hit. Captain France
and Lt. McGuinness were both killed trying to take cover in the roadside ditch. Later I saw their bodies where they fell. Chaplain Griffin's
chin was shot away and Sergeant Caputo was killed.

"Cotton's .30-caliber gun and the tanker's .50-caliber machine gun
fired in tandem during the ambush. Marine air arrived and dropped
napalm on the Chinese. The firefight then came to an end as quickly as
it started. Looking around afterward, a bullet struck my left arm sleeve
and spun my arm completely around, but never hit me. Wounded Marines made their way to Hagaru-ri to be evacuated and Mike Knott was
evacuated from Koto-ri.

"Then Captain Grove told me Colonel 'Litz' had just appointed me
the new sergeant major of the 7th Marines (succeeding poor Knott)."

After the big fight at the reservoir and the long retreat (okay, "attack in a new direction"), Howe said he had enough "points" to be rotated home, but the new regimental commander, Colonel Nickerson,
called him in and told him, "Stay with me. I want you as my adjutant.
I received word you have been commissioned second lieutenant,
USMC."

This is what Howe said in response:

" 'Colonel, sir, I am too tired, I am about worn out, and my wife
and two children are waiting for me.' The colonel smiled, we shook
hands, I gave a salute, did an about-face, and was about to put my left
foot forward, when I turned and said, 'Thank you for the offer.' "

But it hadn't been an offer. When he got back to the States George
Howe was informed he'd been commissioned a lieutenant of Marines.
At the San Diego boot camp when he reported in, he was told by a
lieutenant colonel, "Sergeant, raise your right hand to take the oath."

The light colonel turned out to be the same executive officer who
on Okinawa asked then-Sergeant Howe what was wrong with the

antiaircraft artillery battalion and Howe had responded with what he felt was the truth, "the commanding officer."

George Howe served into the 1960s, the Vietnam era, became a captain in a career that began in North China before the "big war," and finally reentered civilian life. "I tried banking and became a loan officer. Needing to make more money I signed on with the Federal Civil Service, rising from CS-3 to become the chief of position and pay management, in grade CS-13, at the U.S. Army Topographic Command, Washington, D.C., and retired from that command in 1972."

When I last spoke directly with George, he'd just turned ninety and was still shouting at me. Then at Christmas 2006, I got the usual card, signed by his wife and himself. I assume Captain Howe had helped his lady with that chore. That's George Howe. That's the Old Breed.

8

"Iraq is lost," says Colonel Ward Scott, who's been there twice.

To put it mildly, Marine colonel Ward Scott has a rather unique perspective on American wars over the last seventeen or eighteen years. The colonel was in Tampa, being debriefed about Afghanistan by the intelligence people and the brass, when he phoned me out in East Hampton. We hadn't spoken for six months and the fighting had picked up, with the Taliban doing another of their periodic comebacks. "Looks to me like rough terrain. How do you get anywhere, by chopper or jeep or just plain climbing?" I asked. "A mix of the above," he said. "Let me just say it's perfect terrain for counterinsurgency work. I'll tell you about it when I get my leave. I'll come into Manhattan for a day. Maybe we can have dinner."

I told him that would be great. I wanted to pick his brains and maybe use some of what he told me in the book.

The colonel would be leaving Florida the next day for leave in New Hampshire, where his wife and a platoon of (seven) Scott kids all live when the kids aren't away at school (Groton, mostly) or college—an Annapolis first-class midshipman already accepted by both the Marines and Cambridge University (for postgraduate studies), a daughter, Rebecca, teaching in the backcountry of British Guyana, Millicent, the captain of her college field hockey team, and my favorite, Bubba, the ballplayer and historian. Since Mrs. Scott, Patrice (her dad was a Marine sergeant, and she's a lawyer), gets to raise all those kids and maintain a household while the colonel is off gallivanting around fun places like Djibouti, the Hindu Kush, and the Baghdad Green Zone ("We don't travel by road to the airport, we fly in choppers; it's safer," said the colonel), Scott describes his wife admiringly as a mix of Annie Oakley and Jeanne d'Arc. "You'd think he was Irish," Patrice comments skeptically.

Bubba, incidentally an eighth-grader, was recently asked to turn in a short story for class and responded, why should he do that when he was already working on a novel? When I first met Scott he was a light colonel helping organize the Korean War Commemoration in D.C., but he was anything but your usual Washington desk officer, having in 1991 as a captain commanded a Marine rifle company, Bravo Company of the 25th Marines, 1st Mar Div, in Desert Shield and Desert Storm in Iraq. In more recent years he'd alternated spasms of active duty with inactive periods when, among other things, he'd spent a full year at the Naval War College in Newport, Rhode Island, which is where future admirals and Marine generals matriculate, being named the Admiral Mahan Scholar, run (unsuccessfully) for a Republican nomination to Congress from New Hampshire, and been offered a job (which he turned down) by major league baseball working on security for the commissioner's office.

He went civilian any number of times, once until an American outfit, JTS Inc., decided he was just the sort of handy fellow they wanted running their Iraq operation just as the second Iraq war was morphing into a bloody insurgency. Naturally, Ward Scott, on his terms, took the offer. "I headed a company providing information technology support for among others, General Petraeus's command," said the colonel. In a September 2004 letter he reported, "One of our imminent projects is putting in a computer network for the Independent Electoral Commission of Iraq which will oversee the elections in January." Things weren't dull, the colonel seemed happy to report.

"We have been mortared and had some Katushka rockets land nearby but are unscathed here in the Green Zone." Traveling outside the zone was quite something else. Scott had decided to pass up a four-week leave back to the States and to finish out his one-year tour without a break. "I would much prefer to leave here on a one-way ticket never to return. Moreover, traveling in convoys outside the Green Zone, especially to BIAP, Baghdad International Airport, and flying in and out are just extra opportunities to get killed."

And this from a guy who'd been to war before.

On the cheerier side, during his year in Baghdad, Scott was active in the local chamber of commerce, and became "senior church warden to the Anglican Church there, the only time I ever went to church services with a grease gun in my ditty bag."

"Anglican senior church warden" Scott took to that sort of unconventional and nondull civvies job like a duck to ponds. All this while Baghdad was blowing itself up almost daily. But these pleasant detours into civilian life don't always last, and within another year the Corps had called and Ward Scott was back in uniform in Afghanistan, commanding a few Marines and several small warlord armies and running a mountain range or two out in the boondocks around and east of Kabul. More officially, his duties were described as "Commander responsible for leadership of 300 Coalition personnel in advising the Central Corps of the Afghan National Army regarding combat operations, training, and institutional development throughout 11-province area of responsibility, from Kabul to the Pakistan border. Served as personal military adviser to the Corps Commander (Major General)."

"You know you're crazy," I kept informing him during our intermittent phone conversations or by mail, rudely forgetting this was a Marine field-grade officer and I'd never been better than captain. But I had this nasty sneaking suspicion each of us had just so many lives, and that by now, full Colonel Ward Scott, USMCR, was rapidly expending his. I kept thinking about Patrice and their admirable mess of genius children, Bubba and the rest, and not wanting some stupid roadside explosion or ambush up in the Khyber Pass leaving them widowed and orphaned.

"I know," the colonel said, forgiving my impertinence and actually sounding happy. "Most of the people working for me [this was when he was with that technology outfit attempting to rewire Iraq] are former

Marines. So I can rely on them. And I'm thinking of taking up on an offer to become president of the Greater Metropolitan Baghdad American
Chamber of Commerce. It's pretty interesting stuff. Look good on a
résumé."

Now there was another splendid reason Marines went to war and
fought. Looked good on the old civilian résumé. I don't mean to come
off as cynical. But human resources departments love a good résumé,
don't they?

Ward Scott is a native of Manhattan (descended on his mother's
side from the aristocratic von Hohenlohes of an earlier Germany)
whose family moved to L.A. when he was three. He earned a scholarship ("based in part on need") to exceedingly classy Phillips Exeter
Academy in New Hampshire when he was fifteen, and on graduation
joined the Marine Corps hoping to get to Vietnam after boot camp at
Parris Island. "But Nixon closed it [the Vietnam War] down, so after
four years I got out as a sergeant." He briefly attended Princeton, graduated from the Wharton School at the University of Pennsylvania, and,
as a Marine reservist, was sent to Officer Candidate School, earned his
commission, and studied law at Villanova as a Marine lieutenant. "It
was where I met my wife, a classmate in the law school." He was now
in the pipeline to an assignment to JAG but wanted an infantry posting, instead got tanks. At another point he was sent to jump school at
Fort Benning and then run through a Ranger course. "I was promoted
to captain in command of a TOW missile outfit and selected for a regular commission, but I turned it down because they weren't sending me
to the Fleet Marine Force."

For the moment a civilian (though still in the Reserves), the Scotts
settled in New Hampshire. "I knew it from Exeter, rugged, beautiful, a
combination of western mountains and old New England. I loved it."
But his Reserve outfit was mobilized when Saddam invaded Kuwait,
and Scott was finally going to, as he puts it, "smell the cordite." His
New Hampshire unit was a rifle company assigned to Operation Desert
Shield (which would become Desert Storm once the ground war began).

"We were about 200 people in Task Force Troy, a deception unit [a
contemporary Trojan horse?] and we had some scout/snipers across
the border before the official jump-off," in an area where both the 1st

and 2nd Marine Divisions were maneuvering, attempting to confuse the Iraqis. "When the fighting started we went into the oil fields and eventually married up with the rest of our battalion. I wasn't wounded and didn't lose a man and we ended by handling 4,000 POWs. After the cease-fire we languished there for a while and with reservists anxious to get home. I can tell you the volleyball games became increasingly combative." He seemed a trifle disappointed in the war.

Back in New Hampshire, Scott worked for the state attorney general's office as a homicide prosecutor, ran for election to county attorney and won a two-year term, but resigned after nineteen months to run for the Republican nomination for Congress, ending with "a third-place finish and 21 percent of the vote." In 1996 he worked as a field operative for Bob Dole's presidential bid, went back on active duty after that election, and was sent off to Fort Knox to a school for armored officers. He was back in Washington when 9/11 happened and the Pentagon was hit. The Corps then sent Scott to Newport and the Naval War College, where he won a fellowship, and dispatched him immediately to the Horn of Africa, where he did counterterrorism things, polished his French with French officers at the air base, and met the German ambassador ("he knew my family, the von Hohenlohes"). After Djibouti, another bout of civilian life, safely back in New Hampshire.

But along came an irresistibly attractive offer to go to Baghdad to run that info-tech outfit. And off he went for an exciting year, chamber of commerce and church warden and insurgency.

There were plenty of bombs but, says the colonel, "My deadliest moment came when [John] Negroponte's contractor security thugs careered around a Baghdad corner and nearly ran me down" (Negroponte being the U.S. ambassador at the time, guarded not by GIs or Marines but by hired civilians).

No sooner back in the States, reenter the Marine Corps! They needed a colonel for Afghanistan, and Scott re-upped for another tour of active (very active!) duty. "I would lead the 1st Marine Corps advisory team to the Afghan National Army Corps. We had eleven provinces as our area of responsibility, from Kabul eastward to the Pakistan border." How did they cover that vast area? "There were firefights and probes and one major offensive just before I left. I never fired a shot," the colonel said. "We partnered with the Afghans and with the 10th Mountain Division (US Army)."

Scott's Afghan tour was not a happy one. "Corruption was everywhere, just like Iraq. I was told not to turn in Afghan officers we caught stealing. There were the political niceties to observe with the host forces. Just shut up about it." He liked the army's 10th Mountain Division, but of a Florida National Guard Brigade, he said, "They were out to lunch." As for strategy, he said, "The eastern zone of four provinces (closest to Pakistan) was the hotbed of enemy activity but we had no friendly activity up there. No one was up there!"

His outfit had no choppers of their own and when he requested army helicopter assistance was told, "We don't fly in that area." "We had one U.S. battalion in an area the size of New Hampshire and we really needed a full division. All we could do was to have a series of combat outposts. It was very disillusioning, a gross shortage of forces. A sham.

"For a time we were there with a battalion of the 3rd Marines operating with our Corps. We had advisory teams out with each Afghan battalion. Our guys were supposed to handle training and logistics but they were armed and got into firefights. They could also call in air missions and medivacs and fire support. I was in Afghanistan six months. When I first arrived I was told to to take over the team. There was no team."

It was rough country, mountains up to 11,000 feet in the east, so how did Scott's outfit move? "We used trucks and Ford Rangers pickups and that was it, so transport was part of the problem. Our training was truncated. So we said, 'You're Marines, you'll figure it out.' And they did. It was the best group of Marines, and a sailor, I ever had. Mostly regulars. And the Marine chain of command backed us and eventually got us equipment. We [his unit] had arrived off the ships fully equipped, but in the area of operations, we lacked so much. One brigade was handling an area as large as the state of Maryland. And all around were very porous borders."

Aside from praise for his Marines, he sounded disenchanted, a man out of love with war. So the American effort in Afghanistan was being shortchanged?

"Definitely," said Colonel Scott. "It was treated as a backwater. I personally believe we should get out of Iraq and redeploy our forces to stand by in Kuwait and other neighboring areas, and send more of the redistributed forces to Afghanistan." And he was saying so. Trouble was, Colonel Scott kept pushing the envelope. "I'm probably a figure of controversy in some quarters," he told me. "I used 'unapproved means of transport,' flying with my general in a Russian chopper." He also sent in reports, critical reports at that, and copied them to other Marine brass outside the chain of command. None of this made Scott very popular locally and he was relieved by his army general. "FMF [Fleet Marine Force] backed me up but there was a gag order on my reports. The G2 [Marine intelligence] said, 'Hey, finally someone told us what's going on over there.' But I got a dressing down. 'We're not going to buck the army on this,' I was told."

If you think Scott is beginning to sound like a real pain in the ass to the brass hats, like the early Lawrence of Arabia, you're probably not alone.

So he once more shifted from active to inactive status. "Some Marine Corps officers in Iraq are still doing the job, still being good Marines. Others are just riding it out. Not making waves." But isn't this new top man over there, Petraeus, pretty good? "He's the best they have, a real step up from Casey. But don't forget it was also Petraeus whose job it was to train the Iraqi armed forces, and we know how that's gone." He was doing a paper on all this and sending it along to his state's senior senator, Judd Gregg.

When I last saw Colonel Scott he was living in New Hampshire and working as a strategic management consultant and had flown down to Manhattan for lunch. He was eating swordfish and speaking fondly of General George Patton, a rich army officer who traveled everywhere in peacetime with a string of polo ponies, spoke several languages, was convinced he had lived before, and was well read. "He had a book-lined room wherever he lived," said Scott, impressed. "He was crazy, of course, but a real general."

Following our Four Seasons lunch he sent me a a copy of the memo he'd submitted to Senator Gregg, titled, "Iraq and Afghanistan in the General War on Terrorism." It begins with the flat statement, "Iraq is lost." And he goes on from there: "The US can however regain the strategic initiative within the region . . . by withdrawing from Iraq proper, redeploying and aligning its resources for success in Afghanistan." He goes on to bolster his case with details and statistics. While awaiting Gregg's comments Colonel Scott had encountered John McCain at a recent function and sent him the memo as well, after first informing Senator McCain that he (Scott) disagreed "respectfully" with McCain's support for a continued Iraq engagement. At this writing, only Gregg had replied.

The colonel told me he planned "formally" to retire from the Marine Corps in September (of 2007). Which will probably delight his family and be greeted with considerable relief by some senior Marine brass. And which will mean a definitive end to a distinguished military career.

Unless, of course, the balloon goes up somewhere, another place where the Marines "need a colonel."

9

A Dubliner wanders into Times Square, joins the
Marines, and heads to Vietnam.

ONE OF THE MORE COLORFULLY LIBERATED OF THE MANY FREE
souls who follow the seasons trekking from one sun-drenched beach
resort to the next, summering in the Hamptons out on the end of Long
Island and wintering in the islands, living well if not grandly in both
places, is a barrel-chested, still ruggedly handsome, hard-drinking,
chain-smoking sixty-four-year-old Dublin-born Irishman named Cyril
R. Fitzsimons, who as a Marine infantryman fought up in the hill
country around the Tamki River in Vietnam for about eight months in
1966–67, coming out of Charlie Company of the 5th Marines and sec-
onded to what they called CAC, a "combined action company," half
USMC and the other half composed of promising local lads recruited
and trained by the Marines. As a buck sergeant, Cyril commanded one
of those little detachments.

This was a foggy, dank Friday Long Island morning at the end of
April, and when I pulled up in front of Cyril's Fish House, a quarter
mile from the oceanfront Atlantic dunes with the surf pounding just
beyond, they were raising a somewhat wind-tattered American flag
atop the tall white pole in front of the joint. "Where's your Marine

Corps flag, Cyril?" I inquired politely as the great man emerged from
the cool darkness behind the outdoor bar. "We needed a new one," he
said, the soft brogue still authentically Gaelic. "It's an outsized flag
and all beat up and the new one's on order."

Each year for the last sixteen, Fitzsimons goes through this changing of the guard. His other places, the most recent of them being
Zara's Restaurant at Shoal Bay, Anguilla, in the islands, would be putting up the shutters until fall and the freshly painted and gaudy Fish
House at Montauk was shaking down for another season that would
run until about Columbus Day. There was an amiable blonde sitting at
the bar drinking coffee, a yellow kayak lashed to the roof, a big surf-
board labeled "Cyril's" standing on end at the end of the bar, lots of
framed photos of celebrities and pals, many of them, he cheerfully informed me, "dead," and a dozen or so workmen hammering and fixing
and squaring away. God willing, and if the sun came out, it could be a
banner opening weekend, said the proprietor.

We went inside through to a table in the back to drink coffee from
cardboard cups and talk about war and the Marines, pausing along the
way to scrutinize Cyril's framed honorable discharge, "Sergeant Cyril
R. Fitzsimons, 2105487 USMCR, 11 April 1971," and sent to him at
an address in Tipperary, Ireland. "I was there at the time," he remarked pleasantly but without further explanation. This is a man with
his mysterious side. Over the cardboard coffee and at my urging, Cyril
recounted his various journeys, much as Dr. Lemuel Gulliver did long
ago to Dean Swift.

"I was born in Dublin 1943 and came to the U.S. in '64. My family was quite successful but I wanted to see New York and for some
reason wanted to be a Marine. The [Vietnam] war was on and there
was a draft, but Marines were all volunteers and so I went down to
Times Square and joined up. They sent me to Parris Island." And how
was that, a rude awakening? "A nightmare. I was twenty-one and had
been drinking heavily for about five years and these other boys were
eighteen and in shape. After boot camp it was off to Camp Lejeune
where I was picked to go to an army special forces training program in
Panama, about fifty Marines in total. The training was magnificent
with those Green Berets, much better than what we had at Lejeune

and, though I probably shouldn't say it, better than anything the USMC had." And could he get a drink in Panama? "Nothing on the base, but every ten days we'd get a break and go into Colón and get hammered.

"December of '66 I went over as an MOS 0311 rifleman. At Da Nang they sorted us out and I went to Charlie Company, 5th Marines, for a short while, when they asked for CAC volunteers. I was sent up there into the hills at the highest point overlooking the Tamki River. We were about thirty Marines and thirty locals and were supplied mainly by helicopter—ammo, food, everything. I went up there a corporal and after three months made E5, buck sergeant. What we did was go out on patrols during the day and set ambushes by night. We were fighting the Viet Cong, rarely the North Vietnam army. The VC were fearless, skinny young kids coming at you in shorts and bandanas, armed with old M-1 rifles. We were hit one night and they lost maybe 150 and we lost 3. It was suicidal the way they came at us to the wire, carrying Bangalore torpedos to blow holes in the wire they could come through. But that funneled them and the machine guns took them. This was on the Tamki, a wide, occasionally deep but mostly shallow river with fords where you could wade. There were water rats, big as cats. God, how I hated rats."

Did they have close-air support? "Yeah. One morning about three A.M. we called in air and suddenly there was a noise like I'd never heard. Cobras!" You mean snakes? I asked, somewhat dense. "No, Cobra gunships. They came in and kicked ass. When any of our local men were killed we brought their bodies back to the compound where the village Buddhists wrapped the bodies in crepe paper, a lighted candle at each end, and they put down a bowl of rice, stuff like that to see them through to eternity. Good people, respectful of their bodies."

He was in country for eight months, and except for a shrapnel wound to his right big toe, Cyril walked away unscathed. Asked what he feared most in combat, he paused only briefly. And then said, "Booby traps." As for maintaining motivation in combat against the background of antiwar demonstrations at home, he said, "To hell with that. The war was here and I was here and a Marine. What got me through, I think, was that special operations training in Panama." Did his outfit have an officer commanding, or a gunnery sergeant? "No, I was in charge. We carried M-16s and had M-79 grenade launchers, machine guns, and a dozen mortars. When we came down from the hills I didn't get another duty assignment but was shipped home to Quantico. I was told I'd be promoted to staff sergeant if I'd reenlist, and was offered a lot of money at that time." How much? "Twenty thousand dollars. I was so confused that I tossed a coin. It came up tails and I got out. Stayed in the Washington, D.C., area for a while, got a job tending bar in Georgetown, a bar on Wisconsin Avenue, then went back to Ireland (still a Marine reservist) for a while."

In 1969 in Dublin, "I opened my first bar, the Silver Tassie [named for a Sean O'Casey play], and did very well for three years. Then I got in a little trouble." What kind of trouble? "Possession of explosives." IRA stuff? I asked, "Irish Republican Army?" "Yes," Cyril said.

And did he do jail time? Sergeant Fitzsimons sort of tap-danced decorously on that one, spinning a fanciful yarn about how he left the jurisdiction. "My dad had fifty thousand pounds and we went to see the attorney general and the next day I was in Spain. I stayed there twelve years. Had four bars near Barcelona. I had the best Irish bar, I had the best gay bar. In 1982 I was back in the States, living at 60 Sutton Place South [a very classy, very pricey Manhattan neighborhood], the partner of the late Eamon Doran [a popular Easy Side pub owner], and then later I owned Murphy's on Second Avenue." He was by now a well-known local character. "I got to know Jimmy Weston [a former cop and then restaurant and saloonkeeper], and Steve Dunleavy [the *New York Post* reporter and Fox TV News personality], and bought a house in Montauk. That was sixteen years ago. My wife got that [he's got another place now in Amagansett] and the Sutton Place apartment in the divorce. She got it all and she was also my own cousin." Out of an innate delicacy, I didn't pursue that line of inquiry.

Cyril had several earlier BVI establishments but bought Zara's, the Anguilla place, five years ago. When that closes down every spring, three members of the staff lock up and fly to New York to work at Montauk all summer until Columbus Day, living in Cyril's house, and then reversing the procedure to go back to the islands for the winter. His Cyril's Fish House has become a hangout for such boldface names as David Letterman, Christie Brinkley, her former husband Billy Joel, Paul Simon, Keith Hernandez, hockey's Pat La Fontaine, New York newspaper people such as outdoors columnist Kenny Moran. Cyril himself appears from time to time in the columns and on "Page Six" of the *Post*, where editor Richard Johnson is a pal.

His red hair and mustache are yellow-graying now, the one heavy gold earring seems a rebellious 1960s hippie gesture; he hacks away coughing, but assures me he hasn't had a cigarette in two days, two and a half maybe. His two joints are making a little dough, he still looks fit enough to take on most of us. He enjoys his small celebrity with a proper modesty that most of us could benefit from. Sound pretty posh? The sweet life? Well, not quite. There would be one more firefight for Sergeant Cyril Fitzsimons. I mean that literally, one more time under hostile fire.

On July 5 about five years back, a couple of likely lads from Queens, holdup men with an agenda and a gun, drove east on Montauk Highway with a particular target in mind. Following the July Fourth weekend, a joint like Cyril's Fish House would be flush with cash. Eastward they rolled, the pair of holdup men, through Southampton, East Hampton, Amagansett, on to the Napeague Strip and through its stark hardscrabble country, along its narrow, one-lane highway in each direction, the ocean on one side, the bay on the other, and flanked by its famous "walking dunes." (Back in the silent movies of the 1920s those same dunes stood in for the Sahara desert, the camels being shipped out on the Long Island Railroad; there they filmed the adventures of Rudolph Valentino in his two classics, *The Sheikh* and *The Son of the Sheikh*.)

When the gunmen from Queens got to Cyril's and turned in, he was sitting at a backroom table, the same table where he and I talked over cardboard coffees, while he and his bookkeeper, Barbara, a woman in her fifties, went over the holiday weekend's receipts, the bundles of cash collated and stacked before them. "It was 9:15 in the morning when they came in," Cyril said, "one guy a Jamaican who worked for me and I had to fire and the other his brother-in-law. One of them shot at me and missed. Barbara was on the floor under the table and I was ducking and diving, bobbing and weaving. He got off three shots. They all missed, and then the gun jammed. There was money all over the place, scattered about the floor and everywhere. They grabbed some, whatever they could, and they went out the back door. I chased them and we wrestled and when we broke away I had the cellphone and I dialed 911 and East Hampton police answered." It was calling in the gunships time at the Tamki River all over again and Cyril was calling for air support. "I just shouted," he said, "repeating so they understood":

"Cyril's Fish House! Cyril's Fish house! Ambulance! Ambulance! Holdup! Holdup! Two gunmen! Two gunmen! Roadblock! Roadblock!"

The cops got the message, set up a roadblock, and easily (since there was only one possible road the miscreants could have taken, the other direction being Europe) caught the bad guys. Contemporary reports had Cyril being pistol-whipped and seriously damaged, but to me he said, "I just got banged up in the diving and the wrestling around on the gravel, but Barbara got sixty stitches and never came back. Hasn't been in that door since. The two guys are still in jail. They had $28,000 with them when they were caught and the cops held on to that for months as evidence but I eventually got it back. I won't tell you how much money total was on the table."

We went back outside and I thanked him for his time, the old hippie with a massive, laughing dignity, hacking his smoker's cough, recounting with enormous pleasure the details of his last combat, squinting at me with evident delight, his old rifleman's eyes bright as the spring we were all just starting to enjoy. He had been fifty-nine years old at the time and two armed men came in after his money and he fought them for it and then chased them out the back door and followed to wrestle them down, calling in the reinforcements as he did, as the old sergeants were taught to do.

Over his head as I left, I read again a few of the many silly signs hung about the bar, "Once a Marine, always a Marine," and that description of his own joint, Cyril's Fish House, licensed vintners, "A sunny place for shady people."

I've often been back to Cyril's Fish House since then, most recently in mid-July (2007) with the high season underway. The style section of *The New York Times* had just featured the place in a story about summer house romance in the Hamptons. It was late afternoon, an Anguillan steel band was warming up, the parking lot was already filled and spilling out along the sandy shoulder of the Montauk Highway for several hundred yards.

Cyril, grandly costumed and accessorized, held court at a long wooden table with Cronies, happily passing around a savage restaurant review of a rival establishment in that week's *East Hampton Star*. The sun was still high in a cloudless sky, there was a waiting list for tables, sun-tanned young people elbowed for space at the outdoor bar, and all seemed right in the old sergeant's best of all possible worlds.

10

*Mack Allen, a southern gentleman who fought
the Japanese and Chinese*

Washington, D.C., and the countryside around, especially
lovely, rolling northern Virginia, historic sites like Bull Run, Harpers
Ferry, Fredericksburg, and the little Potomac riverfront town of Quantico, with its Marine Corps schools and museum, still reek sweetly of
Dixie, of "Stonewall" Jackson and Bobby Lee, of the doomed Confederacy and the War Between the States, as Southerners still call it. In
some of the bottom land and wooded places, in among the weathered
stones and the churchyards, along the swiftly running streams, especially by night, they say you can still get the whiff of gunsmoke, hear
the marching boots, the echoes of the guns, the Rebel yells, sometimes
see the gray-uniformed ghosts muster.

To a Yankee this can sometimes be unsettling. As it was to me in
1948 when I joined the Marine Corps and found how strange it
seemed even then, after World War II and a mere thirty miles from the
White House, that black Marines and their wives and families had to
sit in a segregated balcony at the base movie theater. But then, the
Corps has always has had its strong Southern accent. One reason you
rarely hear about Marines in the Civil War, with none of the usual

heroics and derring-do, is because back in 1861 the Marine Corps split up, with roughly half its officers and men fighting on each side.

North and South, the Confederate States and the United States, Johnny Reb and the Blue Bellies have, of course, made up since then, which is why I found myself training at Quantico and then fighting beside Marines like Maurice J. Allen of Lynchburg, Virginia, and the famed Virginia Military Institute. Mack wasn't one of those "professional" Southerners forever singing "Dixie," with Confederate flags fluttering from the car antennae, and quoting from the journals of famed Confederate cavalryman Nathan Bedford "Get there fustest with the mostest!" Forrest. But in his quiet moments he was capable of wonderfully moving stories about despairing but gallant last stands by outnumbered Southerners, and tales of VMI cadets as young as sixteen going over the hill to join up with Lee's lieutenants.

Last November (2006) members of Mack Allen's family spoke with me at length about Mack, dead these dozen years, supplied their own reminiscences, and let me page through a bulky dark-green leatherette photo album of pictures and memorabilia, carefully annotated over the years by Allen himself in his own neat and quite legible handwriting. Which is where this family account of why and where Mack Allen fought really begins.

This from his widow Emma to his daughter Janet: "Your father was born August 20, 1925. He never wanted to go to any other college than VMI. After his first VMI year and close to his birthday, he told a fib and stretched the point so that he was able to enlist in the USMC and could go to World War II." As those other VMI undergraduates he so admired had done eighty years before in another war. Daughter Janet Allen Paulovich (her husband is a Marine colonel) picks up the account. "There is a family story that my grandfather, a prominent businessman in Lynchburg, was very upset that my dad was going to war. Apparently my grandfather pulled some strings and tried to get my father assigned as a general's driver, so he would be 'safer.' My father was absolutely furious when he found out and refused to 'take the easy route!' He was going to war as a Marine and he was going to go into combat.

"My dad was a true Marine and was so proud when I told him I was going to marry a Marine. He had a whole treasure trove of memorabilia from World War II and from Korea down in his basement office, so he and Mike (my husband) would go down there and for hours talk about the Marine Corps. When Dad died, we donated his old uniforms and a lot of his memorabilia to the Marine Corps museum in San Diego, where we (the Pauloviches) were stationed. Dad had been a lifelong smoker and he had cancer at the end. We thought at first it was Alzheimer's but then after he died, we discovered the cancer had spread all over."

I met Mack in January 1951 at the Basic School. Except that he had an unmistakable drawl and easy and courteous Southern ways, I knew little of his background. Though he spoke eloquently of the Confederacy and about those young VMI undergraduates marching against superior Federal forces invading their state. Here is how Mack and his album of memories summed up a young man's life in war and peace and war again. Just about everything is in here except the year he spent after the wars at the Harvard Graduate Business School:

In October 1944, the third year of World War II, nineteen-year-old former VMI student, now an enlisted Marine private, Maurice Allen left the east coast for Treasure Island, San Francisco, whence he shipped out to Pearl Harbor, to join the new 6th Marine Division training on Guadalcanal. There he was assigned (a tough little guy with a military school background) to the Reconnaissance Company and the following April 1, Easter Sunday, landed (without camera, alas, he noted) on the big Japanese island of Okinawa, where Mack would fight for the next three months, until the fiercely defending enemy finally gave up or was wiped out.

"In the first Okinawa town we entered," Mack recalled in his album's handwritten notes and photo captions, "an old woman tried to sell Marines some eggs and I met my pal Tom Hawkins from home. Our company attacked Mount Motobu on Motobu Peninsula. We got cut off for three days and they dropped food and water to us. We were beginning to wonder if it was all worth while. We watched the attack on Ie Shima where [war correspondent] Ernie Pyle was killed. We also heard about President Roosevelt's death."

He and the Recon boys were now sent to attack something called

Sugar Loaf Hill. "On the hill the 22nd Marines took and had such casualties that the rifle company [Fox Company] I would later join lost all but four men. From 140 men down to four is rough. I joined Fox Co. [glommed from Recon as a much needed replacement] to finish the operation." Then came the attack and hard fighting at Naha, the principal Okinawa city. Afterward, Mack wrote, "It was hard to believe what I had gotten through without a scratch. After seeing your best buddies killed you could hardly realize that you were still in one piece. You begin to really know there is something or someone, greater than you, watching over you. The operation ended June 30, 1945."

The kid had lied his way out of college and into the Marines, had now been in the worst kind of fighting for three months, and was still a teenager. His account of Okinawa ends with several photos. His caption for a photo of a flamethrower in action reads, "These things were really rough, would turn a man into ashes in a few seconds." Accompanying a picture of several Japanese prisoners being grilled for intelligence by Marines, Mack writes, "They were filthy, shifty-eyed little bastards." He also noted proudly that his outfit earned a Presidential Unit Citation for a night amphibious recon and, with an impressed and equivalent pride, acknowledged the enemy's capacity for hard labor and prodigious digging, "Some Japanese tunnels we uncovered were two to three miles long, and coral is tough digging."

In July the Marines left Okinawa to prepare for the upcoming invasion of the Japanese home islands, where all six of the Marine divisions, about 100,000 men, were slated to hit the beaches six across. You can imagine the thought processes of the average Marine infantryman pondering that very proximate possibility. If the Japanese had fought so ferociously on distant islands, mere atolls and sandbars, places like Guadalcanal, Tarawa, Iwo, and Okinawa, what would they do for the sacred turf of their own homeland?

It was a horrific and terrifying concept. But instead of mass slaughter, on both sides, the empire of Japan capitulated on August 15 and young Americans like Mack Allen breathed a collective sigh of relief. He and the 22nd Marines were shipped off to North China on October 12 to accept the surrender of the last Japanese forces, keep the peace, and maintain a wary eye on bandits and the rampaging Communists under Mao Tse-tung. By now Mack, though still only a corporal, was a rifle company "platoon sergeant." And had gotten hold of a camera and a bottle of Scotch, Dewar's White Label. One photo shows the Marines dug in around Tsingtao airport, believing "the Communists were going to attack. I remember it was cold as hell."

Mack left China for Japan in February of '46 and then home to the States in March. And back to VMI in time to sign up for the new term. A "Brother Rat" once more!

He'd played football in high school but in college was relegated to substitute status. Wrestling, however, was something else. Mack was VMI's starting 155-pounder in winning matches against larger schools like Duke, Georgia Tech, and the University of Virginia.

It was in a football game in October 1948 that he unexpectedly made his mark in football against local power William and Mary. The VMI student paper reported the play of reserve defensive back Maurice J. Allen this way. "Mac [the spelling of his nickname varies from person to person] played a great brand of football against a powerful and experienced machine. Some of the sports writers marveled at his proficiency as they had never seen him in action before. He was all over the field making spectacular tackles, intercepting passes, blocking passes, and just playing a 'whale' of a game."

In the classroom and on the military parade ground, Mack had consistently excelled, and as a senior (first classman) he was named commander of Company B, and on graduation in June 1949 Mack was commissioned a second lieutenant, not in the Marine Corps, but in the United States Army, as were all qualified VMI grads.

The family annals take it up from there. His widow, Emma Allen, since remarried, recalls: "Korea was brewing, and in order for him to go to that war with the USMC, he had to get the commission changed from army to Marine Corps. When the time came (and Korea began) he went to Washington and personally hand-carried his papers to the proper offices to get the transfer done. No time to waste for him. He hiked those halls and saw to it that he was going to war as a Marine officer. He never thought of anything else, because he wanted to serve his country the best way possible and he wanted to be where the action was. Do you remember his story about all the trouble Granddaddy

Allen went through to get an easy job for Mack . . . and he told them in no uncertain terms that his idea of serving his country was other than being chauffeur for the general?"

Mack Allen and I were in the same platoon at Quantico's Basic School and on graduation in April 1951, when most of our classmates shipped out to Korea, we both were held behind to instruct a fresh class of newly commissioned Marine lieutenants, all of these being "mustangs," former Marine enlisted men. These guys, obviously, were more experienced than I was, but Mack more than held his own, having been an enlisted Marine in the war and having fought at Okinawa. In October our turn finally came, and we reported in to advanced infantry training at Camp Pendleton and cold weather exercises in the high Sierras (at 11,000 feet there was already a foot of snow in October). Then, on my birthday in November, Mack and I and a dozen more lieutenants were flown out as replacements to the 1st Marine Division in North Korea, which had recently taken heavy casualties in frontal assaults on enemy ridgelines.

Being lazy, and more than painfully aware the weather had already turned cold in Korea, I left all my summer khakis behind in a locker box, so that when our navy transport plane broke down and we were gifted with a weekend in Honolulu (rooms at the Royal Hawaiian, a guest membership at the posh Outrigger Canoe Club), I had only my winter greens to wear. Mack, being a proper Marine, and generous, lent me some of his spare khakis, both of us tacitly ignoring the obvious, that I was three inches taller but skinnier. And looked like something left over from the rummage sale. The Outrigger Canoe Club members, suntanned, white-haired gents who kept standing us drinks, didn't seem to mind.

In Japan it was Thanksgiving weekend, and Mack and I fell into the clutches of "Mouse" Brydon, a real estate salesman from Philly and a first lieutenant we'd known at Quantico, over from Korea on a liquor run for his battalion's officers, his chest laden with ribbons, including a Navy Cross. "Mouse, the bleeping Navy Cross, where'd you get that?" I demanded. "Borrowed it." he said with typical "Mouse" aplomb. "All the boys threw in their decorations to improve my bargaining position in getting the booze back safe." That night a bunch of us replacements ended up at a posh geisha house Brydon recommended, as catering to Marine officers.

After the usual sake, impeccable service, excellent steaks, and pretty girls playing stringed instruments and singing in foreign tongues, other girls, young, plump, and pretty, were trotted out for more serious scrimmaging, and I will never forget that of all of us, married or single, only Maurice Allen wished us all well, gallantly bade the ladies good night, and went back to our airfield barracks while the rest of us got laid.

In the morning, hungover and guilt-ridden, we all boarded a navy plane and went to the war, wishing I'd been the disciplined, moral man Mack was, and feeling pretty lousy. Mack didn't rub it in; that wasn't his style. A few hours later, in a falling snow, we landed in Korea and, after a night's sleep, were issued rifles and trucked north to the fighting. In the open truck, cold and snow dusted, you could hear the big guns. I had never heard hostile fire before.

On the next morning, having slept warm and safe on the floor of a big bunker carved into the side of a hill, after a briefing and pep talk from two colonels and our assignments, we left battalion headquarters to climb Hill 749 to report in to Dog Company of the 7th Marines. Wanting to make an impression, Mack and I shaved. For once, I was equipped; he wasn't, his razor having gone AWOL somewhere between Japan and North Korea. Repaying him for the borrowed khakis on Waikiki Beach, I handed him my double-edged razor, with which he swiftly, being used to a single-bladed implement, sliced up into his own ear and nearly cut it off, so that he would report in with a bloody, bandaged head and a sheepish look.

By extraordinary good fortune, Mack and I both ended up as replacements in the same rifle outfit, commanded by John Chafee, another wrestler as it turned out. Chafee was a great skipper, and Mack and I both did okay as rifle platoon leaders. After a few months we were promoted, Mack to S-1, or adjutant, me from executive officer to S-2, intelligence officer. "What does an adjutant do?" he inquired. "I dunno. What does an intelligence officer do?"

Mack was three years older, had fought as a Marine in the war, had gone to military school, and I think he was more embarrassed than

I was about our communal ignorance. But we both did reasonably well, became first lieutenants, didn't get killed or anything messy like that.

After Korea, Mack Allen came through New York to visit me at Macy's where I was writing advertising and, incredibly, on his first day in town, he was interviewed on a busy Manhattan street near Penn Station by the inquiring photographer of the *Daily News*. Mack wondered, innocently, "Do they interview everyone who comes to town?" Of course, I assured him. We stayed in touch, I as a newspaper correspondent in Washington and Europe, Mack as an engineer who also earned an advanced degree from the prestigious Harvard Business School (1953–55), and then worked for at least one big Southern town in Alabama and later for a major chemical company, and I eventually got to know his family. When he fell ill at his home in Richmond, Emma and his daughter Janet kept me informed, notified me when he died, and wrote occasionally.

Then last fall, on the Army-Navy Game weekend, Janet and Colonel Mike Paulovich, knowing of my interest in Mack for this book, toted her late father's scrapbook to Philadelphia from their current duty post at Annapolis. On the following Monday their son Mark, a college student studying in New York, delivered the battered but famous old album to me at Elaine's restaurant in Manhattan, where I bought the boy dinner to express my gratitude. Janet had also sent along a little note to put things in context:

"Dad was so very proud to be a Marine. Sometimes we would take him to Marine Corps functions. When they played the Marine Corps Hymn, he stood straight as an arrow and was so proud. When Mike was at the Command and Staff College, he invited Dad to a Mess Night [a formal black tie and dress uniform affair] and had researched all of Dad's awards and unit citations and had miniatures of them mounted, and as a surprise [when he saw Mack in his dinner jacket], he stiffly informed him he was 'out of uniform,' presented Dad with the miniatures, and pinned them on his chest."

Janet's note ended: "Thanks for taking time to chronicle the things that sit in photo albums on dusty shelves in people's libraries . . ."

II

Iwo Jima revisited by the Marines who fought there.

Long before Clint Eastwood released (in 2006) his two splendid films about the battle of Iwo Jima, one from our point of view, the other that of the Japanese, I had once made a brief refueling stop on the island as a young Marine officer headed as a replacement to the fighting in North Korea in 1951, six years after the historic fight and the iconic photograph by AP cameraman Joe Rosenthal. Years later, for the fiftieth anniversary of the landings and the assault and flag raising on volcanic Mount Suribachi, I wrote a *Parade* magazine cover story recalling Iwo, based on interviews with some of the Marines who fought there, a navy nurse who flew in to tend the wounded, and Rosenthal himself.

The stories they told continue to resonate. Here is some of what I wrote a dozen years ago about the Marines who fought there and why.

Iwo isn't much of a place—a small island, ash and sand, stinking of sulphur, bleak and windblown, not a sunny south Pacific atoll with palm trees and blue waters, but gray and chill, a miserable spit of land roughly five miles long and two and a half wide, and within 600 air miles of Tokyo.

Which was why, in February 1945, we wanted Iwo Jima.

It was the fourth year of the war in the Pacific, and we were closing in on the Japanese mainland, island by bloody island. American bombers from Saipan and Tinian flew almost daily raids on Tokyo and other big cities, more than 1,000 miles there and 1,000 miles back—too far for fighter escort. Iwo Jima, astride the route of the bombers, had two airstrips, with another being built. It was from Iwo that Japanese fighters took off to harass and down our bombers. If we could take Iwo from the Japanese, it would move our bombers hundreds of miles and hours closer to a vulnerable Japan.

With both sides aware of Iwo's military worth (there wasn't another damned thing the island had going for it), a collision was inevitable. What no one expected was its ferocity. Our planners called for a five-day campaign; it would go on for five weeks and become, for the United States Marine Corps, one of the most terrible battles in its history: 60,000 Marines landed on Iwo; 23,000 would be killed or wounded. Of the 22,000 Japanese defending the place, only 44 would survive.

Among my sources (the people I spoke with) was one of the men awarded the Medal of Honor for Iwo, a navy nurse, and a two-term state legislator. And Joe Rosenthal, who took perhaps the most famous combat picture in history, the flag raising atop Mount Suribachi by five Marines and a navy corpsman. It struck me that, despite Iwo's horrors, these people returned home and reentered American life almost seamlessly—completing educations, marrying, building families, building lives. They'd come through hell and out the other side.

Some didn't, of course. Ira Hayes, one of those who raised the famous flag and survived the battle, never really shook off Iwo. He became an alcoholic, drifted onto Skid Row, and died at his home, the Indian Reservation at Bapchule, Arizona, at age thirty-two. The other flag raisers are also dead, but were captured forever on Rosenthal's film and in the bronze of that Marine monument in Virginia, just over the bridge from Washington (and of course now in Mr. Eastwood's work). Their names live always in the Corps: Corporal Ira Hayes, PFC

Franklin R. Sousley, killed in action, Sergeant Michael Strank, killed in action, Corporal Harlon H. Block, killed in action, and Navy Pharmacist's Mate 2nd Class, John H. Bradley and Corporal Rene Gagnon, dying long after the war.

But while the scaling of Mount Suribachi and the dramatic flag raising stand out in memory, they were but the overture to another month of killing.

I began my journey back in time by calling on the sergeant major of the Marine Corps, H. G. Overstreet, the highest-ranking noncommissioned office in the Marines (in 1995), who enlisted in 1966 and fought in Vietnam. I asked what Iwo Jima meant to Marines not yet born at the time. Said Sergeant Major Overstreet, "At boot camp we teach Marine Corps history, and Iwo is a part of that history. The Iwo memorial is the most recognizable symbol of World War II and has a lot of meaning for us. I was on Iwo last year for the first time. The commandant and I climbed Mount Suribachi and we raised another flag up there.

"At that moment, hackles rose on the back of my neck, and I was glad I didn't have to speak. Iwo is hallowed ground for Marines and you know that to this day, the only thing Marines ever take away from Iwo is a little bag of sand. The sands of Iwo Jima."

Colonel Joseph McCarthy, eighty-two (when we spoke), one of twenty-seven men awarded the Medal of Honor for their actions on Iwo (seven were still living in 1994), told me: "I'm still alive and kicking. And I'm off now to the pool for my afternoon swim. I'll do fifteen laps or so." A former Chicago fireman who lives in Delray Beach, Florida, he was a captain in command of George Company, 4th Marine Division, when they hit the beach the first day. Earlier he'd landed on Saipan and Tinian.

"I got hit for the third time after we took Hill 382," he said, "and was evacuated March 5. Spent a year in the hospital." What comes to mind when he hears the name Iwo? "I think of the number of Marines and navy corpsmen we lost, and all they could think of was to go forward. I landed with a company of 254 men and when I was hit, George Company was down to twelve of the original men and sixty replacements. Even though I was thirty-three back then, I could run like a deer, and I think that's why they didn't kill me."

Carmine Abaté of New Britain, Connecticut, was an artilleryman with the 4th Division who landed on Iwo the third day. "We went in, in a landing craft, and I jumped off. We were sitting ducks. There was a mortar attack and no place to hide. I jumped in a hole. That was my first ten minutes on Iwo." (Many Marines recalled the virtual impossibility of digging a proper foxhole in those shifting volcanic sands, which slid back into the hole as fast as they were shoveled out.) Abate continued, "Three or four Japs came running at us out of a pillbox, and about fifty guys shot at them. Killed them, of course. I got out unscathed, but one out of three marines got hit the first day."

After the war Carmine served two terms in the Connecticut state legislature, married, had three children, and "ended up in road construction. At the time, it [fighting on Iwo] was the greatest thing I did in my life."

Richard Dougherty, who lives in Florida, was a nineteen-year-old military police sergeant on Iwo. "The Japanese mortars were zeroed in on the beach and we'd wave a tank or bulldozer ahead, and the mortars would drop on it. There were also land mines we could walk on without exploding because they were set for the weight of a tank or bulldozer, and they'd roll over one of the mines, and up they'd go." Later in the battle, "We guarded our 105 howitzers and supply depots and the bodies. There were a couple of thousand dead bodies— American—and the Japanese would sneak in among those bodies at night and snipe at us."

Dave Severance of La Jolla, California, commanded Easy Company of the 28th Marines, from whose ranks came the patrol that reached the summit of Mount Suribachi and raised the flag. "We finally broke through the Japanese lines at the base of Suribachi. The fight was at the base. The Japanese had trenches and pillboxes in depth across the neck. For some reason they didn't fortify or defend the summit."

I thought that the Marines had had to fight their way up Suribachi's slopes foot by foot. Severance laughed. "You saw John Wayne do that in *Sands of Iwo Jima*," he said. "On the 23rd we spent the day blowing up pillboxes. The morning of the 23rd the battalion commander sent a four-man patrol to find a route up, and they got all the way to the top with no opposition.

"When they got back, the colonel thought maybe the Japanese let them through and were waiting for the rest of us. So I sent up a forty-man patrol. The colonel gave the commander, First Lieutenant H. George Schner, a small flag to raise up there. At the top they found a pipe and put up a flag, and that excited a few Japanese who came out and fired some shots. Two hours later, we were told to put up a large flag so it could be seen. I sent men up to wire the summit and sent Rene Gagnon up with radio batteries and the larger flag. Five of the men in the [Rosenthal] photo were in my company."

What happened to Dave Severance after Iwo? You get the feeling that no matter how savage the fighting, some of these guys end up being Marines for life. He became a pilot and stayed in the Marines for thirty years, and seven years after Iwo was flying combat missions over North Korea. He was seventy-five when I interviewed him, twice married and the father of four.

Lincoln Ford Peck, of Huntington Beach, California, also seventy-five when we spoke, "landed with the 25th Marines on Iwo that first day. I lasted the whole thirty-six days and walked off," he told me. "Got out in November of '45, got married, went back to school and took up accounting." He had six sons, one of whom would become a colonel in the Marine Corps, a man I got to know. But Lincoln Peck had more to say about the Iwo fighting.

"You're so damned tired, you see, you don't really register. You're tired, you're dirty, you're hungry." What was the worst part, I asked? "The snipers. They blended right into the background and they were pretty damned good shots. They hit what they aimed at."

A unique view of a historic battle came from one of the few women on Iwo, one of a dozen navy nurses who flew in to pick up the worst of the wounded Marines and to care for them as they all flew back to Guam and proper hospitals.

Evelyn Wisner of Richfield, Connecticut, was one of those nurses.

"I arrived on Iwo on March 8. We couldn't get in until the Marines had taken an airstrip. There was a corpsman, two pilots, an orderly, and one nurse, flying in C-47s, two-engined planes. I noticed everyone was armed with sidearms but me, and I wondered what we nurses were supposed to do—run? We left Guam about midnight, arrived at

Iwo about 7 A.M. There was shelling. We could see it and hear it. I was young and frightened.

"The wounded had already been given first aid in caves or wherever by the corpsmen. Brains and chest cases were high risk for flight. No doctors—just one nurse and eighteen or twenty wounded. These planes weren't pressurized and that first flight, I almost lost a patient, because at 7,000 feet he started to bleed, and I got the pilot to drop down to 3,000, even though it was bumpy. We had plasma and narcotics aboard—we used morphine to deaden the pain. I made four trips [to and from Iwo]. One of our planes was hit but didn't go down."

Wisner was a lieutenant junior grade then and would go on to serve during the battle of Okinawa, another major Marine fight, before getting out of the navy in 1946. "I continued to work as a registered nurse and got married. Widowed now. I'm seventy-four and find I don't have the energy anymore." Then she laughed, and said, "Though I was washing the windows when you called."

It takes two sides to make a great battle. What of the 22,000 Japanese on the lousy island? Tokyo had sent its best to defend the place, a brilliant, courageous three-star general named Tadamichi Kuribayashi, who deployed his men in blockhouses and caves so they could survive the month-long saturation bombardment and shelling that preceded the landings. His strategy worked, with most of the Japanese still alive and ready for a fight when the Marines came ashore. In the Japanese martial tradition, Kuribayashi did not survive the defeat. Whether he committed ritual suicide or was killed is unclear. His men never surrendered. Only 44 were found alive. Out of 22,000.

The Marine commanding general was the wonderfully nicknamed Lieutenant General Holland M. Smith, known to his gyrenes as "Howlin' Mad" Smith.

Was Iwo worth its terrible cost? Six thousand dead Marines, 23,000 casualties. Is any stinking piece of ground worth a single human life? But the official Marine Corps history tells us, "By the war's end, 2,251 heavy bombers carrying 24,761 American airmen had found refuge on Iwo Jima during the course of raids on Japan."

I mentioned having once landed on Iwo, six years after the fight. It was just to refuel, not a pilgrimage. But you couldn't be a Marine and

not remember what had happened there. I walked around, a young officer who had not yet ever fought, a college boy searching this sacred
ground, questing perhaps for its ghosts, looking at the hill, at the beach,
at whatever little else there was. I recall thinking that Suribachi was only
a hill, that beyond the airstrip and its scatter of buildings, there was
nothing much, no people, no structures, nothing. Only an emptiness,
spare and raw, no sound but the wind blowing up from the Pacific and
across the beach. But a lot of Americans had died here. Iwo once had really been something—a place where, as Admiral Nimitz put it, "uncom-
mon valor was a common virtue."

I was a kid going on to another war but at that moment in November of 1951, it was Iwo that grabbed at my imagination and shook me
to my soul.

12

He fought at the "Chosin" and later joined the cast
of Romper Room.

K EITH ROBBINS OF TOWSON, MARYLAND, DIDN'T JUST PASS
through the boot camp at Parris Island and come out the other side
thirteen weeks later as a full-fledged Marine, as perhaps a half-million
young Americans have done. He was literally born there, in the Parris
Island base hospital.

I'd never heard of Robbins until last November when I got a letter
from him. He'd seen a story in *Leatherneck* magazine about this book
and how I was looking for Marine combat veterans who could and
would be willing to talk about why they joined up and why they thought
that we fought. And usually fought so well. It was an intelligent letter,
well written, crisp and brief, intriguing in the hints it dropped but did
not explain or elaborate on. Mr. Robbins (I am being formal here, not
at that point having even spoken to him) began like this:

"Why did I join the Corps? Family tradition back to 1815, pugnacious as a child, Navy/Marine Corps Junior, Marine battles in World
War II. Joined 1949—Parris Island, South Carolina (birthplace)."

If a punchy, staccato opening like that doesn't grab at your imagination, you're not much of a reporter. Nor should you be reading

Hemingway. Consider, as well, the man's timing. If he joined the Corps in 1949 he didn't have to wait very long for the next war. It began in June 1950. Korea. So I phoned Towson and asked for Mr. Robbins, a man who entered this world at boot camp, and for his own good reasons then joined the Marine Corps and went to fight a war. This might be a man of parts, someone with a few thoughts and ideas I could use. So I left a message on the machine and got a call back the next day.

I got a question in, and then Keith Robbins began talking, a man who admits he's naturally "loquacious." First, that tantalizing hint of a really Old Breed, what was that 1815 connection? "Well," said Robbins, "the first Marine in my family was Major Parke Goodhall Howle, commissioned as a second lieutenant in the U.S. Marine Corps by President James Madison himself. Howle was seagoing and served on a frigate commanded by Admiral Perry. He served in the Corps for forty-seven and a half years and was the author of 'Howle's Regulations for Marine Corps Recruiting,' published in 1847, and served at various times as adjutant and inspector general of the Corps. I believe there was also a family member who was a lieutenant during the Revolution but can't document that one."

Robbins's mother's father and a great-grandfather also served, and his dad was in the Nicaragua campaign. The 17th commandant, General Thomas Holcombe, was related to Keith Robbins's mother. "My father was a career Marine officer and my mother's father was a career naval officer. My father was at sea when I was born in September of 1931 in a little old wooden building at Parris Island. I grew up [living at Parris Island until he was ten] to be the only enlisted man in the family, joining the Marine Corps in 1949 [photos show a tall, good-looking kid] just out of high school. I had played four years of football and my grades were B minus, C plus. I was thinking of college but decided to join up instead, going through boot camp at P.I. I was in communications school at San Diego when the North Koreans attacked June 25 of 1950. We scrambled to gather up what would become the 1st Marine Provisional Brigade. We landed at Pusan and went into the fight up at the Naktong [River] where we took a hell of a hit."

Leatherneck magazine records his adventures this way. "Robbins remembered that his first experience in combat [he was eighteen] was a 15-minute bout of Marines firing at each other [a fairly normal occurrence—JB]. On his second day in South Korea, Robbins's company was to relieve a U.S. Army outfit near Chingdong-ni. On the way the Marines were ambushed. At that time Robbins did not know that he should get down under cover [he must have cut class that day at Parris Island!]. Experienced Marines shouted at him, 'You damn fool, get down. We're getting shot at!' 'I was born and bred a Marine, but I was still a little naïve,' said Robbins. He realized that while going up to Chingdong-ni, fierce fighting, ambushes, and mortar and artillery fire. Even though it was his first experience with combat, Robbins says he wasn't afraid. 'I didn't think a bullet was going to hit me, but then I saw people I knew get hit. It started me thinking about self-preservation and put into effect the training I had.' Robbins said that he realized you fight for the guy next to you. 'I was thinking that you don't let down another Marine and that I hope I do my job so that no one gets hurt.' "

The kid's distaste for the American army dates back to those first fights along the Pusan Perimeter. *Leatherneck* wrote, "The early bitter feelings between Marines and soldiers . . . are still fresh in Robbins's memory. 'It was one hell of a fight . . . we took the objective a lot sooner than expected.' Disappointment set in when the U.S. Army lost control of the hard-won gains a few days later. The Marines returned to push the North Koreans back again, take the same ground a second time. 'We were mad (Robbins goes on) because there were a lot of Marine casualties. Often there would be fisticuffs whenever we passed the army on the road.' "

Keith Robbins told me, "The [American] army wasn't really prepared for war. They were Occupation troops [from Japan], out of shape and not ready. There was a lot of animosity between us and it didn't quite endear me to the army. We found 105's [cannon] just abandoned and the 24th or 25th Division [of the U.S. Army] going away from the enemy and not toward 'em.

"For the whole time I was attached to Dog Co. of the 5th Marines as a forward observer from Baker Co. of the 11th Marines [artillery], but by the time we got up to the Chosin [Reservoir], everybody was a rifleman."

Here is how this articulate enlisted Marine summarized his combat experiences and motivation in his own pithy style:

"First combat experience, on road from Pusan to Chindong-ni. Took intense mortar, small-arms and machine-gun fire. Followed by action at the Naktong River, twice. Also Inchon, Kimpo airfield, capture of Seoul, and Chosin Reservoir. Between Inchon and Kimpo airfield our unit knocked out five North Korean tanks and killed at least 250 enemy. Spectacular action with no Marine casualties. Intense combat from Yudam-ni to Hamhung, North Korea.

"As there is nothing more intense than being faced with a gun, combat is certainly the ultimate test of one's character, commitment, and courage of yourself and your combat team. In action I was more anxious to prove to myself I could suppress fear and turn it into courage than I was of being injured or killed. I did not blindly advance in face of enemy fire when told to do so. It was an automatic reflex as a result of my training, faith in my leaders, and the Marine next to me. And, yes, a hatred for an enemy that proved how brutal they were to a number of army people and several Marines as well when captured.

"There was certainly a feeling of excitement in combat that was fulfilling in a sense. In boot camp there was a touch of uncertainty. However, after boot camp and further training, I went into combat somewhat undaunted. I was willing to face the uncertainty, to uphold the traditions of the Corps and my family, to become an effective member of my unit. I and WE wanted to win each battle and we did."

His toughest combat experiences came at the "frozen" Chosin. Here is how *Leatherneck* of March 2001 recounted it. "In November 1950 Robbins's unit headed north. 'We didn't know where we were going.' As they headed north, the temperatures plummeted. Many suffered from frostbite because they did not have the proper gear. Robbins, himself, still suffers from complications associated with frostbite in his fingers. At Yudam-ni, the farthest point north, Dog Co. made up the rear echelon and was the last company to pull out. Robbins was wounded by shrapnel in the face and leg. Later he also suffered a gunshot wound to the shoulder. 'It knocked me down. I remember going to an aid station with another fellow, and they were going to evacuate us but I didn't want to go.'"

But Young Robbins must have been rethinking some of his earlier conclusions about battle, also recorded by *Leatherneck*. "I felt somewhat indestructible. I had been shot at and developed an 'I don't care' attitude. I wasn't cocky, I was becoming wise. You hear a shot fired and know how far away it is."

In March of '51, Sergeant Keith Robbins was rotated home, but remained a Marine until 1954, taking some courses, earning a few college credits, and mulling the university option. He enrolled at the University of Maryland, got married, dropped out before graduation, and then, but let Robbins tell it: "On a dare I answered an ad for a job at *Romper Room*. It was a syndicated program and I was loquacious and I thoroughly enjoyed it. There were ninety-one shows in ninety-one cities. Each show had a formula and a format and they were to adhere to it strictly. I interviewed the girls who were to be the *Romper Room* 'teachers.' I hired the talent, I directed, I filled in sometimes if a teacher called in sick. I didn't know the lessons, so I'd announce to the class, 'I'm the new teacher, so you'll have to help me.' I was at *Romper Room* three years and I loved it. Then I took a radio job, on-air on an FM station in Baltimore. Next I went to station WTOP in Washington, D.C., not on-air. A sales and marketing position I wasn't too enthusiastic about. I had a friend at the privately owned Shoreham Hotel in D.C., started there as a salesman and after six months was sales manager. Then I met and married a girl from Tahiti (a second marriage) and went to live in Paradise for four or five years."

"Paradise" wasn't forever, apparently, and Keith was back in the States working at the historic Greenbrier Hotel at White Sulphur Springs in West Virginia, a place so lavish and well appointed one might think of it as a paradise all its own. Except that, "One day it snowed and my Tahitian wife looked at the snow, and then at me, said, 'Uh-oh,' and we got out. I was hired by the Fairmont Hotel in San Francisco and then moved to their new hotel in Dallas. I live now in Towson and my daughter has three kids, eleven, nine, and three, and I'm helping her raise them."

"Pugnacious, are they?" I inquired politely of a guy born at Parris Island boot camp.

"They can sing the [Marines'] Hymn and salute," Robbins said happily, "and I think the oldest could take a fire team up the hill right now."

13

Coleman of the Yankees who played in World Series and flew in two wars

Lieutenant Colonel Gerald F. Coleman, USMCR (Ret.) was an all-star major leaguer with the New York Yankees, playing in six World Series (once the Series MVP) in nine seasons, and is today, at age eighty-one, in his thirty-fifth season of broadcasting San Diego Padres games, but when Jerry Coleman looks back on all that, he says, "To me the height of my life, the best thing I ever knew, wasn't the Yankees, wasn't baseball or broadcasting. It was the Marine Corps."

There's a little of the hero-worshiper in all of us and here I was talking with a New York Yankee second baseman who played in World Series, a Marine pilot who battled Zeroes in one war and Migs in the next, and lived to talk about all of this.

Born in San Jose in 1924, Coleman's Marine career began as an eighteen-year-old college kid and promising athlete in October 1942, the early years of World War II, when he became a naval aviation cadet in the navy's V-5 program, which was then training, testing, and pumping out young flying officers for both the U.S. Navy and the Marine Corps. I asked Jerry if cadets could opt for one or the other or if they were simply packed off to whichever service needed pilots most.

"We had a choice. Joe Foss came through and right away I knew I wanted to be 'Joe Foss Jr.'" Foss was one of World War II's first aces, a Marine who flew his F4F Wildcat against the Japanese and shot down twenty-six of their planes in forty-four days, matching the twenty-six kills of ace Eddie Rickenbacker in World War I. Foss was awarded the Medal of Honor. He eventually became a general, governor of South Dakota, president of the National Rifle Association, commissioner of the American Football League, and TV star on the ABC show *The American Sportsman*. But the only thing aviation cadet Coleman knew or cared about at the time was that Foss was a top gun and a Marine, and he wanted to be just like him.

"Later," said Jerry Coleman, "a Colonel Mangrum, you'll have to look up his first name, who was the first Marine aviator to land a plane on Guadalcanal, came through to talk to the cadets, and he growled at me, 'Do you want to be a Marine?' and I can't remember what I told him, but it worked."

Coleman's training took him from San Francisco to Colorado, Texas, and North Carolina, and culminated on April 1, 1944, at Corpus Christi's Naval Air Station where he received his gold wings and his second lieutenant's commission in the Marine Corps Reserve. Advanced training in Douglas Dauntless dive bombers followed at Jacksonville Naval Air Station and then brief duty at both Cherry Point, North Carolina, and El Toro, California, before being shipped out on a troopship to the Pacific war as a replacement pilot. I asked Jerry, who was twenty-one years old at the time, about that first combat experience.

"I went to Guadalcanal first"—the Marines had two years before defeated the Japanese and secured the Canal after a long, bloody battle—"and then what we called Green Island, only about three hundred yards long. We went up against Rabaul and other Japanese bases on raids and against Japanese shipping." That casual, offhand mention of Rabaul stopped me. I believe that Rabaul was where Admiral Yamamoto was flying to or out of all the time, and where the Air Corps sent a squadron of Lightning P-38 fighter planes to ambush and kill him. Rabaul was the key to the Central Pacific, their biggest and most powerful base, said to be the fiercely defended, the most formidable enemy stronghold this side of the Japanese home islands. And that was where a twenty-one-year-old second lieutenant flew raids over and over again in his first combat.

Coleman went on. "The Dauntless was a dive bomber with a two-man crew. My crew mate was Irish and was called 'Stretch,' and he died only recently, but I think I nearly frightened him to death back then with my flying. Mostly we came up against Japanese flak and not their Zero fighters. I ran into them later over Luzon [the Philippines]. It was Japanese carriers that had destroyed our fleet at Pearl Harbor, so I was out to get a carrier. But of course I never did."

The official records tell us that brief, laconic, and self-deprecating account doesn't quite tell the entire story. Jerry joined a squadron designated VMSB-341 but nicknamed "the Torrid Turtles," and he flew combat missions through the Solomon Islands and later the Philippines. It was over Luzon that he saw his first Zero, and as Jerry recalls it, he wasted very little time "getting out of there." His squadron became the first ever designated specifically to supply close air support to Marine ground troops (something he was to do a lot more of years later in Korea, when he was no longer a twenty-one-year-old kid).

Bad as Rabaul was, his Luzon fighting was more colorful.

"On dive-bombing missions it was mostly flak." But on one raid he encountered several Zeroes, the Japanese fighters that were clearly faster and more maneuverable than Coleman's reliable but sluggish dive bomber. "I ran right into a waterspout trying to get away from them. At night in Luzon it was the Fourth of July every night, all the firing. Fireworks in the sky. They said guys on the ground got hit sometimes sitting on the edge of their foxholes just to see the excitement. I had my worst experience flying when my roommate, a major named Harper with three kids, blew up right in front of me. Years later at Yankee Stadium I was playing a game when Harper's brother-in-law called me. He was in New York with his sister, Harper's widow, mother of his kids. And since they'd never found the body, she wanted to meet me and ask if he was really dead. So I told him to bring her up and I had to tell her he was really dead. That was the worst time."

In July 1945 all Marine and navy pilots were called back to the States for carrier-based training in preparation for the planned invasion of the Japanese home islands. When the A-bombs were dropped

and the war ended suddenly that next month, Coleman was training at
Cherry Point. The Marines released him from active duty in January
1946 and the baseball aspect of his life resumed seriously, though in
the minor leagues. By 1949 he was in the majors, for a cup of coffee
the previous September and then as a full-fledged pro playing for what
would be that year's World Championship New York Yankees. It stuns
me as it does Coleman, even now, that five years earlier, he'd been a
Marine pilot in combat, flying bombing missions against Rabaul,
dodging Zeros, and now he was just another ballplayer playing a
child's game. But on the storied Yankees.

That first season, he wasn't bad. Not for a rookie. He played 128
games and batted .275, became an All-Star. In 1952, after four winning seasons, and as he was batting an extraordinary .405, Jerry was
called back into the Marine Corps on active duty as the Korean War
bloodily, endlessly ground on. The Marine Air Wing needed replacement pilots and there was Jerry lounging around at second base. His
next two seasons would be impacted, on the team only long enough to
play eleven games that year and eight games in '53.

"Those were at least theoretically your best years, your biggest
earning years, how bitter were you to be called back after having already fought in one war? Lots of other reservists bitched about the situation being unfair, life being unfair," I asked.

"I had a career, I had a wife and two kids myself, so I understand,"
Jerry said. "But I really did think I was going to come back, that I was
going to play ball again. So I didn't protest. I just went. And it worked
out okay."

I'd fought in Korea on the ground with a rifle company. What was
the fighting like in the air? I asked Jerry to tell me about Korea, about
his second war. What did he do and what was it like?

"I was flying Corsairs then [you know, the Pacific war's workhorse
fighter-bomber the Marine grunts loved for its close-air support, Pappy
Boyington's Black Sheep Squadron plane]," he said. Was he flying off
carriers? "No, we flew out of K-6 [one of the South Korean airfields]
mostly flying interdiction [bombing raids on railroads, roads, bridges,
cutting enemy supply routes], but also on TAC call, close air support
for the troops. We dropped napalm, but not very often. Usually it was

bombs. We flew almost as far north as the Yalu River [the border with Red China] and sometimes we flew into 'Mig Alley' where our jets fought their Migs [most Marines believe the Migs were actually piloted by Soviet Russians]."

What kind of bomb load could a fighter carry, five hundred pounds? That drew a laugh from Coleman.

"Lindbergh"—Charles A. Lindbergh, then a Reserve colonel in the air force—"nearly killed us all during the war. He was in the Pacific as a flight expert for the American military and told the brass the Corsair could be used as a bomber. Sometimes we carried three thousand pounds of bombs. Three thousand pounds of bombs! If it was a job close to the lines in air support, we carried even more, up to 3,500. It was all Lindbergh's fault. Think of getting off the ground on a 5,000-foot runway with a load like that. It was so heavy we could never fly higher than 10,000 feet." So spoke a Corsair driver, still resentful about Lindy, "the Lone Eagle."

In Korea he flew another sixty-three combat missions with what they called "the Death Rattlers" squadron. After that, they gave him a break, sent the poor guy up to the trench lines and bunkers, the barbed wire and outposts of the main line of resistance to pull forward air control duties, in effect, a flyboy transferred to the infantry to give him a break, a little R&R from flying. Just imagine that, kiddies. I shook my head and asked, Had he ever been shot down or wounded?

"No, but I had two bad accidents. In the first of them we were on a raid and my radio went out. There were varying cloud layers and I couldn't find anybody to follow home and with no radio couldn't have someone talk me home. I finally found K-6 and came in for a landing without radioing in, but I assumed everything was clear for a landing, else they would have fired up a Very signal to warn me off. And an F-86 [jet] nearly hit me.

"The other, second accident, it's a miracle I'm even here. The K-6 runway had a bump in the middle of it, and this time on takeoff when I hit it my engine stopped. And I was suddenly airborne, upside down, heading for the end of the runway. I dropped my bombs. They hadn't been armed so I knew they wouldn't explode. But my own bombs hit my tail, my knees were up behind my ears, my helmet slipped, and I was choking on the chinstrap, and was unconscious when they pulled me out."

Did they send you home after that or, in the grand old guts football tradition, send you up again right away? I asked. Coleman didn't hesitate. "Next day at four A.M. I was back in a plane and going up again."

Americans are, with ample reason, forever boasting of our technological edge on the rest of the world, smug in the assurance our stuff was usually better. Yet Jerry Coleman flew two warplanes demonstrably less advanced, inferior to what the enemy had back then, the hostile fighters that tried to kill him in two wars, the Zeroes the Japanese used in the Pacific and the Russian Migs the North Koreans and Chinese flew. Makes you wonder why we are surprised to learn Toyota is now larger, and a lot richer, than Ford. And has General Motors in its sights.

Two other rather famous Marines also flew in Korea, future astronaut and United States senator John Glenn and Ted Williams of the Boston Red Sox. Did Coleman fly with either of them? "No, Glenn was there before me, and Ted was flying jets then and flying out of K-3. I was still in Corsairs." I told Jerry I'd heard from other Marine aviators that by the time Korea came around, Williams's reflexes were shot and he was getting to be a danger to himself in the air. That fellow pilots and Marine brass were afraid he might kill himself and bring down a righteous national fury on the Marines and Marine aviation.

"I don't believe that," Coleman said. "I was twenty-eight or so and Ted was six years older, thirty-three or thirty-four, so the reflexes may have been slowing, but jet pilots wore blackout suits, so you can fly a jet older than you can flying prop planes like Corsairs." I take his word for it, since Coleman's an aviator and I'm not, and that was what Jerry said. Later I read a piece by writer J. David Truby in a magazine called *Flight Journal,* an interview of Williams by Truby, in which he quoted Ted about his Korean combat. After thirty-nine missions a bout of pneumonia put the great man in the hospital and damaged the hearing in one ear, a problem resulting later in total deafness in that ear. But when Truby asked if he were bitter, Williams told Truby, "Any guy who has been in combat knows that bitterness vanishes quickly when you gamble with death and win. From there on, you're just grateful to be alive."

On being mustered out, he returned to the Red Sox. And much later, in 1988, Ted Williams said, very nearly echoing Jerry Coleman's remarks to me, "I was a United States Marine pilot. It was the greatest experience of my life. The two things that I am proudest of are that I was a Marine and that I was lucky enough to play the game I loved."

After Korea, Coleman, too, was back in the majors, again a member of the Yankees. Getting into a couple of games at the end of 1953 and 107 games in '54, having 300 at bats and batting only .217. His second war had taken a toll.

"My eyes were shot. I was frowning a lot. They sent me to the doctor and he asked, 'Have you been under stress lately?' I thought, oh, nothing much, Doc. Just a war. But he gave me some pills and some exercises and eventually the eyes came back. I was still pretty good, but just not as good." He played major league ball into 1957 and then hung up the spikes. His record reads rather well. Most Valuable Player, 1950 World Series (Yanks sweep Phils!), Baseball Hall of Fame (broadcasters' wing), Ford C. Frick award for Broadcasting Excellence. His USMC record is okay, too: two Distinguished Flying Crosses, thirteen Air Medals, three Navy Citations. But we know how "Airedales" pile up the medals, don't we? To me, the most impressive stat: The guy flew 120 combat missions (120 missions! Remember that the air force boys treasured the so-called fifty mission-crush uniform cap, how all the girls flocked?) and is probably the only major leaguer to have fought, really fought, in two wars, not just playing ball on the base team, selling war bonds, and doing PR.

He and wife Margaret (Maggie) and daughter Chelsea live in La Jolla. When we last spoke he thought he might be coming to New York to broadcast a Mets-Padres playoff series. He was pleased about that but grouchy about one thing. "I'm getting to an age where people call me 'Mister' or 'Colonel.' I hate that. I'm Jerry, Jerry Coleman."

Aye, aye, "Jerry."

14

A Long Island detective with a Bronze Star and three Purple Hearts

IN 1965, AS VIETNAM WORE ON, WITH MORE AND MORE YOUNG Americans being drafted to feed the increasingly insatiable needs of the American military, nineteen-year-old Dennis Delaney, who had graduated in June from Lindenhurst High on New York's Long Island, was working as a plumber and looking over a shoulder at the draft process. "For me, the draft was about to ring the bell and one day when I was feeling particularly funky, I called them and asked, Well, when? They looked it up and said, December 27, two days after Christmas. I had this idea I didn't want to be drafted but wanted to go to the Marine Corps. I admired their tradition and what I'd heard about the training. So the Marine Corps lured me. But there was an argument at home. My father said, Why not go into the army, do your two years, and you're done? My mother said, 'It's his life.' But my father was opposed to the four-year Marine enlistment.

"So I went to Bayshore to the recruiting office and they said, Take a seat, look around, while they finished up with another fellow. I looked around at the pictures and was reading everything on the wall, and then I saw a decal on the recruiting officer's desk. It said, 'Join now, get 120 days deferment, and a two-year enlistment.'

"I was ready to sign up for four but I asked, Sir, is this still available? I think he was disappointed because he wanted me for four, but he said yes and I took it. When I went home with the news my dad was quite pleased."

His 120-day grace period ended, Delaney was sworn in April 13, 1966, and off he went to Parris Island. "After boot camp they moved us very quickly, up to Camp Geiger at Lejeune for advance training. Then we got leave and orders to Camp Pendleton. I went over [to Vietnam] as a private; my three promotions were all over there—to PFC, to lance corporal, to corporal. I was assigned to India Company, 3rd Battalion, 5th Marines, 1st Marine Division. That was in Chulai. My MOS was 311, basic rifleman, but when I arrived in-country I was told to go to 'rockets.' 'What the hell is rockets?' I asked. You know, bazookas. So I went up to the 3.5 rockets and protested. 'There must be an error. I'm a 311.' Their response: Now you're a 351 [rocket man]. The footnote is, you start out as a private humping ammunition but within a few months I was running the squad, seven or eight men, as a lance corporal."

Young Delaney's promotion sounds swift. But wait until you hear about what happened those first weeks in Dennis's war.

"We were part of a truck convoy Chulai to Da Nang. It was very easy for the enemy to learn a very large convoy was coming and to set up an ambush. Which began with a land mine that exploded under the first truck and wrecked it and hung up the rest of the convoy." Realizing this was the first time the kid had ever heard hostile fire, I asked what happened then. Everyone bail out of the trucks and start firing back?

"Exactly, we all emptied out on both sides of the road. You could see the bright flash of the mortar tubes. We fired back and the firefight went on for quite a while and then Puff the Magic Dragon showed up in the sky." Puff, Delaney explained, was a C-130 rigged out as a gunship with a very heavy volume of fire. "Their effectiveness in aid of ground troops was enormous." He earned his first Purple Heart in that fight, but to me sloughed it off as "only a burn mark on my arm." But his Bronze Star citation, dated March 24, 1967, for the same fight, goes into some more colorful detail.

"PFC Delaney, serving as an assistant 3.5 rocket gunner, was providing security for the convoy when it was ambushed by an estimated company of North Vietnamese soldiers using automatic weapons, recoilless rifles, and mortars. Reacting instantly and with complete disregard for his own safety, he leaped from the truck and assisted his rocket team leader delivering a heavy volume of accurate 3.5 rocket fire at the enemy while the other men in the convoy deployed from the trucks. Although wounded by mortar fragments, PFC Delaney maintained his position. After the rocket rounds were expended, he obtained an automatic rifle and dauntlessly continued to bring accurate fire to bear on the enemy. Upon receiving the order to re-board the trucks, PFC Delaney provided covering fire while the rocket team leader evacuated the wounded across thirty meters of fire-swept terrain. Subsequently he assisted in delivering deadly fire on the enemy with an M-30 machine gun as the convoy moved out of the hazardous area. His heroic actions were responsible for the destruction of an enemy mortar position and were instrumental in saving numerous Marine lives."

Dennis has been "in country," as the jargon went, for a few days and in his very first ever firefight jumps out of trucks, gets wounded, wrecks an enemy mortar, saves Marine lives, fires in turn a rocket, a BAR, and a machine gun, and is written up for a Bronze Star with combat V for valor. A year or so earlier he was a high school grad learning the plumber's trade.

When Dennis and I spoke over my lousy coffee early in 2007 on the patio of my house in East Hampton, I asked him what happened next.

"We went out on a number of good-sized operations. On 26 May we were on an operation when a firefight started the afternoon of the day before and continued through the evening. Fighting the NVA, North Vietnam Army, not the Viet Cong [VC], and next day we were still battling. I had just put a bipod onto my M-16 when they skipped in a lot of automatic fire and it was lucky I had the rifle there or I would have been hit directly in the chest. Instead, the shot hit the elevation reel of my rifle. It shattered like slate and I took small pieces like bird shot all over, nearly taking my thumb and hitting my hand, arm, and shoulder. And my chest. The corpsman bandaged me up. I was bandaged from thumb to shoulder and you remember how they tagged the wounded for evacuation. They put a shipping tag with wire on me to signify I was to get on the next helicopter out of there.

"But they were shorthanded and I decided to stay."

That was his second Purple Heart. But Delaney hadn't quit quite yet. "We were out on another operation and there was a fire on a hill-top we didn't know what it was, and then something exploded and I caught pieces in the left ankle. This time I had to be taken out and had to do surgery. I couldn't walk. They did the surgery in the hospital at Chulai." And that was his third and final Heart.

With the antiwar movement growing at home I asked Dennis Delaney how he kept up his own motivation and that of his squad.

"I was certainly well aware of antiwar bias when I got home, and in country we knew about it from men who came back from leave." Grumbling among his men? "I recall no issue from my standpoint. We had our assignment from the lieutenant and that was my concentration. I didn't worry about what was going on in the States or wonder about why we were in Vietnam. There was never any hesitation under fire from any of my men. One of the things I was so grateful for was that, here I am, twenty or twenty-one years old, and I'm running these men and I have a responsibility to get not only me, but them, home safely, and that was my greatest concern."

"Ever lose any men?" I asked Delaney.

"Fortunately, none of them were lost." And then, a month short of a year in country, he went home. But the Marine Corps wasn't going to let slip a Dennis Delaney before his time was up. "After liberty, I re-ported back to Camp Lejeune and then they packed up the entire 2nd Battalion (of the 8th Marines) and shipped us off to Gitmo [slang for Guantánamo Bay, Cuba]. It was wonderful, tropical weather and we had escaped winter at the base [in North Carolina]. We maintained the fence [between the Marines and Fidel's Cubans], held two- or three-man bunkers along the line. By then I was the company commander's driver. We were there several months, then back to Lejeune for another

few months, and I was mustered out and went back to Long Island."
The family happy? "Very happy," he said."

When did Dennis first think of becoming a cop?

"I was still in the Marine Corps when I began writing to everybody I could think of, the New York P.D., the State Police, and so on. Everybody responded, saying, well, you have to take these tests. When I got home I began to apply officially. And the Suffolk County [Long Island] test came up and I took it." That was thirty-seven years ago and Dennis is still on the Suffolk County force, these days as a detective in the Criminal Intelligence Section. He's a very fit-looking six-footer (a serial runner, Mrs. Delaney tells me) with a full head of close-cut dark hair, and he and his wife, a retired social worker, have a thirty-seven-year-old daughter and a home in Sag Harbor.

Since he was now sixty I asked, "Think they'll retire you one of these days?"

"No, I don't think so."

I guess maybe they know they have a good man. We ended up our talk by my asking Dennis his feelings now about the Marines. Any regrets for all those wounds? Or about having been sent to and having to fight an unpopular war?

"No. The Marine Corps meant a tremendous amount to me. And even today I gain momentum from it. The Corps is one of the prime reasons Marines are so successful in whatever we do—because we refuse to quit."

15

A "proud mustang" who was in three wars and ended up a general.

THE MARINE CORPS HAS A GRAND TRADITION OF PROMOTING outstanding enlisted men and NCOs to commissioned officers, many of them through field commissions under battle conditions. All such officers, battlefield or not, are called "mustangs," even and proudly by themselves.

But in the spring of 1951 an extraordinary group of several hundred "mustangs," brand-new Marine second lieutenants, reported in to the Basic School at Quantico, Virginia, to be formed into a unit called the 5th Special Basic Class, where they would be trained in what young Marine officers were supposed to do. A rapidly expanding Korean-era Marine Corps needed lieutenants, and these fellows were themselves very special, all of them having been enlisted Marines of various rank for several years and many of them having fought as Marines against the Japanese during the big war. As a young officer assigned as a platoon leader over them, and to help educate these already quite savvy and very salty gyrenes, I found it a bit unnerving to be commanding about forty of the mustangs, men my own rank (I was also a second lieutenant but one with only thirteen weeks of active duty and absolutely no combat), and trying to teach these old-timers stuff they knew far better than I.

In a quite real sense, they were not only older and seasoned, but they were men and I was a boy, just a year out of college and looking it. I should have been learning from them. Instead, not by choice, I was their commanding officer. I was hardly stupid, but when I goofed, and I did from time to time, they must have enjoyed it. But being Marines, at least while I was around, they kept their laughter to themselves. All in all, they were pretty good guys and I think most of them appreciated the awkward situation I was in, commanding men older and, probably, better.

One of those brand-new lieutenants, those former enlisted men, now suddenly anointed commissioned officers, actually ended up a general. Which was why last Thanksgiving (of '06) I phoned retired brigadier general George L. Bartlett at his home in Potomac, Maryland. He was about to leave for two weeks' skiing in Aspen, Colorado, but promised to get back to me before Christmas to tell me more about the background and origins of that very special Special Basic Class, and their history of combat in World War II and Korea and, for some of them, Vietnam. Bartlett and I had met again in September after half a century at a preview of the new Marine Museum being dedicated in November of '06, and I was down at Quantico to write about it for *Parade,* and a handful of us former officers ended up having lunch.

I asked Bartlett to detail just who made up his bunch and how they were selected. "They brought over five hundred of us to Quantico for the fifth Officer's Screening Course, many of us staff NCOs. I can remember several master sergeants in the group. I would guess that more than half of us had been in World War II and had been called back for the Korean War. They commissioned 293 of us, and of that total about 75 made the Marine Corps their career. I forget the number of officers who made colonel, but three of us made flag rank [general]. Several actually stayed on active duty until they had their thirty years of active duty as an officer, and then retired. I think the Marine Corps more than got its money's worth."

Bartlett himself was born in Idaho. "My dad was a civil engineer who worked on the Panama Canal and met my mother down there, an

English girl, and through her family he was offered a job in Pocatello, Idaho, which then was way out in the woods. I always wanted to be a Marine, and when I graduated from high school my dad was in Alaska on a surveying job, and when I told my mom I wanted to enlist, she said, Well, let's wait until your dad gets back, but by then I was drafted and chose the Marines and went to San Diego, 'the real boot camp,' and was sent to Miramar, a little administrative base.

"I scored high on tests and applied for navigation school but I wasn't nineteen yet and they sent me to a twenty-six-week aviation machinist course and I graduated number one in the class. An old Marine with Nicaragua time, Colonel Evans, asked me what I wanted. I said to be a pilot. But they sent me to navigation school instead, and I went out to the Pacific to fly in B-25s as a navigator-bombardier. Never saw a Zero, never bombed their home islands, the Pacific air war being by then pretty much a thing of the past, mostly flying around the Solomons and down in the Philippines."

At war's end, George would have had to sign up for six years in order to be sent to flight school, so he got out instead and went to college at the University of Oregon. In 1950, with the Korean war buildup, and still in the reserves, he was activated as a staff sergeant navigator. "I told them it was six years since I'd navigated, but they told me, 'It's like riding a bike. You never forget.' And soon I was flying back and forth over the Pacific. Then a Marine Corps order came out saying anyone with a college degree or able to pass a GED test could apply for a commission. I went for my physical and was flunked for a cavity. I told the doctor, 'Well, why don't you fill it?' He said he was too busy. But when I told a senior officer what happened, he went to the doctor and ordered him, 'Just fill the goddamned thing,' and I was in.

"Five hundred of us reported in to mainside at Quantico [for the screening process]," and on graduation (and surviving me!) Bartlett was dispatched to Cherry Point to become an air controller and shipped off to the Korean War. Where he was assigned as an air controller to Chodo Island, with a garrison of 250 Marines sixty miles north of the line, off the Korean mainland.

"We sent up fighters to fight Migs. Best job I ever had."

In 1965, by now a regular career officer, but apparently doomed to stateside staff and technical assignments of one sort and another, dreading the very real possibility he would inevitably be labeled "a desk officer" (something no Marine wants to be considered), Bartlett wangled himself a transfer to the infantry, and went out to Vietnam with the 7th Marines, an infantry regiment, only to find himself assigned to logistical support. His screech of outrage got him sent to the Philippines, where he was assigned to a naval task force sailing off the Asian coast. More sightseeing? Not this time.

"We had a special landing force with helicopters and we made about fifteen amphibious landings in Vietnam." So you were finally getting shot at, I wisecracked, not as respectful as I should be to a general officer. "Finally," Bartlett conceded without kvetching. By now he was a major. "And I knew this was going to be my career. I was seven or eight years older than my contemporaries and thought I'd better get cracking, and [after Vietnam] went to night school to earn a master's in personnel management. A Marine officer today needs at least an MA. The days of becoming a Marine company commander with a sixth-grade education are over."

I wanted to know more about those "fifteen amphibious landings" and George called me back from another ski trip to Aspen. "I was a staff officer in what we called a Special Landing Force, what is today a 'Marine Expeditionary Unit.' It was a Marine infantry battalion, reinforced, with a squadron of helicopters, engineers, and landing craft, and we worked with Westmoreland's staff, and made landings in all four Corps areas, landings on hostile beaches and on every one of the fifteen we got opposition of one sort or another, and, hopefully, we killed people. Not much hand-to-hand stuff and I was so far back I was pretty safe. Our flagship was an old carrier and I usually spent a lot of time there, but the colonel would let me go ashore because I didn't want to be left out or miss the fun, and I carried a .45 and never got shot but did some shooting of my own."

Bartlett ended up a brigadier general having served thirty-seven years on active duty, a guy who wanted to be a pilot and then an infantryman, kept being turned away, but wouldn't be turned down. After his retirement, he bought a bicycle and rode it from the Atlantic Coast to the Pacific at Oregon in a carefree fifty-five days, and then for the next ten years, he ran the Marine Corps Association. What became of his fellow mustangs who would be gathering again in late May 2007 for what they expect may be their "last post" at Quantico, where their story began. How did that special class of Marine mustangs turn out?

Said George Bartlett: "The 5th Special Basic did pretty well. Good men, good Marines. Three of us ended up generals, two of us were killed in Korea, one in Vietnam. And all of us are getting old." Here was a guy older than I was, just back from skiing at Aspen, and he was talking about getting old.

I promised Bartlett I'd be going to their "last" reunion in Quantico where we first met. Virginia seemed appropriate, where so many Americans of both sides died in the War Between the States, in Virginia where Lord Cornwallis surrendered to Washington and the French, and as the redcoats marched out of Yorktown their band played a jolly English tune, "The World Turned Upside Down," and where in 1951 a clueless college boy tried to tell some old Marines how to do their job. Or as George referred to himself and his mates, "the mobsters you had to deal with as a brand-new second lieutenant."

And I ended being the one who learned from them, about the honorable and deadly trade we all, those aging mustangs and the rest of us, were intended to practice.

16

Jack Rowe lost an eye and other parts and now grows avocados and chases rattlesnakes.

I WAS THE FIRST IN MY FAMILY TO GO TO COLLEGE," SAID JACK ROWE. And that was what got him into trouble, also known as the Marine Corps, when he joined the NROTC at Villanova University. "The Korean War was on and in my NROTC unit of about thirty, a dozen of us picked the Marines over the navy. The Marine major on campus had to get a dispensation because only about ten percent were supposed to go Marine and not navy and I put in with them because I didn't want to spend my time picking lint off a navy blue uniform." Rowe went on active duty in the spring of 1951 not as a reserve but as a regular. Having been a Reserve officer myself, and experienced all the usual Marine snobbery toward the Reserves, I asked how he pulled that off. It seems that a priest at Villanova cleared the way for Rowe to take a competitive exam for regular status so that his college costs, books, room and board, tuition and uniforms were "on full tab, paid all the way through" college. "That was important," Jack said, "because we didn't have family dough, didn't even have a flush toilet at home until I was in my teens."

At the Basic School in Quantico Jack was put into the ninth Special

Basic Class along with a sizable influx of Annapolis graduates, Class of
'51, some VMI grads, and others, an impressive, rather classy lot, and
he arrived as a replacement in Korea in the winter of '51–'52 to join
Dog Company of the 7th Marines. Which was where I got to know
Jack and do some fighting alongside him. He remarked that being a
"regular" won him at least a tentative, early acceptance by the men. "I
overheard one Dog Company Marine say to another, 'Well, at least he's
a regular. So he must know something.' " My own early Dog Company
nickname, it pains me to report, was the somewhat less impressive,
"Shit-Trench Brady."

On Memorial Day of '52 Jack lost one eye, some fingers, and other
useful parts in an entertaining firefight and grenade-tossing contest (he
lost) with some ill-tempered Chinese soldiers on a minor sandstone hill
called Yoke, north of the Imjin River in South Korea near the so-called
Panmunjom truce corridor.

Half a century later, he and his wife, Laura, the mother of his children and a former United States Navy nurse, raise avocados out back
of their lovely, sprawling one-level house up in the hills of Fallbrook,
California, forty or fifty miles northeast of San Diego, conveniently
close to the back gate of Camp Pendleton, and I was up there visiting
them and having lunch last September (2006) and listening to Jack explain to a city boy how you grow avocados, and telling me how you get
rid of rattlesnakes. The snakes being a hell of a lot more interesting
than cultivating vegetables (or are avocados fruit?), I asked rattlesnake-
killing questions.

"I've got a couple of old shovels in the garage," said Jack, "that do
the job very well. But what you've got to remember is to cut off the
head and bury it." Bury it? What was this, some sort of local religious
ritual, a snake spirit cult totem at work?

"No, you bury the head so a dog won't eat it and get poisoned."
The Rowes, I might make clear, may have a dog or two around (as well
as plenty of snakes) but no cats. The local coyotes have eaten the cats.
And every so often there's a mountain lion scare up around Vía del
Gavilán (the Way of the Hawk) where they live. And where Jack drives
maniacally up and down mountain roads that have no guardrails protecting drivers from the steep ravines on either side, and at occasional

stretches aren't even paved. And I suspect that if you hit a loose shoulder and spin out on the gravel and go into one of those ravines by night or when no one is watching, you may not be found until spring. Rowe is also a licensed pilot who at one time owned a share in two private planes. Though how with only one working eye you handle the depth perception aspects of flight, or even of fast driving, I cannot say.

Until he was retired a few years ago Jack taught high school in Fallbrook. He is an otherwise quite civilized gent who grew up in the Wilmington, Delaware, area, where his dad worked for DuPont (one of Jack's more successful books was about the Du Pont clan and was once optioned as a miniseries by CBS).

Rowe briefly was employed as a schoolteacher and assistant football coach after graduation from Villanova before going on active military duty, and came into my life early in 1952 as a replacement rifle platoon leader joining Dog Company (I was by now the executive officer) of the 7th Marines up on the Kanmubong Ridge of North Korea where we were fighting the local lads and had been doing so during the fall and winter. "I showed up and bunked in with you and Charley Logan [the company commander] for one night until I was given the machine guns."

I can't say I can remember sleeping with Jack that long ago night in North Korea but I can testify that Rowe distinguished himself once that winter, by rolling down a steep Korean hillside with members of his platoon in a six-by truck that overturned in a heavy March snowstorm while the 1st Marine Division was being transferred from the mountainous eastern front to the low sandstone hills of the west where, for something of a change of pace and for variety's sake, we would be put to fighting the Chinese.

"I remember that truck," Jack said, "and inside it we were all bouncing around yelling and cursing as it rolled down the hill while machine guns and ammo boxes and BARs and cartons of rations and hand grenades came down on our heads and bounced off our shoulders and backs and I thought we would never stop rolling." Small harm, however, was done. They righted the truck and Rowe's gallant, if bruised, little band resumed its journey. It was in May of that year, during the early stages of what would become known as "the outpost

war," with U.S. soldiers and Marines grappling through a nightly series of murderous scrimmages with the Chinese near Panmunjom, that
Jack Rowe forever set himself distinctly apart from the rest of us.

The thing began innocently enough. I was by now intelligence officer of the 2nd Battalion 7th Marines when one morning Colonel Noel
C. Gregory, a gentle soul who'd fought on Guadalcanal and other
places, sort of suggested I might go out to reconnoiter a hill called
Yoke to discover if there were Chinese on the hill. "Division [meaning
the general] would like to know," the colonel remarked. Being that
Gregory was a lieutenant colonel and I a mere first lieutenant, I said I
thought that was a swell idea. I should have become suspicious when the
operations plan drawn up by Major Dennis Nicholson stipulated that
my half dozen intelligence scouts and I would be accompanied on our
patrol by about sixty Marines, a reinforced rifle platoon plus a section
of light machine guns. If there were no Chinese on Yoke, we hardly
needed almost seventy Marines to go out there to stare at the silly place
and report back. But being an amiable sort, I issued no protest. It was
Jack Rowe's Dog Company rifle platoon (reinforced) that would be my
escort.

We gathered on that particular evening in the Dog Company position atop Hill 229, I got a few hours sleep, and just after midnight we
saddled up and moved out. Rowe was somewhere up near the head of
the single-file column of Marines. Dog Company exec Stewart Mc-
Carty, who had a new Bell & Howell movie camera he wanted to try
out, was also on the line of march. My scouts and I wandered along
with the machine gunners near the stern. Here I was off on a night patrol again but not uptight about it. Maybe because it was Jack Rowe's
patrol and I was just along for the ride. A passenger. Or maybe after
seven months I was finally getting used to the dark. It was pushing
maybe two A.M. on a chill spring night.

I don't remember a moon but there were plenty of stars to see by
and we straggled along, making too much noise, as Marines always do,
not stupidly talking aloud or issuing shouted orders, but just carelessly,
the creak of leather and metal and 782 gear, the scuff of boots on un-
even ground, the occasional stumble and curse. Just an ordinary route
march down the forward slope of 229, then across the flats between the

MLR, our lines, and the Chinese positions, with Hill Yoke looming dark ahead of us, the ground rising imperceptibly and then more steeply as the column began its ascent. Behind us on a low ridgeline the squad of two machine guns and their gunners had dropped behind to set up, and if necessary to support us with overhead fire. Then, suddenly, shockingly, came the angry crack of an explosion and a brief flash lighting the blackness, blinding us momentarily in the flash.

"Oh, shit! They hit a mine." Maybe that was it. Wasn't a shot. Gunfire sounds different. Could have been a grenade. If it was a grenade, that meant there were Chinese up there. A mine could have been left over from a year ago. There were shouts up ahead. No point in maintaining approach-march silence now. The world knew we were there, knew we were coming. In the east the first hint of false dawn. I turned to my sergeant. "Let's get up there. See what's happening." Jay Scott, Rudy Wrabel, a couple of other guys. Good men. Other Marines were double-timing ahead as well, humping uphill fast, and now we could hear the first shots, another couple of explosions.

Sounded like a pretty good firefight was starting. The machine gunners set up on a low ridge behind us were firing their light guns now, the shots whistling overhead, hitting the hilltop I assumed, a few shots hitting the wreckage of the long useless steel high-tension tower that was the key feature of Yoke from a distance, the whine of the ricochets winging off somewhere harmless. And day was breaking, true dawn. We humped ahead, up the small hill. As usual, I felt very calm now that the fight was on.

I didn't know it yet, but up ahead, the point man was dead. He'd been killed by that first explosion, the mine that alerted the Chinese defenders or a grenade thrown by them. (Which it was, to this day I am unsure.) Stew McCarty saw me coming. "Rowe's down," he said. We talked about which of us should take command. "It's your company. You're senior to me and you know the men," I said. That seemed to make sense to McCarty, too. I told him to tell me what to do. "Take the right flank," he said. "We're going to attack the hilltop." Sounded okay to me. I didn't ask questions about Jack Rowe. At a time like that you have other things on your mind than the sick and the dead. That isn't callous, just sensible and the way it is, the way the brain works in a fight. You only ask questions or talk about stuff you have to do to win, to stay alive. No social chat.

I took the right, my scouts and I, with those of Rowe's men over there, and we went for the top, getting through the barbed wire but not much farther. The Chinese weren't firing much, just tossing grenades from their trenches or hidey holes, the grenades tumbling and bouncing downhill toward us, stopping us dead. They must have had a stack of the damned things. I didn't think there were that many Chinese, maybe a squad or so. McCarty said later he thought it was at least a platoon. There were now so many of our men hit or down, if this kept up we wouldn't have enough people left to get the wounded back off the hill. Our walking wounded kept up fire very nicely, but they weren't going to be much good at attacking. We sure weren't going to overrun the Chinese at this rate since they were sheltered in holes and our rifle fire wasn't very effective. A 60-mm mortar would have been handy.

It was full daylight now, and overhead the first black shells of the 105 guns roared overhead to smash into and explode on the hilltop ahead, thirty or fifty yards uphill. I was very nervy again there for a moment, thinking about the possibility of a short round exploding among us, the artillery having joined the party. Woooeee! That's all we needed, a short round. I was more afraid of friendly fire than I was of the Chinese. The grenades continued to fly, some of them familiar, others old-fashioned potato mashers with a wooden handle, from World War I. Antiques, maybe, but they did the job. I was packing a rifle now, dropped by one of the wounded, figuring it would be a lot handier than the damned .45 in my holster. For some reason, I was feeling fine and I remember Rudy Wrabel, in his first firefight, was grinning at me. Very happy, Rudy was.

But this is Jack Rowe's story, not mine. I didn't know it until later, but this is what happened to Rowe, what he told me last year at his house in Fallbrook where the rattlers are, and later on the phone.

"I was up in the point because I had a new platoon sergeant who didn't know the ground and I was right behind the lead fire team. I didn't know the source of the first explosion. Later, on the hospital ship we had bull sessions and talked about it once I could walk a little and I'm almost certain it was an inertial grenade, a grenade hung in the

barbed wire. My point had told me, 'Hey, there's a booby trap up there
in the wire.' I knew then we were in trouble." Putting it in context, in
1952 there were forty divisions of Chinese Communist regulars in Korea, six U.S. divisions, five army, one Marine. Rowe and his sixty-man
patrol were out there a mile from our lines, confronting no one yet
knew how many hostile Chinese on the hill, and he thought, "We
might be in trouble."

Rowe went on. "Then I saw a thing flying through the air and I
yelled, 'Smitty, grenade!' I picked up a few fragments, and you know
how guys don't always fire at first, so I stood up and sprayed the hill
with my carbine and said, 'You guys start shooting!' then everyone
was firing. But it was mostly grenades, not small arms. I was dancing
around and a grenade went off and hit both legs. There was a god-
awful burning in my legs. I'm not sure of the sequence but I counted
five distinct grenades. Another grenade nicked my head and knocked
off my helmet. Then a big one blew up my carbine and radio and then
one blew me up in the air. There was a really bad burning in my face
and hands. I took a half-inch-square metal fragment in my eye socket.
They told me later it first went through my hand and my cheekbone,
otherwise it would have gone right through my head. They made an in-
cision later and sucked it out with a magnet. It's not true that I was
catching grenades and tossing them back, and that one exploded. Good
yarn, but not so. Another grenade then got me in the butt [getting his
pelvis and buttocks].

"I was still conscious, but it was about then I told my runner, Earl
Lofthouse, to tell McCarty, 'It's your patrol now.' I knew I was about
finished. Earl could tell you more. He lives now in Elkton, Maryland,
runs an auto repair shop."

I listened to and took notes on all this and then I said, "When I saw
you on the stretcher, you seemed to be out. I was shouting at you, saying, 'He's a Villanova wildcat. You can't kill a Villanova wildcat,' stuff
like that, hoping you could hear, trying to will you to stay alive. But
you looked bad to me. You weren't reacting, though maybe you could
hear me. Could you?"

Rowe laughed. "I was probably enjoying my morphine by then. It
was really the corpsman who saved me."

"Who was that first guy killed by the grenade?" I asked. Rowe told me to hold on and went away for a moment.

"Edward R. Bosch," Rowe said then, without hesitation, after checking a note. "I'm pretty sure it was a shaped charge that got him." Both of us remembered that the Chinese were throwing those old potato masher grenades such as Lew Ayes and his other Germans like Slim Summerville tossed in *All Quiet on the Western Front*. And I reminded him of other grenades packed in socks with additional gunpowder to increase the impact but inadvertently smashing the metal fragments so small the grenades were less effective. Which we agreed may have been why so many Marines were hit but not disabled, the fragments were broken up so small.

Here we were, a couple of Catholic boys a year or two out of college in the States and we're suddenly experts on the killing power of fragmentation hand grenades. I guess both of us appreciated the irony. Forty-eight Marines went up the hill called Yoke that morning and thirty-two or thirty-three were hit.

All I knew was this. Once his point man was killed, Jack led an attack uphill against the enemy. There was a pitching duel. With hand grenades. When one exploded he lost the eye and some fingers. But what the hell, he had another eye and lots of fingers, and he continued to shout orders and direct fire, by now lying on his stomach and firing off a shot or two himself. He was hurt but very much in control up there at the head of the column with the rest of us still moving up. "What kept you going?" I asked, wanting a useful reply for this book.

"Well, we were just a few yards below the top of the hill, and I figured, why not?" Then another grenade hit him, landing in the small of his back and breaking his pelvis, shredding his buttocks. By now he looked pretty bad, I guess, and some of his men dragged him back down the hill, where a corpsman took over, and McCarty kept things going until I came up and we talked over the situation. Would have been nice to have a 60 mm mortar handy, we agreed.

By now, our artillery had taken up the cause of the righteous, 105-mm shells coming in, low and fast and black against the blue spring morning sky, smashing into the ridgeline of Yoke, presumably into the

Chinese trenches, helping stop their grenade tossing, enabling us to take a moment or two to think about where we should go from there.

Which is where Jack's story leaves off and mine begins. But at Fallbrook, I wanted to hear more from Rowe, what led up to his adventures on Yoke.

When Jack first joined Dog Company up in the Taebaek Mountains of North Korea, he said, "For about forty-eight hours I had the machine guns and then they gave me [Bob] Simonis's rifle platoon. It was a difficult time for me to take over because a machine gunner had just killed [in a friendly fire accident] two men in Simonis's and now my platoon." Yeah, I said, "And that machine gunner was a minister's son that later raped a couple of South Korean women. Beat the rap, too."

Much of what Jack told me in Fallbrook last year, I knew already, though not in detail or in his voice. To me the real surprise was this: Rowe already knew the enemy held Yoke before our ill-starred reconnaissance patrol ever stepped through the barbed wire that midnight in late May.

"I knew there were Chinese on Yoke. I used to go out late at night [on the high ground of the ridgeline of Hill 229 held by his rifle platoon] to have a cigarette and coffee and look through the glasses over at the Chinese lines and, specifically, at Yoke. And there was activity over there. I could see it. And by day I could see the barbed wire over there, their aiming stakes, could see that the Chinese were doing things."

"Jesus, I wish you told Colonel Gregory that. We never would have had to send a sixty-man patrol out there."

Rowe responded, "I reported what I'd seen. And what I suggested was that they send me out there with Nichols and one other guy and come back to report on it." Who was Nichols? "He was one of my squad leaders." And why didn't they let you do that? "They said, 'No, we're not sending an officer out there with two men. We'll send a real patrol.'"

Which was how I got sent out to reconnoiter Yoke and how Jack got shot to pieces and Ed Bosch was killed and thirty more hit.

After the war I lost track of Rowe. Knew he'd survived, been awarded the Navy Cross, and was probably still alive. Then, in 1990,

I got a phone call. My memoir, *The Coldest War,* had just been published and was getting some ink. Rowe was on the phone from San Diego. Some old Marines out there were having a cocktail party and after a few lubricating drinks thought they might as well call me. You know, cocktail party stuff. "Let's call so-and-so and break his chops." I was "so-and-so."

"Rowe, last time I saw you, you were nearly dead. What happened?"

When you've been in combat with a guy, there's nothing you can't ask. Jack didn't resent my curiosity.

"I spent a year in the hospital. Fell in love with and married my nurse. One of our kids had asthma, so we moved to California and I went back to teaching school and coaching football. Wrote a couple of books. Got a private pilot's license. Had ten kids."

Here was a guy I thought finished and instead he lived a life most men only dream of.

Then he stunned me, by putting Colonel Gregory on the horn. He was having cocktails, too! In *The Coldest War* I'd written about Jack and McCarty and John Chafee and the others, including "old" Colonel Gregory, who at the time of Korea was probably only thirty-nine or forty, and describing him as having a skinny, turkey neck and cackling when he laughed. I was sure, of course, that I was safe, that the colonel was long dead. So it was something of a shock when Rowe handed Gregory the phone.

"Brady, I've seen your book."

"Yes, Colonel."

"And my attorneys will be getting in touch."

"Yes, Colonel."

"And I want you to know, Brady. I do not cackle when I laugh."

There was a brief silence, and then a kind of wheezing that swiftly morphed into something else, something familiar.

"Hell, Colonel," I said, "you're cackling now!"

I believe Colonel Gregory now really is dead and I'm safe writing this.

17

Combat engineer captain Lauren Edwards and her first firefight

WHEN MARINE CAPTAIN LAUREN EDWARDS WAS A COLLEGE undergraduate at George Washington University who ran varsity track and majored in radio and television, she thought the attractive and really nifty thing after graduation might be to work at ESPN and go into sportscasting. Somewhere along the line those ambitions were side-tracked and she joined the Marine Corps instead and in 2003 found herself commanding a combat engineering unit under hostile fire along the fluid, rolling front in Iraq during the first days of the ground war. How do things like this come about?

When I began this book I made a point of saying it would be strictly about Marines in combat, men who fought in our various wars and what they remembered of and what they thought about the experience. It was retired Marine Colonel Walt Ford, the editor of *Leatherneck* magazine, who pulled me up short. Colonel Ford remarked that while he might not himself be a poster boy for the politically correct, he thought I was making a mistake in not speaking with women Marines who had actually seen combat in Iraq. "Several of them have quite extraordinary stories to tell, if they choose to do so," he told me. Not being either doctrinaire or stupid, I didn't need to mull that one over. "Find one of those women, Walt, and ask her if she'll talk with me."

Many of us, I don't need to tell you, old Marines like myself, long opposed any relaxation of restrictive, and some felt unfair, laws and rules intended to keep American women soldiers and women Marines out of combat situations. Remember how Jim Webb's stance on the question became something of a "cause célèbre" in his Virginia senatorial contest last November? Since then, with the changing nature of combat, women have been killed in Iraq combat. In the fall of 2006 I spoke several times with Captain Edwards, a combat engineer, with whom Colonel Ford had put me in touch, a woman Marine who was there at the start of ground warfare in Iraq and had spent more time serving in that unhappy and recently more chaotic country than I would care to do, and agreed to talk to me about it.

Captain Edwards, who had turned thirty-one just before we spoke, was born and grew up in a small Kentucky town called Smiths Grove. When she was in high school, she lost a Marine cousin, an aviator, in a crash, and she speaks of how moved she was, a kid, at his funeral with all its customary Marine pomp and ritual. "Later, one of my best friends was also killed in a training accident. These deaths, those funerals, moved me to do something, just what I didn't know. I went to college in D.C., George Washington University. I ran track, cross-country and two-miles and the distance relays." And at some point, perhaps with those two deaths of young men close to her working on her motivation, she enlisted in the Marine Corps' Platoon Leaders Class, a college-based officer candidate program I had gone through myself half a century before. But before PLC summer training even began, Lauren suffered a stress fracture and dropped out on medical grounds. Later, recovered, seeing another opportunity and still interested in the Marines, Lauren signed on for another sort of officers' candidate course at Quantico the summer of 1998, did well, and in August was commissioned a second lieutenant.

"My first duty post was Okinawa. I wanted to get out of the country, see the world. I'd never been abroad except for Mexico, a one-day trip to Tijuana. I was now a combat engineer by trade (MOS, military occupational specialty, 1302). And for an exercise I took eighty-eight

Marines and sailors to the Philippines." She also learned to scuba-dive while in Okinawa and after a few more years on active duty, in November 2002, Lauren was promoted to captain. It was then the situation in Iraq started to heat up.

"By then I was with a Marine Air Wing support squadron and we were in San Diego on a long weekend when they got in touch with us. 'Come on back. We're going to deploy. You're leaving on Thursday with the advance group.' It took a few days more actually to get away, but we flew over, with a stopover in Spain, and about seven or eight days later we were in Kuwait. It was my first time there, though a year earlier I'd done a project in Bahrain [it struck me as she spoke that the girl from Smiths Grove, Kentucky, really had begun to see the world].

"At that time, January of '03, there was no war yet (the actual fighting would begin in March) but on the first day of the ground war, my unit, which was a Forward Armed Refueling Center (FARC), sort of like a giant gas station for helicopters, was alerted. There I am, in command of 150 Marines, sailors and a few soldiers, including eight or nine women, when we got our orders. We're leapfrogging with other units, driving along the battle's edge, jumping back and then jumping up ahead again, everyone moving fast. Then they [the enemy] decided not to attack the grunts. They didn't want to face Marines. So they decided to attack the convoys instead. Which was when we got into it.

"It was near Nasaria and it wasn't a giant attack, small arms and snipers. It was the first time I was ever shot at. The mortar attack was first. A very helpless feeling because you can't see who's shooting. They were using pickup trucks with tubes in back, and launching rockets. I never did get into a really dire situation in Iraq. But during my time there we came under attack all the way up and down our convoy." How big a convoy, I asked. "It was a sixty-five-vehicle convoy with a fuel cargo of about forty or fifty thousand gallons."

All of it fairly flammable, I assumed. Captain Edwards didn't go into much detail on that, but described how "we were looking to move on with our little Beverly Hills convoy. I was in a HumVee, the soft version, but I took care to keep my door shut. Back then, in '03, we weren't under the same kind of pressure or necessity to be armored that the convoys did later on. I was in the area about six months during which I got ordered to be a monitor in mid-June and we handed over to the army in the fall. We had one Marine KIA and some wounded in our convoys. God was with me, and on Easter I remember thinking it was good to be a Christian."

Sure, but what was it like being shot at that first time?

"You look to the right and the left. Marines ask, 'What's next, Captain? What's next, ma'am?' That's when you fall back on your training. It's like an out-of-body experience. I thought, Hey, if I've gotta go down, you go down. Out there are mothers and fathers hoping that you care for their kids. The responsibility is on me. I had a very experienced gunny, eighteen or nineteen years in the Corps, and she said, 'Hey, ma'am, are we supposed to be this far forward?' Another guy came up to me and said, 'Hey, it worked out all right.' I took that as a compliment."

Captain Edwards's colonel, also a combat engineer, later told her, "Eddie, I don't think women should be here, but I'll keep you."

Did the captain believe the legal and other restrictions on women in combat had so far inhibited her own professional career as a Marine officer?

"No, it hasn't. But on today's battlefield you can't legislate women out of combat. And you can't stop using women in war. We need women for the numbers we need in today's wars. It's a women's world," Captain Edwards said.

And what is she doing in today's Corps? "I'm a student again. In the expeditionary warfare school, a nine- to twelve-month course, and after that I hope to get a command again. As a Marine I've seen fifteen countries and been to great places. I've visited Iwo Jima and Belleau Wood. There's been a lot of sacrifice and there's been a lot of energy. Yet there are still some combat engineering jobs I'm not authorized to work on."

What might they be, mine laying and mine clearing, that kind of traditional combat engineer's job? "It's more where I can be assigned. I can be sent to an air wing but not to a combat engineer battalion."

One of the more dreadful moments of the war's early days involved an army convoy ambushed by the enemy and the killing and wounding of American soldiers and the capture of a wounded young

army enlisted woman. The usual fanciful rumors immediately surfaced, that the heroic young woman had fought it out with her attack-
ers, firing her weapon until she was out of ammo and overwhelmed.
The fight had begun to resemble those last moments at the Alamo with
Jim Bowie and Davy Crockett by the time the truth came out. The
young woman soldier, undoubtedly a brave young American, was res-
cued from the hospital in a commando raid and promptly debunked
the legend, told the truth about what really happened. She not only
hadn't shot it out with anyone but didn't even know how to fire a
weapon. She'd never had a lesson, never fired the range.

Recalling that incident, I asked Lauren Edwards to clarify what
weapons training she and other women Marines get today.

"We get as much marksmanship training as any Marine except for
the infantry. We're required to go to the range annually, even MPs, to
fire pistols and rifles. [Women] officers have to qualify with the pistol
and the rifle. Others [women Marines] actually get heavy-machine-gun
training in case one day they're assigned to a unit with heavy guns and
they might have to join a heavy-machine-gun team."

I told the captain I always enjoyed "firing the range," as they call
those qualifying bouts of firing exercises on the rifle range. "The range
is fun," she agreed.

Yeah, but I was a city boy who never even owned a Daisy BB gun,
while Captain Edwards was a girl from Kentucky. Had she grown up
capable of using a Kentucky long rifle to pick off a squirrel from a tree
branch two hundred yards away? She said she hated to explode my
fanciful theories about Kentucky. but then Lauren laughed, and said,
"I never fired a weapon until I joined the Marine Corps." And her own
weapon in Iraqi combat?

"I carried a pistol, a 9-mm Baretta. I like the weapon but, then, I'm
not an expert."

Our conversations had all been by telephone, so I admitted curiosity. I had a romantic vision of Captain Edwards as a strapping, armored Valkyrie striding right out of Wagnerian opera into battle, the
Gods looking down smiling from Valhalla. Any merit in that portrait?

She laughed. "Mister Brady, I'm five-two in my Harley boots."
And what are "Harley boots"?

"The boots I wear when I ride my Harley."

My faith in the Marine Corps' judgment in choosing and promoting its officers was reinforced yet again. A five-two woman, qualified on the rifle range with pistol and rifle, packing a Baretta, and riding a Harley motorcycle, sounded terrific. Hooray for our side! Any criticisms of the Corps she hadn't yet mentioned?

"I criticize my brothers and sisters," said Captain Lauren Edwards, USMC, "but I still love them."

The winter after Lauren Edwards and I spoke, in February 2007, I was skiing in Vermont and there on the front page of *The Boston Globe* was the photograph and story of the funeral of another young Marine captain, Jennifer Jean Harris, a Naval Academy graduate from Swampscott, Massachusetts, killed in Iraq when the rescue helicopter she piloted as one of the Marine Corps' elite flying units, the "Purple Foxes," crashed while ferrying wounded Marines from the battlefield. At Jennifer Harris's funeral, her former commanding officer, Colonel Michael Hudson, said with a brief eloquence, "There are so many people who are not gathered at a place like this because Captain Harris flew."

As of this writing, April '07, seventy-one American servicewomen, Marines and others, have been killed in Iraq.

18

Bestselling author "Mick" Trainer learned his trade in Korea and lectured at Harvard.

I KNEW FROM THE BEGINNING THAT I'D HAVE TO TRACK DOWN AND interview "Mick" Trainor.

Bernard "Mick" Trainor started as so many of us did, at the Basic School in 1951 and then as a replacement rifle platoon leader in Korea. And we fought over some of the precisely same ground, at first in the Taebaek Mountains of North Korea by winter, then in the so-called outpost war just north of Seoul following spring and summer. He was 1st Battalion, 1st Marines, I was 2nd Battalion 7th Marines and we never met then, but each time my outfit moved on, it seemed Mick's outfit was coming up to replace us. But there were differences. I chewed cigars and ended up a captain in the Reserves. Unlike most of us, Mick was a dedicated pipe smoker, stayed in the Corps and served to lieutenant general, became military affairs analyst for *The New York Times,* and an associate at the Kennedy School of Government at Harvard. In 2006 he and coauthor Michael Gordon of the *Times* wrote a bestseller about Iraq titled *Cobra II.*

More pertinent to my purposes, Trainor wrote other books, most specifically a slim monograph just three chapters long that he called

On Going to War, published in three different issues of *Marine Corps Gazette* in 1996, '97, and '98, and then republished by the Marine Corps Association. We'd both written about our mutual war, and I knew I wanted to talk with Mick about this new book of mine.

He was a New York Catholic from the Bronx and Cardinal Hayes High School. An older brother had joined the Navy ROTC during World War II and become an ensign, and in his senior year as the war ended in 1945 and over parental protest Mick enlisted in the Marines, his active duty to start on high school graduation. "My parents didn't want me to enlist at all, but if I did, why not become an officer? I was called up July 5, 1946, and went to Parris Island. In November my mother [still ambitious for the lad] sent me a clipping about something the navy was starting for high schoolers and enlisted men. It was called the Holloway Program, named for an admiral, Jim Holloway." Mick "went to see the first sergeant. In December I took a test and forgot all about it. I was in a draft to go to China when they called me in to say I'd been pulled off the China draft, and they were sending me to Holy Cross," a small Catholic college in Worcester, Massachusetts. "I was commissioned in 1951 and sent to Quantico, arriving in North Korea in December."

His rifle company first succeeded mine that month near a piece of high ground still controlled by the North Koreans that we called "Luke the Gook's Castle," on Hill 749, a rocky outcropping that it took two regiments of Marines to assault and take in September of '51 at a cost of nearly a thousand casualties in a four-day firefight. We (Dog Company of the 7th) held it and a parallel piece of high ground, Hill 812, at various times that fall and through the winter, and in late February we came down off the line and it was again Trainor's and the 1st Marines' turn. Mick wrote about it in simple but strangely nuanced words, signaling the strong, subtle writer he was to become.

He was still a kid, not long out of a Navy college program, but he was already thinking, analyzing what lay ahead, even in those confusing and somehow intimidating first days on the line. He'd just been given command of Charlie 2, the second platoon of Charlie Company, 1st Marines, with a seasoned gunnery sergeant as his platoon sergeant (most platoon sergeants are staff sergeants, not gunnies). When Mick expressed interest in touring the line, the gunny said, "Be my guest, Lieutenant." That was all. Trainor's new platoon had just been assigned a supporting-fire role for a night raid about to be mounted by Baker Company. Mick had scouted out the position his men would be taking to provide supporting fire and he asked the sergeant, "This looks pretty good, Gunny. What do you think?" The sergeant continued to stare straight ahead toward the enemy lines and without looking back to Trainor simply said, "I guess so, Lieutenant. You're the platoon leader."

When I first read that passage, I knew that in a similar situation, I would have been pissed. Would have expected at least some minimal guidance based on the Gunny's obviously superior local knowledge and experience. And not just a curt equivalent of "You're on your own now, sonny." But Trainor strangely seemed to take encouragement from it, from what I thought of as his sergeant's surly attitude, bordering on insubordination. Maybe that's why he ended up a three-star general and most of us didn't. As Mick wrote about that North Korean moment half a century before, "It was my epiphany! I had arrived. He had just relinquished command to me. While I had won my bars earlier, it was at that point I won my spurs."

Last fall when I told Trainor my subjective interpretation, that the sergeant had failed him, he swiftly assured me I was wrong. "When I took over the platoon," Mick said, "the sergeant felt responsible. Then, when we went out, he was handing over that responsibility as his was relinquished."

When I asked Mick about his first firefight, he said, "It's in there." In his book. And it was. A brief, modest account of a mortar exchange, the tossing of grenades, an argument between two Marines over the grenade supply, some shouted orders by the gunny into a phone to warn against firing automatic weapons since that's what the enemy was doing, seeking out their positions. But to a wide-eyed young Trainor, the new boy on the block, "Here was the fiercest battle since Iwo Jima taking place and they're bean-counting grenades?"

I read on in Mick's monograph, and what Trainor wrote later in that same passage got no further argument from me but an authentic nod, a mute appreciation, of what I considered very nearly eloquent good sense. This is how the once-young platoon leader went on:

"A rifle platoon is much more than just a map symbol. It is a flesh and blood organization that is in the most dangerous of businesses. There are lots of things and people behind it that make up a war machine . . . there is nothing in front of a rifle platoon but the enemy and possible death. Its members must care for one another. Its leaders must cherish the men in every fire team and squad. For a rifleman, a leader's misjudgment, ignorance or inexperience can be fatal—no second chances. No rerunning the exercise until you get it right. When the word 'go' is given, there is no turning back from the consequences. It is the monstrous burden of command that my platoon sergeant felt when I stuck my head into the C.P. He knew, loved, and sought to protect Charlie 2. Nobody else out there would do so. He didn't know me. He didn't know if I was prepared to assume his burden, and he wasn't about to oversee its transfer until he had measured me for size. I hated and was silently humiliated by the process, but on that day overlooking the Soyang-gang [the meandering North Korean stream that ran between our front line and the enemy's], when he had judged I was fit to command, and willingly turned over the reins, I was grateful for my apprenticeship at the hands of a master."

I still would have resented the gunny's condescension, but Mick didn't.

The gunny's name was Harold Wagner of West Virginia, and he was hit by a burst of burp-gun fire later that year on the Hook, a topographical feature of the outpost war. Mick Trainor writes, "We pulled him and the other casualties back through the wire. Wagner was dead by then. Before his body was hauled to the rear, I had the privilege of closing the lids over his sightless eyes." A graceful, poignant little symbolism of how young platoon leaders mature and grow.

I questioned General Trainor about combat, about fear, about motivation. He called on his time on Hill 749 for illustration, but even more so, cited the bad summer fighting in the outpost war, when Chinese mass attacks by night on Marine positions were the big deal, the terrifying reality.

"As a lieutenant if you were on the defensive, the fear was that we were going to get overrun. It was strange, I had trouble on the defensive using my land line, the EE8 [calling in fire support and calling his own NCOs]. My throat would constrict and I had a tendency to hyperventilate; my voice went up an octave and I had trouble speaking. Going out on patrol never bothered me. What bothered me was going out on a raid. But only until the firing began. Then I was fine."

As for motivating the men? And himself? What was it, tradition, training, concern for the next guy, or just what? "All of those things, with a mix of patriotism. But we're a different breed, wild and wooly. There's a challenge and we want to prove ourselves, show that we're hot stuff. The Marine Corps brainwashes you at boot camp, breaks you down and then builds you back up. It transforms you, builds a bond. Will I measure up? we ask. Dammit, I hope I don't fuck up. Then in a firefight, the training kicks in. At first you're in a state of shock, but then the training comes through."

After his retirement Trainor returned in 1988 to tour the old Korean front at Hill 229, looking out at Yoke, hills on which we both fought only weeks apart. He gives us his thoughts in a piece for the *Times,* "A Return to No-Man's Land."

"It seemed incongruous to look across at a North Korean strongpoint on a hill we knew as 'Red Hill' whose soil had been churned ochre from shelling and bombing, and see a bored soldier staring back at me while two of his comrades played Ping-Pong. In my time we did our level best to kill every living creature on that hill. When we got near Hill 126 on the eastern boundary of the 1952 Marine zone of action, I saw the spot where Gunnery Sergeant Harold Wagner, my platoon sergeant, was killed in a firefight."

I remembered Wagner as the guy who welcomed Trainor to the war in what I thought a cavalier manner. But more significantly, that wasn't how Mick recalled him.

"The thrill of returning to scenes of my youth evaporated," he wrote. "Until then my recollections of Korea were largely anecdotal and humorous—time has a way of submerging ugly memories. But as they resurfaced on 126, I felt like a burn victim whose raw nerve ends are suddenly exposed to air. Though nobody else on the hill with me could smell the stench, see the shattered landscape, hear the whoosh of incoming or the popping of machine guns, I became increasingly aware of them as the day wore on.

"It was time to bury the past."

After the Korean War, Trainor stayed in the Corps, fought two tours in Vietnam. "There was a special covert operations outfit with a water and an air component, the air being solely Vietnamese, but we went in boats. That was '65 and '66. Then in 1970 I went out there in a command job, recon, taking over a recon battalion eventually." Other postings followed, and Trainor retired as a lieutenant general, which is an important rank in the Corps, with its relatively few generals, becoming a military affairs correspondent for the Washington Bureau of the *Times* (coincidentally, publisher "Punch" Sulzberger had also been a Marine and in Mick's class at Quantico), and a consultant for NBC News and the job at "Fair Harvard." Not bad for a Catholic high school kid from the Bronx.

I congratulated Mick on his book, the one about Iraq he did with Michael Gordon of *The New York Times*. How's it doing? "It's selling very well." (It had made the *Times*'s bestseller list). "The paperback comes out in January. The hardcover has been bought for foreign editions in the United Kingdom, Italy, Spain, Egypt, Poland, and, get this! Estonia!"

Estonia! Wow! "But why did you need a collaborator? You're a good writer. Why share the dough with someone else?" I asked the question jocularly, but his reply was a surprise.

"I take no royalties," Mick said. "All the money goes to charity." Even the big bucks from Estonian royalties, one presumes.

There was no chichi to Trainor, no pose, only the self-deprecating and amused laughter at himself. Not all Marine general officers were like that.

19

General Smedley Butler, "I could have given Al Capone a few hints."

I KEEP ASKING, WHY DO MARINES FIGHT? HERE IS YET ANOTHER theory not frequently plumbed.

In the third year of the second Persian Gulf War, a number of American generals, including several Marines and all of them no longer on the active duty rolls but retired, issued statements critical of the Bush-Rumsfeld-Cheney management of the Iraq war, their strategy and tactics. The generals' language was forceful but courteous and restrained. Even that of the Marine officers among them. In the following year, with things getting worse, Washington sacked the top army generals in the Middle East, Casey and Abizaid. Both of these gentle souls took their medicine without plaint. When Harry Truman sacked Douglas MacArthur for insubordination in 1951, the general (with an eye on history and a possible GOP presidential nomination in 1952) promptly and impudently seized on an invitation to address a joint session of the Congress to air not only his differences with Truman but to issue his eloquent though self-serving oration, "Old Soldiers never die/ They just fade away . . ."

Not every general officer debating the rightness or justification of an American war has been quite as stylish or poetic. Especially not every Marine general.

In 1933, the depths of the Great Depression, the first year of Franklin Roosevelt's presidency, the police commissioner of Philadelphia made an astonishing and pungent speech. It was quite a moment.

"War is just a racket," the commissioner began. "A racket is best described, I believe, as something that is not what it seems to be to the majority of people. It is conducted for the benefit of the very few at the expense of the masses. I believe in adequate defense at the coastline and nothing else. If a nation comes over here to fight, then we'll fight. The trouble with America is that when the dollar only earns 6 percent over here, then it gets restless and goes overseas to get 10 percent. Then the flag follows the dollar and the soldiers follow the flag."

Who was this subversive fellow before he became commissioner? A Communist Party organizer, a lefty rabble-rouser? Some home-grown Trotskyite?

The orator was in fact a distinguished career soldier, Smedley Darlington Butler, former general of Marines, a holder of the Congressional Medal of Honor, and familiarly known throughout the Corps as just "Smedley." Now, as the police commissioner in Philadelphia, he went on with his rant.

"I wouldn't go to war again as I have done, to protect some lousy investment of the bankers. There are only two things we should fight for. One is the defense of our homes and the other is the Bill of Rights. War for any other reason is simply a racket.

"There isn't a trick in the racketeering bag that the military gang is blind to. It may seem odd for me, a military man, to adopt such a comparison. Truthfulness compels me to. I spent thirty-three years and four months in active military service as a member of this country's most agile military force, the Marine Corps [I like that "agile"—JB]. I served in all commissioned ranks from second lieutenant to major general and during that period, I spent most of my time being a high-class muscleman for Big Business, for Wall Street and the bankers. In short, I was a racketeer, a gangster for Capitalism.

"I suspected I was just part of it at the time. Now I am sure of it. Like all the members of the military profession, I never had a thought of my own until I left the service. My mental faculties remained in suspended animation while I obeyed the orders of the higher-ups. This is typical of everyone in the military service.

"I helped make Mexico, especially Tampico, safe for American oil interests in 1914. I helped make Haiti and Cuba a decent place for the National City Bank boys to collect revenues in. I helped in the raping of half a dozen Central American republics for the benefit of Wall Street. The record of racketeering is long. I helped pacify Nicaragua for the international banking house of Brown Brothers [later Brown Brothers Harriman] 1909–1912. I brought light to the Dominican Republic for American sugar interests in 1916. In China I helped to see to it that Standard Oil went its way unmolested.

"During those years, I had, as the boys in the back room would say, a swell racket. Looking back on it, I feel that I could have given Al Capone a few hints. The best he could do was operate his racket in three districts.

"I operated on three continents."

Well, you can't complain that Smedley didn't give you value for money in a speech. He didn't just pussyfoot around. But was old Smedley right? Were those wars all "just another racket?" It was widely known he'd been passed over as commandant of the Corps in favor of a more temperate rival, John A. Lejeune, and was this screed simply an aggrieved Butler spouting his resentments? Was it just the same old untamed Smedley? During his long career he'd once been the commanding officer of the Marine Corps schools and base at Quantico, Virginia, where he created a Marine football team that played every Saturday afternoon and drew large crowds of spectators to the Quantico stadium, many of them congressmen and their families, a fan base it was in General Butler's interest to delight, divert, and entertain. Which he certainly did, personally leading the band onto the field, leading the cheerleaders as he capered along the sidelines and whooped it up through a large megaphone, grand in polished boots and his Marine Corps blues under what looks in the snapshots to be a luxuriant fur coat, perhaps sable.

On one occasion, following an obvious foul by the opposing team, and suspecting dirty play, a righteously indignant Smedley turned to his own grandstands and ordered, *ordered!* Marine spectators watching the game to charge the opposition stands on the other side of the gridiron. Now there was a Marine who understood direct action.

When in September 2005 I interviewed Marine four-star general Peter Pace in his Pentagon office as the newly anointed chairman of the Joint Chiefs, we discussed Smedley and the long-held notion that Marines were wild men, and couldn't be trusted to exercise cool, mature judgment in the higher realms of command. General Pace thought we, as a Corps, had moved beyond that.

That, in effect, we weren't all Smedley Butler or Gregory "Pappy" Boyington or even the sainted Lewis B. "Chesty" Puller, of whom all over the South you still see bumper stickers GOOD NIGHT, CHESTY. WHEREVER YOU ARE. Incidentally, that passing mention of Boyington may get me in difficulty. In 1991 following the publication of my Korean memoir, I received a letter about the book from George A. Tehansky of Hummelstown, Pennsylvania, who signed himself as "a proud dogface, 23rd Infantry Regiment, 2nd Indianhead Div." His letter follows: "I read your book and I think it stinks. This book will definitely go in the garbage can. No, I think I will burn it. I have nothing but contempt for you and the Marines. There was only one Marine who wrote a good book and that was Pappy Boyington's *Baa Baa Black Sheep,* and you are no Pappy Boyington."

"Proud Dogface" Tehansky had fought at the Pusan Perimeter and had every right to raise hell with me, so I wrote back saying so, and still have a framed copy of his letter on my living room wall, to the delight of my three grandsons, who love me but are secretly pleased when someone bold chews me out. So not everyone agrees with my conclusions on just about anything. Though Jerry Byrne, longtime publisher of *Variety* and a Vietnam Marine officer, is fond of declaring, "All Marines are crazy." Of course, when you consider Major General Smedley Darlington Butler, you understand Byrne's remark.

Not that we don't all, including General Pace I suspect, still revere old Smedley.

20

New York Police Commissioner Ray Kelly cites the USMC's "principles of leadership."

NEW YORK CITY POLICE COMMISSIONER RAYMOND W. KELLY chose to become a cop of his own free will thirty-one years ago. There were no such options available about his becoming a Marine; he never had a chance not to. We were sitting over coffee on a sunny autumn afternoon in his fourteenth-floor office at Police Headquarters overlooking downtown Manhattan and City Hall and I was asking just why Kelly joined the Corps.

"I grew up on the west side of Manhattan, Ninety-first and Columbus, and at fourteen I was engaged in gang fights, Puerto Rican kids versus white kids, just like *West Side Story*, and I had three older brothers who were all Marines. Our dad was in World War II but in the army. I remember seeing the *Guidebook for Marines* around the house, about fieldstripping a weapon and the principles of leadership and small unit tactics and . . . Wait a minute . . ."

The commissioner got up from the coffee table and crossed the room to a bookcase. "Here," he went on, "is my older brother's copy [of the *Guidebook*], so I grew up with this, and in the back of my head I was always thinking about the Marine Corps. One brother was in both World War II and Korea and our house had 782 gear [military web belts, knapsacks, and the like] all over the place.

"I went to Manhattan College [a small Catholic men's school in Riverdale from which I also graduated] and joined the PLCs, the Platoon Leaders Class [an officer candidates' program], and spent one summer at Quantico in 1962."

"But wasn't it still a two-summer deal?" I asked.

Kelly broke into a grin (he's not a big smiler, but when he gives you a grin it's a good one). "Yes, but one summer I had to go to summer school. I don't precisely remember the details but you know how those things go. I graduated from college in '63 and Vietnam was on, but it was early. The intensity wasn't there, the size wasn't there, or the bitterness. Not yet. I went through the Basic School at Quantico and I was an 08 [MOS], an artilleryman, and they sent me to Fort Sill [artillery school] and in '65 I went to Vietnam."

Being an infantryman, I sort of don't take the artillery very seriously, but Kelly soon set me straight on that. "I was an FO [forward observer] with the infantry, most of the time with the 2nd Battalion, 1st Marines, going out with them on patrol. Then I was a fire control officer, later did liaison work, was executive officer of the battery and then the CO. I was in Vietnam for a year, never wounded, and was promoted to first lieutenant."

And how did a young officer in combat keep his men motivated at a time when the Vietnam war was so unpopular back home? I wouldn't have known how to do it, but the dilemma didn't exist in the Korea of my time. Kelly's experience turned out to be not so different.

"It wasn't so bitter an issue yet, and when I came home I was surprised there was so little interest in the war. It wasn't yet as big a story as it became later."

While he was serving as an FO with the infantry, did he remember his first firefight?

"Yes, I'd been in several landings, but when the first firefight came along, there was a phenomenon I remember. I don't know whether you felt like this, but for me the worst part was when you were anticipating something. Then, when it happened, you were calm, the anxiety was over. Here it is! Almost relief. I remember talking to my sergeant about it and he said, yes, he agreed with me. But of course I was the officer and he was the sergeant, so I don't know if he really meant it." Since I'd experienced that same phenomenon, I wasn't dubious at all about Kelly's sergeant. Anticipation was the worst part for me, too.

And why are Marines good fighters? I asked. Why do we run toward the guns?

Kelly said, "Discipline, training, esprit, all of those, but another thing, even more so. Peer pressure. You don't want to look bad in front of your fellow Marines. 'I'm going to make certain that I'm not less than my fellow Marines.' As for officers, pressure from below is very much a factor. It gives you adrenaline, gets you going. You [the officer] can't get tired. Others may get tired, but you can't."

In Vietnam young lieutenant Kelly served alongside such significant figures as Chesty Puller's son, and future Marine commandant Charles C. Krulak. "I was with him when he was wounded in the hand." (Krulak's father, "Brute" Krulak, was one of my commanding officers a generation earlier, in Korea. Such is the intimacy of the Corps.) "Puller's boy was a tragic case, maimed by a mine, life in a wheelchair, eventually a suicide. He wrote a book about it, sort of a guilt feeling, and bitterness, but he never bad-mouthed his dad. Krulak did a great job as commandant. In our time, the Marine commandant was God. Now we have [former commandant] Jim Jones commanding NATO, we have a Marine [Peter Pace] as chairman of the Joint Chiefs, so the commandant is just an operations guy."

Obviously, no longer God. Which I think both Kelly and I as aging Marines regret.

Since artillery was his military MOS, and I knew nothing about big guns beyond having been targeted by them a few times, we talked about artillery for a while and I told him how stunned I was to realize you could actually see American 105 shells in the air coming in your direction as supporting fire in a fight. And how scared I was of a short round, friendly fire, landing right in the small of my damned back and what it might feel like before I realized I had been blown up to hell and was by now probably dead. "Yeah," artilleryman Kelly agreed, "even when you've got the map coordinates right, you can still get a short round. It's scary in the fog and chaos of war. A short round is always possible. Of course, naval gunfire is the worst. Don't ever get in the line of fire of naval gunfire. Five-inch shells," Kelly said half to himself, as if remembering the damage those babies could do. I said, "Yeah, an American cruiser just offshore on the Sea of Japan was once giving our battalion supporting fire up in North Korea and sent over a volley of eight-inch shells. Only they got the ridgeline wrong. They were aiming at one ridgeline south of where the North Koreans were, and shelled us with eight-inch shells, bracketing our position. Fortunately, no one got hit, but Marines were cursing out the goddamned navy for a week." Kelly laughed, as if to say, "Those things happen, Jack," the old artilleryman in him scoffing at a mere infantryman.

There we were, two old Marines from different wars, talking war stories, being happy about it.

Raymond Kelly is the only man ever to serve two separate tenures as police commissioner of New York, and under two different mayors, the first from 1992 to 1994 and currently under Mayor Mike Bloomberg. He is a lifelong cop with thirty-one years of service, a trim, solid, conservatively dressed and clean-shaven no-nonsense executive with a close-cropped haircut and martial demeanor suggesting another line of work, the Marine Corps. Outside his office, there is a spare but pleasant waiting room for visitors, decorated with badges, emblems, uniform caps, souvenirs, and the like from other police forces around the world, gaudy little tributes to New York's Finest, but the waiting room's principal (and most impressive) decoration is a gallery wall of black-and-white photos of another city police commissioner, Teddy Roosevelt. I was there for a few moments, waiting to be ushered in to Commissioner Kelly, with my only company a burly, polite, soft-spoken young detective, a black man born in Haiti who came to New York as a child.

Well, I said, here was another commissioner who had fought a war and then, after running the New York police, went on to greater things. Yes, the detective agreed, nodding his head tactfully when I suggested perhaps there were parallels here, Ray Kelly occasionally being mentioned by the media in connection with bigger jobs, elective offices, maybe even, one day, the White . . . Well, let's not get carried away.

Above our heads Teddy Roosevelt, in his khakis and on safari, his top hat and his cutaway, his spectacles shiny and his mustache bristling, pranced and speechified.

Kelly is hardly as flamboyant, but an impressive figure, cool, controlled, conveying strength and authority without any of the usual preening and posturing. Solid man, conveying a little depth, considerable spine, "a good pair of onions" as prizefight managers and trainers say of a gutty boxer. I got him talking again about his beginnings, those early days that shape us all. "While I was at college I was already thinking about the police and became a police cadet." The Vietnam War was on, and while he waited to be admitted to the Marine Corps' Basic School for young officers at Quantico, Virginia, "during that time I was actually in the [Police] Department for a few days." In the Marine Corps he served eventually to full colonel in the Reserve, and was again activated for duty in another shooting war, the first Gulf War in 1991. No firefights this time. "I was called up for prisoner handling, but the war ended before they could put me to work. Back then I wanted to be on top of the job and even bought myself a global positioning device so I'd always know where I was."

"But you never got to Baghdad," I wisecracked. Kelly was swifter than I. "Nor did anyone else, if you'll recall." That's right, our forces pulled up short of Baghdad, the first Bush, Colin Powell, and Schwarzkopf and their people convinced we shouldn't go in. Not all the way. Not into that mess.

Thinking of all this stuff going on, where Kelly had served, the things he'd done, I asked, "Isn't there a book in you about all this?"

Tapping his temple with his fingertips, he said, "I've got a lot of stuff in my head, but when you do a book you leave yourself open." "To critics?" I suggested. Kelly nodded, "Open to anyone."

He got that bachelor's degree in business admin from Manhattan College and a law degree from St. John's, an advanced law degree from New York University, and another advanced degree from Harvard's Kennedy School. In between his two tours as police commssioner, he served as commissioner of the U.S. Customs Service, was undersecretary for enforcement at the Treasury Department. There he supervised the department's enforcement agencies—Customs, Secret Service, Bureau of

Alcohol, Tobacco and Firearms, among them. He also served in Haiti as director of a U.S.-led force responsible for ending human rights abuses and establishing an interim police force in the troubled nation. He and his wife, Veronica, have two grown sons, one of them an officer in the Marine Corps Reserve.

Before I left the office, Kelly showed me his daily planner. Inserted in it was a list from the *Guidebook for Marines*, the fourteen principles of leadership. "Page 27 of this edition of the *Guidebook*," Ray Kelly said, paging through it to show me. "My refresher," he called it, the man responsible for the safety of a great city and its eight million inhabitants. We finished our coffee, and his detective, the young native of Haiti, took me downstairs in a private elevator and I was back out on the sidewalks looking into the late afternoon sun glinting off Police Headquarters in downtown Manhattan.

A few minutes' pleasant walk from where the Twin Towers of the World Trade Center once stood, where for New Yorkers there are still ghosts.

21

A Browning Automatic Rifleman on the day he became "a real Marine."

Last September ('06) I flew out to San Diego for the annual reunion of the Dog 7 Association, our old rifle company, met some old pals, had a few drinks, walked the beach at Mission Bay, talked to a couple of men about a book I had just begun to write, made the after-dinner speech, a mildly ribald affair, and, after a couple of days of doing television talk shows and an interview with the local paper, flew back to New York.

A month or so later I received this letter from John C. Seaman, a chemical dependency consultant in La Jolla, a fellow with a master's degree and other impressive initials following his name. He was also a Marine. A guy who in the North Korean mountain winter had toted a Browning automatic rifle in combat, a wonderful if hefty weapon of great range and extraordinary accuracy, that gave your simple, dozen-man Marine squad of that era much of its lethal punch. An army squad carried one BAR; a Marine squad had three! If you have ever been a BAR man, as John Seaman was, you'll know what I mean. Herewith his letter:

"I was at the Dog Seven reunion and received an autographed copy of your book *The Scariest Place* . . . I also had lunch with Bob Simonis in Oceanside. I am a member of Dog Seven, being asked to join by [Chuck] Curley. I went out and bought *The Coldest War* and had to write to you.

"I was involved in the rescue action of Bob Simonis' patrol of January '52."

Mr. Seaman grabbed me with that single sentence, had my rapt attention from then on. Simonis was a rifle platoon leader in Dog Company, a man I knew at Quantico, quiet and unassuming, slightly older and nothing like a fire-breather, yet he had the previous November led an outstanding raid on enemy lines, descending with his men down the steep and snow-covered forward slope of Hill 749 about two thousand feet to the valley of the Soyang-gang, a small stream dividing us from the North Koreans, climbed their forward slope (all this by night), raided their trenches and bunkers, and killed or captured several soldiers and led his people back safely.

Having succeeded at that, naturally, the Marine Corps suggested in January that Bob pull the same stunt twice. This is what some less-than-nimble thinkers call strategy and what most of us consider idiocy.

On this second occasion, heading back home across the stream, the Simonis patrol had been hit by enemy fire, including mortars, had lost several dead and had others wounded, and some of us (all the enlisted men were volunteers, it's important to say) had gone down shortly after first light with stretchers to try to help get Simonis and his men out. We would start the long climb back, under enemy fire, mortars, and small arms, about eight in the morning, lugging both the wounded and the dead. When I first got down there to the valley Bob Simonis seemed happy to see us, but his navy corpsman began cursing me out. "You stupid bastard, take that fucking thing off!" I thought this guy had flipped out but realized he was pointing at the gold bar on my fatigue cap. "They aim at those damn things!" he shouted again. I was still pretty green and thought maybe I was doing something wrong. When I looked around I noticed Simonis was wearing bars and some of the men had pinned on, for amusement's sake, souvenir South Korean badges of rank. I ignored the corpsman as probably being shaken by all the casualties around him. The hell with you, Jack.

We began the climb back, Simonis and I both taking our turns at a corner of the stretchers. We all did, exhausting work on an incline that steep, in foot-deep snow. Seaman's letter continued:

"I was a PFC, a BAR man, and when they asked for volunteers our whole squad volunteered and we got down the hill about 11 A.M. or maybe noon [it was earlier than that as I remember] and I was with Caulfield's stretcher until he died, in my arms. I knew him from the ship, the USS *William Wiegel* on which he and I came over. I didn't really know him but he put on a Christmas song & dance act on the ship and I remembered him from that. I didn't even know his name until I read it in your book."

Caulfield was a very tall, maybe six-foot-six young African-American Marine whom I knew only by sight. (You could hardly miss a black guy that tall in what was still an only sparsely integrated and nearly lily white Marine Corps in Korea.) When I wrote my memoir, "Caulfield" was the nom de guerre I gave him, since I didn't want to inflict additional pain on his family or friends by describing his dying hours. Caulfield had been terribly hurt, with shrapnel wounds all over his lanky body, and was being carried by stretcher back toward the Dog Company lines, a long, cruel journey that cold, sunny January morning. Marine John Seaman resumed writing his memories with these poignant lines about how it was to be a raw newcomer in a combat unit:

"I was also a new replacement . . . a stranger to the entire company. The only guys I knew were in my squad. Some guys weren't interested in getting to know me, which made for a fairly uncomfortable way to go into combat, but after that battle, my squad patted me on the back and said, 'Well done.' I finally 'made it,' and was a 'real Marine.' "

How many of us felt that way after a "first firefight," officers and enlisted men both.

"When I got back to my position about midnight," Seaman went on, "my bunk mate, Ray Pelletier, gave me a break and took the watch and let me sleep for four hours. Getting back to Caulfield, I remember how he kept slipping off the stretcher and losing his mittens, his hands dragging in the snow and I kept trying to put them back on his hands but to no avail. His hands were frozen. I also remember the corpsman.

He was a real 'prick' and I was ticked off when he 'gave up' on Caulfield. I saw Caulfield gurgling and muttering when we put down the stretcher in a little flat spot. I knew he was dying. I held him in my arms and held a frozen hand feeling his pulse. He was crying for his 'mama.' I whispered in his ear, 'I'm here, son.' He smiled weakly and died. We then put him in a poncho and tied a rope around his feet and pulled him up the rest of the way."

That's all Seaman wrote about the Simonis patrol and the "rescue," which by my reckoning took thirteen hours. But being a Marine, Seaman had something else to say about our war and its charms. We had been on the line for forty-six days straight at that time and had never bathed or changed clothes from January 10 until February 26 of '52, when we went into reserve. He wrote about it:

"Only a Marine who was there could relate to 'dingleberries' and when we finally got to take showers. I remember throwing our clothes into that big pile of stinking underwear and will never forget the smell and the heated drums of hot water at the mess tent and the showers. They burned fuel oil from 55-gallon drums. I could not share the 'dingleberries' story [from my book] with my wife, as she would surely think the story was 'disgusting.' Only another Marine would understand. Well, Jim, I could go on and on but I did want to share my part in the rescue of Bob's patrol. I'll never forget that day." He remembered a Marine's slow death in the snow and the stink of filthy bodies and our dingelebrries.

I phoned Seaman the following week. There were questions I wanted to ask. Needed to ask. He called me back on a Saturday afternoon and filled in the blanks.

"I grew up in a small company town in Roebling, New Jersey, a steel town with mills and blast furnaces where they made steel wire and cables. My father and grandfather both worked there and I did for a time. My father was an alcoholic, not the nicest guy in the world, and I had a lot of anger. He loved my little sisters but he pushed my mother around and I got into it with him. I rebelled against authority in general and got kicked out of high school. The local police by now were keeping an eye on me. So one day in 1951 I went into Philadelphia and joined the Marines. They sent us down to Parris Island by train, a three-day trip, and for some reason put me in charge of the seven of us and we raised a little hell on the train. But I felt they must have seen some leadership in me. Maybe they'd even make me an officer, I thought. I was nineteen and a cocky kid. It didn't take them long to knock that out of me. But in the end, we were the honor platoon."

Seaman joined Dog Company when we were still in reserve over Christmas and New Year's and were getting ready to go back up on the line. He recalls that first night he reported in with the other replacements. "I met my new squad for the first time and we stayed in big tents and they served us tough steak and black coffee. That was dinner. A few days later (January 10) we went up to the line in helicopters. When we jumped out of the choppers up there on the ridgeline there were explosions all around us and someone shoved me down into the snow. Then someone else said, 'Okay, on your feet. We're moving.' I didn't understand that, because the explosions were still going on. But I got up."

They were incoming mortars, I said. I remembered them, too. Seaman went on. "The odd thing on the trail to our new bunkers I met a guy from my high school and we were relieving his outfit. I was only up there on the line a few days when word came one morning that a patrol was out there and had been attacked and they asked for volunteers. As we were going down in deep snow to Simonis most of my squad dropped off to set up a base of fire but I kept going down and a mortar came in and blew me up, threw me against a rock. Knocked my helmet against the rock and rang my bell. I thought maybe I was badly hurt and looked down but not a drop of blood, so I got up and went the rest of the way down. There were gooks coming, they said, and I could see a few across the way and they put me on one corner of the stretcher with Caulfield on it."

Our battalion and Dog Company were on the line forty-six days that time without a break or a change of clothes, and Seaman was with us. "Do you remember that time we pretended we'd pulled out and tried to draw the gooks in? "Yes," I said, "Operation Mole or something like that. We couldn't show ourselves, weren't supposed to fire a shot or light fires or make noise for five days."

"Mole" had been pretty much a bust, as I recall, with a few

trigger-happy Marines breaking fire discipline but very little action on
the part of the North Koreans, who must have been as puzzled by the
whole idiotic operation as we were. But BAR man Seaman absolutely
remembers a good firefight. "We got hit really hard. There were gooks
at the wire and my buddy and I fired up every single round we had.
Threw every grenade."

Who knows? Each man remembers his own war.

John Seaman stayed with Dog Company those forty-six days on the
line but later on was pulled out. What happened? I asked. "My father
had died some time before and then my mother fell ill and was in the
hospital and needed help with my baby sisters. A neighbor who advised
my mother wrote to the Marine Corps telling them of the situation and
I got sent home in the spring. I was sort of angry, but it was a compas-
sionate thing, and I went home and got out of the Marine Corps so I
could take care of the family. I was angry, ashamed, too, about getting
pulled out of combat. I loved the Marine Corps, I came to love the
BAR. I was still a PFC, and now I was going home. Hey, I'm not a
hero, but I'm still sore about it."

After Korea, Seaman worked for the New Jersey Department of
Corrections as a day-shift commander at Bordentown Reformatory, a
maximum security operation, was promoted to lieutenant, moved to
Arizona for his daughter's arthritis, became a parole officer ("I had
some pretty hard cases along the border"), later was a Scottsdale policeman and joined the sheriff's office. At some point a first marriage
broke up and he was drinking.

"I got sober twenty-three years ago" and remarried, a solid situation this time, John said. He's earned a master's degree and California
state certification and works as a counselor. His title is chemical dependency consultant for Scripps McDonald Center Intervention Services
in La Jolla. And what does that mean? I asked.

"Scripps has a group of hospitals and every Saturday I give lectures
for families with a family member in denial. They write up a history
and we confront that individual and try to get him to face the problem.
Over the last twelve days I did nine interventions. It's not always that
busy."

He later sent me a short story he'd written. "The Bus Stop" was about a boy going to war, and saying goodbye, perhaps for the last time, to a father from whom he was estranged. In part, it reads like this:

"It was July 1951, and I was a nineteen-year-old PFC in the U.S. Marines. I just completed boot camp at Parris Island and had received orders to report to Camp Pendleton for advanced combat training, following a short leave at home. I would then join a ground unit in Korea as a rifleman. The sun was hot in my small hometown in New Jersey as we waited on the corner, neither saying very much and avoiding each other's eyes. What was there to say? "The trees sure look nice this time of year," my Dad said unconvincingly. His eyes were glassy, a big tear running down his cheek which he embarrassedly wiped away with a big fist. A fist I felt more than once. I just couldn't talk, my mind swimming with memories of this town, of my father and mother and my two little sisters, Mary Jane and Pat, still looking out of our living room window, frantically waving.

"Dad and I never really got along and I knew it was my fault as it was his. I never even tried. I resented his drinking and the hurt my mother suffered. What I never thought or cared about was the utter frustration he must have felt, twenty-seven long years in a steel mill, coming home dog-tired every single day, his face greasy and his hands calloused and sore. Only once in all those years did he receive any kind of promotion and then it was only one small step from the bottom. The years of hard work showed in his face, as did the hurt. Without saying so we both knew this could be our last goodbye. Things were going badly in Korea, with casualties mounting. Replacements were desperately needed and were being shipped over as quickly as possible and being sent directly to the front lines. I would soon be one of them. The bus would be coming.

" 'Here it comes,' Dad said. I dragged my seabag to the curb. I extended my hand but he ignored it, embracing me instead. I felt his whiskered face, wet with tears. He looked me in the eyes, saying in a look words that were impossible to speak. Words of love and regret. Hours spent together catfishing in the Delaware or watching baseball. I remember watching him, very proudly, as he played for our hometown 'Blue Center' team, a winning home run he hit and how I cheered and yelled in delight as he ran jauntily around the bases. He ran right over to me and threw me into the air to the delight of the crowd and, most especially, me. The bus pulled up, started with a lurch, and I looked back to see Dad waving. I wondered what lay ahead for me as the green New Jersey country slipped by.

"A few weeks later, near the end of my training on a Sunday evening, two friends and I returned from liberty. It was late and I was tired. I threw my liberty card on the counter and turned to walk out of the sergeant's office. Noticing my name, he called out. "Hold it, I think I have a message for you. I think your dad died, or something.""

And so it was, through the chill, uncaring afterthought of a duty sergeant checking in some drunken liberty men, that nineteen-year-old John Seaman learned his father was dead. That was how they sent him to the war.

The Saturday half a century later on which Seaman and I spoke was a beautiful, sunny day in San Diego. The cocky kid from a troubled family in a tough steel town, kicked out of high school and eyed by the cops back in New Jersey, who joined the Marines, got into a couple of firefights, didn't influence the course of the war, but would always remember that last view of his dad at the bus stop, never forget a big, black Marine who died in his arms on a snowy hill in North Korea, is today straightening out other troubled lives in California.

"You know," he said, and without any urging or even a question from me, "I still love the Marine Corps." Yes, I told Seaman, I know. Few can explain it, but that's how plenty of us feel.

22

Gunnery Sergeant Milks and his Afghan adventures

ALL I KNEW ABOUT AFGHANISTAN I OWED TO KIPLING AND HIS
nineteenth-century stories and poems for boys, Gunga Din and all that,
gallant redcoats, elephants and Scottish pipers, spunky kids named
Kim, and fierce tribal warriors just the other side of the Khyber Pass,
that exotic, rugged little kingdom. Back then, in Victoria's time, Afghanistan was a pawn of the czar's Imperial Russia and the British Empire in the so-called Great Game the two world powers played for
leverage and strategic influence somewhere on the other side of the
globe. Then, in 2001, following the World Trade Center attack, Americans were suddenly fighting in Afghanistan and the Great Game took
on other, contemporary dimensions. No more redcoats or kilted Scots
pipers or regimental beasties like old Gunga Din. This time it was American Marines and U.S. Army mountain troops and "special ops" boys,
all of them searching for Osama bin Laden, and beating up on his Al
Qaeda and its Taliban allies. Following a rather easy if only partial win
over the bad guys, Washington lost interest, targeted Iraq instead, and
with our national attention focused there, Afghanistan became a sort

of backwater. Which did not mean the fighting ended; it just took on a different look.

Marine Gunnery Sergeant Keith Milks filled me in on phase two of the current Afghan wars.

Milks was born on a naval air station in Tennessee where his father, a navy man, was then stationed. "I was a graphic illustrator and joined the Marine Corps in 1990 at the age of nineteen. After boot camp at San Diego, I was sent to a graphics specialist course, and moved on to a USMC air station in Yuma. From 1993 to '96 I was in Atlanta, working as a Marine photographer and illustrator." Did he just pick up photography along the way? "No, my wife was an active-duty Marine as well and a professional photographer and she taught me. Then I pulled drill instructor duty at Parris Island. I was the DI for the former heavyweight champ Riddick Bowe, if you remember him. He was in the Marine Corps for exactly six and a half days. His enlistment was not precisely a well-thought-out move on anyone's part. He was a bigger, dumber recruit than normal, and he tried hard, but it was mutually decided this just wasn't going to work.

"I left the drill field and moved into public affairs in Washington, spent three years at the Pentagon. I was there in 2001 on September 11 when the plane hit, and I was soon transferred to the 22nd Marine Expeditionary unit and we shipped out." The Horn of Africa, Djibouti, Pakistan, and considerable intensified and stepped-up antiterrorist training all followed. "I became a combat correspondent and made gunnery sergeant about then in 2001." Having never understood them, I asked Milks about the rules of engagement for combat correspondents. "We carry weapons, can fire them, we're embedded with infantry units, we go out on patrols. In 2004 I finally went into Afghanistan.

"At that time most Marines went to the eastern border with Pakistan to do patrolling duty (looking for infiltrators and Al Qaeda). It was rough country, mountains from 10,000 to 12,000 feet. I never went that high. Our patrols were lower down. We didn't run into any firefights there in my time. Then they threw us into south central Afghanistan, a province north of Kandahar, where we set up a forward operations base at a place called Tarin-Kowt. The first few weeks we were there were difficult. We went out patrolling and got into a few firefights, but they [the enemy] wouldn't stand and fight. Just vanished into the country. We took only one KIA in that time. Then on June 2 of '04 that changed. We launched Operation Asbury Park (named for a Springsteen song). Our commanding officer realized the present patrols weren't doing us any good. They (the baddies) just melted away.

"We had a helicopter scouting for us. They took some fire and landed. Just a few holes. They patched them up and they took off again. We moved up and that's when eight days of a running gunfight began in rough mountainous terrain, and we went as high as about 6,000 feet as we chased them. It was tough. We had come from Camp Lejeune and then on the ship coming over all our exercises and training took place at sea level. We realized we couldn't wear the usual body armor. It was just too heavy to carry climbing the hills. Truck drivers and men back at the base could wear armor but the infantry couldn't. A local craftsman fabricated a kind of vest with some armor fore and aft. It was only about twelve pounds and didn't give as much protection as the full body armor, but you could move with it.

"We moved up in a column of Humvees, 270 men in the unit including some Afghan militia forces with us, men in their late thirties and forties who had fought the Russians—maybe some of them were ex-Taliban—and they knew their stuff. They could outrun us and outfight us. They were something. Even the forty-year-olds. They carried no equipment, no water, and were just superb mountain fighters. I was lugging a camera and an M-16 rifle. I had been a Marine for fourteen years and had never been under fire before. Most Marines in our outfit hadn't either. A few had been in Desert Storm, but no one took that seriously as a war. The photos I took during those eight days appeared in *Leatherneck* magazine, the *Marine Corps Gazette, Soldier of Fortune* magazine." I said I was surprised about *Soldier of Fortune*. Milks explained, "Well, our pictures are government issue and they get them free. So they use a lot of USMC pictures. But otherwise it's a lot of posturing and conspiracy theories."

How did he feel about being in combat, his initial reaction?

"The realization sank in. Things were popping overhead and people are trying to kill us. Those were my first thoughts on it. We'd pounded a lot of miles, chasing ghosts, and now here they were, in front of us. I was in Iraq later, but Afghanistan was very personal. Because I'd been at the Pentagon on September 11 and now finally I had a chance to get back at them. The camera sort of shielded me from what's going on. I'm taking pictures of the other men and concentrating on them and on the picture, not worrying about myself but about the images I got. That helped me in that first firefight.

"That first day of the eight, we got ambushed. The next day we killed five of them. Then we chased those guys to a village and there were fifteen or twenty guys hightailing it and they ambushed us again. We took two WIA. One of our sergeants went forward and destroyed one of their placements with a grenade. We couldn't get a chopper up there for the wounded. Terrain too tough. So we had to carry them on our backs down the mountain. We also carried wounded prisoners, trading off on the carrying. The History Channel tonight"—this was early 2007—"is supposed to run a segment on that firefight. Also about one of our men we lost, a corporal named Ron Payne, six foot seven and about 270 pounds. I'm six one and 230 but this guy dwarfed me. We ran a night patrol and were ambushed and Payne killed a Talib and then he was hit and died. That was a little while after Pat Tillman was killed [by friendly fire]."

I realized it sounded stupid, but I asked Gunny Milks if he'd found combat in some way satisfying.

"Yes, knowing I was in the war after so long. I could put the camera down and helped with the patrol. For me it was more satisfying than it might have been for the average grunt. I get calls all the time from guys around the country who've seen themselves in one of my photos. I should mention we had women with us, too." Why? "They were women Marines who were our searchers of women when we took prisoners. They were there along with us on every firefight." Armed? "Oh, yes, they carried weapons."

I am continually being surprised by stuff these guys lay on me.

And Milks still had war stories to tell. "After that fighting died down, Geraldo Rivera came out. I was a public affairs guy assigned to Geraldo. He was forced on us. A lot of people were hesitant about him. Remember that drawing in the sand he did? But he turned out to be the most gregarious person, the friendliest guy, and by the end, Marines were swarming him wherever he went. On June 27 we launched Operation Thunder Road (more Springsteen), our last op in Afghanistan, a push west with a combined anti-armor team." But the enemy had no armor, did they? "We used Hummers to surround a village. They were our workhorses. Not heavily armored. The terrain was too rough for that, just as it was for the men to be armored. We were in Afghanistan three months and got out of there in early August by ship. And we had one more deployment in November of 2005 to Iraq, another three-month deal, mostly patrols. Our base was a city called Hit in Anbar Province. That's the bad place. But when we [the 22nd Expeditionary unit again] got there a massive operation had pretty much cleaned out the place. During our time we had three KIA and thirty-nine WIA. I was shot at a few times but no real firefights and I only fired on one occasion. Then I was medically evacuated."

The guy is a public affairs specialist, which is next cousin to a Madison Avenue PR man, and he's medically evacuated? What happened? Gunny Milks sounded slightly baleful. "I was helping a guy with his gear, using my knife to cut off a pouch he couldn't reach that had his sunglasses. While I was cutting he moved and swung around and I stabbed myself with my own knife, cut through my hand, cutting all the tendons. The first sergeant was just standing there looking at me bleeding. 'What the hell, Gunny—' I was pretty ashamed to be evacuated by plane with guys with really bad combat wounds. I'm still doing rehab on the hand but it's about 50 percent healed."

These days Keith Milks is on the staff at Fort Meade, Maryland, which is an army base but the Marines train their public affairs people there. Which is what the Gunny is doing. "Most of these people are young and they look at me and know I've been overseas and I have a bad hand and if they ask about it, I just say, 'Iraq, happened in Iraq.' Which is true enough. With most of them, I don't go into detail. My wife, Barbara, is a commissioned warrant officer now and we have a ten-year-old son who's in a good civilian school and doing very well. I have three years to go and then I'll retire. If we didn't have our son, I might re-up. And just today I was notified I'd been chosen for master sergeant."

I congratulated him but said with regret, and meaning it, "I hate to lose a good gunny." "I know," Milks agreed. He felt the same way. "My favorite ranks were sergeant, not staff sergeant, and then gunny. But I've been a gunny for a long time and I guess it's time." He finished up with a little salesmanship:

"Don't forget to watch the History Channel tonight. At nine Eastern."

Old Marine lieutenants do what gunnies tell us, so I promised I would.

23

A Marine who wouldn't have missed the "Chosin"
"for a million dollars."

"DEAR JIM BRADY," WROTE GEORGE R. LIPPONER, "I WAS BORN IN
Patchogue, New York [1931], and after graduating from school I
wanted to be a ballplayer or a Marine. Well, the ballplaying didn't
work out that well so several of us decided to join the Marines; after
all, we'd been seeing *Sands of Iwo, Guadalcanal Diary* flicks. The others backed out, and the job scene being what it was, I was off to the recruiting office at Hempstead in January 1950. The Marine recruiter
was off that day so a navy chief took my application after trying to
steer me to the navy. I was sworn in at NY City by a most impressive
looking officer. It was Lewis Wilson, then a major, a Medal of Honor
winner [Guam] and later a commandant of the USMC. We spoke at
length and he sought my advice on opening a substation at Patchogue,
which they did later in 1951. So it was off to boot camp, all three of us
from the NY area that week.

"After the rigors of boot camp, which I did enjoy, as June '50 arrived and after a short leave home, I was assigned to Camp Lejeune at
end of June. I was a supply clerk and hated it, went rather quickly to
see the CO for a transfer. He said he might send me on a Med

[Mediterranean] Cruise sometime [it is enormously comforting to know that, in whatever era, Marine officers are still sweet-talking gullible young Marines—JB].

"Then the Korean War began and the army wasn't holding up that well and the call went out for the Marines. A roster of men going to Calif. and to the 1st Mar Div was posted. My name was missing. Back to the CO who said he wanted me to remain behind . . . unless I could arrange a switch with another PFC. I did find one in the company who was engaged and madly in love. We went back to the CO, explained the situation. He [the lovesick Marine] stayed behind and I was put on the roster. It was a troop train across the USA and along the way I ripped up all of my mail and girl pictures and tossed them into the winds of the Ozarks."

Was that a burning of the bridges or something more complex, I wondered? George Lipponer didn't elaborate but went on, taking us with him to Korea and then north to the borders of great China and an uneasy and deadly rendezvous no one expected.

"We trained at Pendleton for a short time and as the army was being pushed further and further south we were rushed along, down to San Diego, boarded a troopship on to Kobe [Japan] and another APA and landed at Inchon, on to Kimpo airport and the capture of Seoul. Boy, we kicked ass then; the gooks were on the run. I was reminded of the gunny who asked me if I was ready to die for my country . . . and I said, no, but I'm going to make some gooks die for theirs. Now they wanted us up north, so we boarded ship and landed at Wonsan and battled our way up toward the Reservoir and another enemy . . . the cold which we weren't prepared for at all.

"November 1950 had us driving to the Chosin area and a new enemy. The Chinks had entered the war and they seemed everywhere, they kept on coming and kept on coming, like a giant army of ants. It turned cold and colder and windier. We froze in our protective gear . . . and the Chinks in their padded outerwear and rubber sneakers had to be colder. I wondered . . . the stronger would surely survive, the best survive. And it got colder. Upon emptying one's bladder, the piss froze before hitting the ground. On one particularly freezing night while I was on watch, I had to urinate and rather than getting out of the sleeping bag, I decided to unzip my bag part ways and piss into my canteen cup which we didn't use anyway and tossed the bladder contents over my shoulder into the swirling winds. In the morning my foxhole buddy commented, wondering why there were frozen yellow beads on our weapons and field packs.

"But we were fortunate. B/1/7 [Baker Co., 1st Battalion, 7th Marines] was part of Chesty Puller's outfit on the Canal and we got the tales of his exploits from the reserve vets of World War II that served with him. I recall one such training lecture where an old salt, giving a machine-gun lecture advised letting the gooks know who they were fucking with. We took his advice. We were together in spirit and action, had great leadership, confidence in our mission, and unit cohesion even though the lines to either side of us were in full retreat and already fifty to eighty miles back (army and ROKs). We kept our canned rations in our crotch or under our armpits for a bit of warmth and were even able to find some humor on occasion. We sang to the tune of 'Bless Them All':

"They asked for the army to come to Korea
But General MacArthur said no
He gave for his reason, the doggies are freezing
Besides the Marines are gung ho.

"And it got colder and colder, our hands stuck to the metal receivers of weapons, canteen water froze solid, shoe pacs we wore were suboptimal, trigger-finger gloves seemed useless, the gloved forefinger didn't fit the housing. Bowel movements if one had any, or the common runs, were dealt with a tiny wad of paper tissue in with the rations, and never enough of them. But we drove on and on.

"On one occasion after taking mortar rounds and suffering numerous casualties, we were rushed off our hill leaving behind our packs and sleeping gear. We engaged the enemy, moving into position through low ground centered on a frozen stream. As it was late afternoon the firing ceased and we pulled back. Myself and two other BAR men were to cover our company's withdrawal. The main body of the company led the withdrawal and we started to take heavy fire from the high ground on either side of us. The firing loosened and cracked the stream's icy surface, and being the last to cross, all three of us fell into the waist-deep stream. With darkness having set in, we never made it back to our beginning point and so the three of us BAR men, soaking from the waist down, in absence of our sleeping bags or a change of pants, stood around all night trying to keep the circulation going. With the first light of day we returned to our starting point and recovered our gear. That was the start of my cold injuries with the Veterans Administration, who after years of denials [that] they existed, finally have cold injuries entered into their files. On one such exam of mine to establish a claim with the VA, their doctor asked me why I didn't just go to a warming tent. A warming tent? I explained to him there weren't any in our area. The VA doctor found that hard to understand."

Having fought in North Korea in winter and served with men of the Chosin Few, I share Lipponer's incredulity. He finished his letter to me with these words.

"All in all it was a great experience, one I wouldn't trade for a million dollars. It is mine and mine alone. We endured a great deal but with training and esprit de corps we persevered. When the word came to move out, we did with fine leadership from the NCOs and officers, whether from OCS or the halls of Annapolis. We moved forward toward the enemy determined, and the enemy knew the Marines, the troops with the yellow leggings, wouldn't back down. And all we got for it was another battle star on our presidential unit citation. I was proud of those four battle stars I wear on my PUC for action from Inchon through February 1951.

"The Marines I served with didn't ask for anything in return. We knew we had each other . . . just give us more ammo so we can finish our mission. That's how we felt. Semper Fi, George R. Lipponer."

Lipponer today lives half the year on Long Island, at Lake Ronkonkoma, and winters in Florida near Orlando with his wife. They had six children, one of whom died. When we connected on the phone last fall, I asked if George had been evacuated from the Chosin Reservoir because of frostbite. "No, there were too many guys much worse off. The Chinese were coming and we did a lot of damage to them as we came out. They didn't get away free. Or undamaged. We walked out all the way to Hungnam, where we took ship. Happy? I'll say. There was a great deal of exhilaration that we got out at all."

Recently the VA increased his frostbite disability to 100 percent, "a total disability based on being unemployable."

Since he'd carried a BAR I asked if he were a big man or small, because the BAR is heavy and by some strange Marine alchemy, it is usually assigned to the little guys. "No, I'm average in size but I hung on to the BAR. After the Chosin we went down to 'the bean patch' near Masan. I think they called it that because they grew beans there. We were billeted in tents with lots of room because Baker Company had so many casualties. We were down to only one officer, Woody Taylor [a rifle company usually has seven officers], and they said the 1st Marine Division wouldn't be ready to fight for another six months. But suddenly replacement drafts began to come in and the tents filled up. We had tents all up and down what began to look like a company street and not a 'bean patch.' Soon we were a full-strength company again."

It was supposed to take half a year before the division took the field again. But, Lipponer went on, "Then in January and February"— not six months but one or two months later—"we went up to Pohang for the 'great guerrilla hunt.' There was a whole division of North Koreans trapped somewhere in the hills up there and they sent all three rifle regiments up there, the 1st, the 5th and the 7th. We went in after them. The orders were to flush them out, go in and draw fire! That's some order, 'Draw fire!' " Lipponer snorted derisively. "But that's what we did up and down those hills. We were worn down and worn out. Then the first rotation draft of Marines went home, mostly guys who fought in World War II. Then a second came along and it was my turn." The troops going home were to turn in their weapons just before embarkation, but his company commander, appreciating the value in firepower of every single Browning automatic rifle he had, called George aside. "I remember the captain said, 'Be sure your BAR stays here in the company.' So I went to a guy I knew and I gave him my BAR. I said, Here, this is yours now. Take care of it. He didn't want to carry it and griped for a while, but he got over it and I left."

After Korea George did three more years in the Corps. "First I was stationed at Portsmouth, Virginia, then back to good old 'Swamp

Lagoon' [Camp Lejeune to the rest of us], and then a year or so of re-cruiting duty in Baltimore. I loved it! We'd march the kids down to the railroad station while a band played. Before we took them we had to check the police blotter and the courts to be sure they weren't wanted for anything.

"When I got out, I bartended one summer on Long Island and then I started a construction business and I stayed in that until I retired." Now George Lipponer summers on Long Island and as a good "snow-bird" should, winters in Florida. There's apparently very little frostbite in either place. And wherever Lipponer is, up north or down south, summer or winter, "I always wear the eagle, globe, and anchor on a cap or shirt, a car window or bumper, and in return I receive a toot or a wave. It bothers me that we had to leave some of our Corps in that frozen hell of North Korea as their final gravesite . . ." In his own small, personal nod to those men, "I donated and placed a 'Chosin Few' monument at the Veterans Plaza, Hauppauge, New York, a few years ago in memory of those we left behind."

Speaking with George Lipponer and the others, it struck me as re-assuring that no matter how much hard fighting some of these guys were in, under what punishing conditions they fought, killing and be-ing killed, and no matter how badly hurt they were, how well their postwar lives had turned out. How most of them, of us, had reentered society, how the severely frostbitten Lipponer, who couldn't find a warming tent in North Korea, found himself a trade at home, going into construction work, building houses for others to stay warm.

24

A sailor, a Marine, and now a U.S. Senator, John Warner of Virginia

SOMETIMES A BRIGHT IDEA JUST DOESN'T WORK OUT.

Senator John Warner, by now considered one of the powerful and respected "old bulls" of the Senate, longtime chairman of the Armed Forces Committee, and as of 2007 its ranking minority member, would surely have a grand story to tell of his Marine service and his World War II navy tour.

The onetime husband of one of the richest young women in America, the gorgeous blonde, wealthy, but shy Cathy Mellon, daughter of billionaire Paul Mellon, and later wed to actress Elizabeth Taylor, still later, after several divorces, the beau of Barbara Walters, Warner was a Korean-era Marine officer who had enlisted in the wartime navy at the age of seventeen. Why? And how had he ended up in the Marines?

Surely with all that time in uniform in two services during a couple of wars, there were tales to tell.

I knew the young Warner casually because we both gobbled cheap but filling breakfasts of sausage and eggs, hot breads and steaming coffee (for less than a buck as I recall), in a Wisconsin Avenue joint called Britts in the Georgetown where we both lived as young men. I was a

Washington correspondent covering the Senate and he was a big, hand-some, dark-haired young lawyer people knew as "Big Chief." His kid brother, "Little Chief," was also studying law, but when *The Washington Post* and *Washington Times-Herald* announced the engagement of "Big Chief" to the heiress Mellon, "Little Chief" promptly and prag-matically changed his academic track from the law to "estate manage-ment." There was, over breakfast at Britts, considerable levity, a wink and a knowing nod, over this career move by John's kid brother.

"Big Chief," a secure and self-confident young man with an innate serenity, took no note of our capering.

Born in Amherst County, Virginia, in 1927, Warner enlisted in the navy in January 1945 and served on active duty in the final months of World War II and until September 1946 when he was discharged. Then it was off to college at Washington and Lee and law school at the Uni-versity of Virginia, a stint interrupted by another war (Korea), and a second military tour, starting in October 1950 as a Marine officer, a first lieutenant in communications, and a ground officer's billet with the 1st Marine Air Wing in Korea. Finishing his law studies after his discharge, he was selected as law clerk to a chief judge of the U.S. Cir-cuit Court of Appeals, appointed assistant U.S. attorney, and went into private practice.

His press aide, John Elliot, himself a former Marine officer, sent along the senator's military bio. It began during the final year of World War II, "when in January 1945, at age 17, enlisted in the U.S. Navy. He served on active duty until the summer of 1946 when he was hon-orably discharged as Petty Officer 3rd Class, electronic technician's mate. Following the war he attended Washington and Lee University on the GI Bill and was awarded a B.S. degree in 1949. He then entered the University of Virginia Law School.

"At the outbreak of the Korean War in the summer of 1950, Warner interrupted his law studies and commenced a second tour of ac-tive military duty, beginning in October of 1950, this time as an officer in the United States Marine Corps. A year later in October 1951, as a first lieutenant in communications, he volunteered for duty in Korea, and served as a ground officer with the 1st Marine Air Wing. Following his active service in Korea, he remained in the Marine Corps Reserve and was promoted to the rank of Captain."

I asked Mr. Elliot about that "active service." "He served stateside in the navy." And in Korea? "He was a communications officer, but he went up to the front line from time to time. He was not a forward air controller. I don't believe he was ever in combat, ever in firefights." Which rather effectively shut down my hopes of getting a good war story from the senator.

In 1969 "Big Chief" left private practice to serve as undersecretary of the navy and in 1972 to become navy secretary. In 1978 he won the first of his five consecutive elections to the United States Senate from Virginia. Great résumé. Good man. Looks like a fellow who would have enjoyed a fight.

Too bad he missed out on the fun and I missed out on yet another bloodthirsty yarn.

25

After the war, Ramon Gibson plays it safe,
becomes a test pilot.

As a child, Colonel Ramon James Allen Gibson had already lived more swashbuckling adventures in more exotic places than some Marines have in an entire career.

He was born in Argentina, son of an American diplomat, Raleigh Augustus Gibson, and his wife, Lucille Snell, his dad Raleigh being so popular throughout his Latin American tours that local people said of him, "Es muy simpático," called him "Rolly," and newspaper caricaturists made something of a character of him on the editorial pages with his pipe and hat. The affable, colorful Rolly apparently was anything but the stuff of "Yanqui go home" posters and the direct antithesis of our latter-day "ugly American." Ramon and his brother, Raleigh Snell Gibson, grew up at different postings throughout Latin America, and in Mexico got to know Anne Morrow, daughter of the American ambassador Dwight Morrow, and an aviator herself who intrigued the impressionable Gibson boys with her tales of high flying. She would become the wife of Charles Lindbergh, the famed "Lone Eagle," whose baby son was later and tragically kidnapped and murdered.

It was also in Mexico where Ray Gibson and his brother narrowly escaped their own kidnapping. It seemed the Gibsons lived near a golf course in Guadalajara and therefore were thought to be wealthy, and not the offspring of a mere career diplomat on a government salary. The Gibson boys had become friendly with a local farmer turned itinerant fruit vendor they called Don Pedro. The vendor was often called on to help find young Raleigh when he toddled off. In this way, Don Pedro became a Gibson family ally and resource. But when the Jalisco Federal Police uncovered a plot to identify, kidnap, and hold for huge ransoms some of the rich children in the neighborhood, it turned out that friendly Don Pedro was himself a terrorist, second in command of the kidnappers, the guy who cased the joints, and had personally crossed off the names of his young amigos, the Gibson kids, from a roster of potential victims. The Gibson boys were still living in Mexico when Kremlin thugs hatcheted to death Lenin's and Stalin's old bête noir, Leon Trotsky. And as a boy, and capping those adventures, Ramon flew for the first time ever, a noisy but otherwise pleasant experience. Gibson decided on the spot to learn to fly.

He became a flier, and while in a wartime V-5 college program set up to train future naval aviators, chose the Marines over the navy because he assumed they were "the elite." Ray was flying fighters in Korea when we met.

After the Korean War, when most of us settled down, Ray Gibson began a new career in Texas as a test pilot, and until his death (in his early eighties!) was still test-flying planes. As a boy his first flight was in a Ford Trimotor with an affable pilot who permitted the kid to sit in the copilot's seat, and a yen to fly was hatched. After three years at Texas Military Institute, a high school, Gibson chose aeronautical engineering as his field of study at the University of Alabama. He played freshman basketball and, with World War II now on, qualified for the Navy's V-5 program, which would lead to a commission and a chance at flight school. Ray had an edge on classmates in that he'd already done civilian flight training in Columbia, Georgia, in a forty-horsepower Piper Cub used generally for crop dusting.

Naval flight training was at Glenview Naval Air Station, north of Chicago. There was additional training at other bases, then combat flight training at Corpus Christi, where Ramon Gibson was commissioned in

June 1944 as a second lieutenant in the United States Marine Corps Reserve. Among others in the same training cycle, Hollywood's Tyrone Power, then a Marine first lieutenant and Robert Taylor, a navy lieutenant. As Gibson remembered it later, the term "media" had not yet been invented, but there was plenty of "press" swarming around the stars, trespassing on the airfield, interrupting training, and arousing in young Gibson an antipathy that still seemed to be eating at him years later. Ray ferried aircraft for a time, was promoted to squadron leader, and had just received orders about the upcoming invasion of Japan when he ran out of war.

Oh, damn, no combat for gallant, swashbuckling Lieutenant Gibson.

Korea would make up for that. After World War II Gibson returned to college and to a Marine Reserve air unit at Cherry Point, North Carolina. During one two-week summer stretch of active duty, Gibson's Corsair lost power over the Atlantic and, with his craft on fire, he coasted back to a pancake landing on relatively calm Pamlico Sound. The Coast Guard fished him out. In 1951, with the Korean War grinding into its second year, Ray Gibson, like Ted Williams of the Red Sox and Jerry Coleman of the Yankees, was recalled to active duty as a naval aviator in the United States Marine Corps. After the usual refreshment brushup of technique, Gibson was in a transport plane being flown across the Pacific to join the Marine Air Wing, then in action in Korea.

His squadron, VMF-212, flew not jets but old Corsairs, for a reason. They were the best close-air support craft in the business, and that was one of many reasons for the fighting effectiveness of Marine infantry. Corsairs had four 40-millimeter cannon mounted forward, could carry 2,500-pound bombs (Coleman, as noted, claims 3,000), and deliver a load of napalm on enemy trenches, dugouts, and other positions. The big bombs were reserved for North Korean bridges and railroad terminals, that sort of target. Starting in March 1952, Gibson's squadron flew daily combat missions, ducking Mig interceptors and taking heavy ack-ack fire. His description of those sorties in his book *As I Saw It* conjure up imagery like that in Jim Michener's *Bridges at Toko-ri,* and the subsequent film starring Bill Holden as a carrier pilot shot down during a similar bridge attack. According to Ray, Corsair jocks, as the Marine pilots were known, were sworn to an informal pact that any other Corsair driver who by some fluke shot down a Russian-built Mig would himself immediately be shot down by his buddies lest word get back and the Pentagon enthusiastically order another thousand antiquated Corsairs for the next interplanetary war.

I mentioned close-air support. The army relies for that on the air force. And you know all about interservice rivalries. In combat in my time, each Marine rifle battalion had two Marine fliers temporarily assigned as forward observers, men who, being pilots themselves, knew that end of the trade and, being Marines, were supposed to have at least a passing appreciation of infantry warfare and tactics. That's where tactical close-air support came in. The infantry loved it. The pilots . . . well, they tried hard to be enthusiastic, all the time lusting to get back in he air and back to the airstrips with their hot meals, showers, flight pay, and more couth companions than we crude fellows in the infantry.

In the spring of 1952 our battalion had two air officers, Bob Baker and Gibson. Baker, also a captain, wore out his welcome early. Every morning the colonel held an officers' meeting (I was by then battalion intelligence officer), a casual, outdoor affair sitting around on logs or sandbags, giving brief reports from our area of competence as Colonel Gregory listened and then issued orders. On one early May morning Baker stood up to deliver the daily air report. It was very brief.

"Hurray, hurray, the Fourth of May / Outdoor fucking starts today."

The colonel, something of a stickler, got rid of Baker that very day, sending him back to the air wing, leaving the somewhat more cultured Gibson our lone air officer. There was a coda to the Baker Saga, however. Some weeks later he playfully buzzed our battalion area at treetop level, sending all of us, including presumably the colonel, diving for cover, but in so doing Bob Baker clipped a power line and crash-landed, drawing on himself the usual angry screech from high authority for destruction of government property.

Clearly, a vestige of Pappy Boyington's spirit yet survived.

Air officers tried to get in their hours of actual flying each month (to qualify for flight pay, I guess, or actually to maintain their skills). Ray Gibson's scam was to fly an OY, a small, two-seat observation plane, to the nearest air force or Marine airfield to scrounge ice for the officers' mess. To keep him company I went along, claiming I wanted to see the enemy lines from the air to report back enemy movements and such to battalion. I don't believe anyone actually believed me, but there were no protests. To amuse himself, Ray let me drive for a time, issuing casual instructions. The landing and takeoff he handled, fortunately. During one of my flying lessons I noticed what I thought was firing from the Chinese lines.

"Can they reach us?" I inquired, trying not to sound nervous. "Oh, probably not," Gibson said casually. "That's small stuff without the range. They won't waste the big stuff on an OY because then we could call in counterbattery fire on them. Or call up an air strike."

The Chinese kept shooting and we kept flying, Gibson more relaxed about it than I. And he continued his flying lessons. One thing he stressed, "Never be ashamed to take a wave-off. If the landing officer on the carrier deck waves you off, take it and go around and come back another time." I promised solemnly that if I was ever landing on a carrier, I'd take a wave-off, and cheerfully so.

The fighting went on all that spring and summer, and Ray Gibson stayed with us, a popular figure but one of the least martial looking Marines we had. He was tall and lanky, but slouchy, and wore his .45 automatic in a loosely slung leather holster that was forever slipping around from his hip to front and center, approximately over his buttoned fly. The colonel would stare at Gibson's crotch and shake his head, but no one ever bothered Ray about it and he didn't seem to care. There was then and still may be a memorable saying about navy or Marine top guns: "The average Navy pilot, despite the sometimes swaggering exterior, is very much capable of such feelings as love, affection, intimacy, and caring. These feelings just don't happen to involve anyone else."

None of us ever felt that way about Ramon Gibson. He and I remained in touch over the years and visited from time to time. He read my books and was forever threatening to write his own (he did, finally), and unlike most Marines home from the wars, whose lives become less risky and adventuresome, taking on a new, more placid rhythm, he never settled into a more sedate existence.

Not Ramon Gibson. He became a test pilot.

When Ray died in January 2006 at age eighty-three, *The Dallas Morning News* obituary page gave him a typical down-home Texas adios: "The Silver Fox [his blond hair was by now gray], Ramon James Allen Gibson, took off from Irving, Texas, for the Lord's Airport." Until a year or two before his death, Ray was still certified and a working test pilot, flight-testing aircraft in Texas, and was by then a colonel in the Marine Corps Reserve, and had only recently published his hardcover memoir, *The Way I Saw It: From Fighter Pilot to Test Pilot.* Shortly after his death, the usual Christmas parcel arrived from Dallas, the two excellent fruitcakes Ray sent our family every year. He'd shipped them just prior to that final hospitalization and his last flight "for the Lord's Airport," and the parcel crossed in the mail with his obituary notice.

26

Medal of Honor winner Hector Cafferata says, "I was a Marine-happy kid."

THIS WAS A FEW YEARS BACK AT CAMP LEJEUNE, THE BIG MARINE base in North Carolina. Secretary of the Navy Gordon England, commandant of the Marine Corps James Jones, and other great men had gathered in the football stadium to mark some anniversary or other of the Korean War. There were plenty of us who'd been invited or just showed up, including, memorably, three men who wore the distinctive pale blue ribbon of the Medal of Honor, one of them a Marine general; another a naval aviator who would rise to four-striper, a navy captain; and Hector Cafferata, a mere private when he earned his medal.

Big, bulky guy with a bad gimp; his hips needed work, and Hector said he might have both replaced at once so he'd miss only one hunting season and not two. I assumed on our first meeting this was some unbridled and ferocious western ranch hand or southern farm boy who'd grown up with shotguns and rifles, a born gunslinger like Jimmy Ringo. Or William Bonney, a.k.a. "Billy the Kid." The medal commendation said Hector and two of his mates had killed more than a hundred attacking Chinese regulars, with Hector doing most of the firing (one of the other Marines had been blinded, the other badly wounded), so this

Cafferata couldn't be a city boy. I was wrong. Hector was a New York, born November 4, 1929, a couple of weeks after the stock market crash, who grew up in New Jersey, and joined the Marines because "I was a Marine-happy kid."

We went out for a drink that night at the Lejeune officers' club. Emily Post isn't any more particular than the Marine Corps about such things: Marine officers don't barge into enlisted men's clubs; nor do sergeants frequent officers' clubs; the only enlisted men in an officers' club are mixing drinks behind the club bar. Marine privates or corporals (as Hector had been and ended up) aren't welcome. But that night at Lejeune, it was Hector, big and noisy, who led us into the club, one general, a couple of colonels, a couple of company grade officers like myself trailing in his luminous wake. And no one raised an objection. It was the medal he was wearing, of course, but also the way in which Cafferata carried himself, bellying up with a swagger to the bar as grinning enlisted men put down their bar rags to shake his hand and ask his order. And it was definitely Hector who did the ordering, even the general acknowledged that. It must have been something like that in 1950, the night of November 27–28 on that hilltop in North Korea when the Chinese came up the hill and Hector rolled out of his sleeping bag to pipe them aboard, trot out the hors d'ouvres and adult beverages, and get the party started. Oh, yeah, being understandably in a hurry at the time, Hector left behind his parka and boots and fought all night in his wool socks.

I spoke briefly earlier about ill temper and belligerence possibly being contributing factors when calculating why Marines fight. My pal Joe Owen told me this story from his days recuperating and rehabbing at St. Alban's Naval Hospital in New York following the Chosin Reservoir campaign. It involved Hector.

"One night we jumped ship and ended up in a gin mill just outside the main gate. Dick Brennan came along, both of us in uniform and with one arm each in a sling, and there were some enlisted men in the bar as well, all of us drinking hard and with wounded flippers, bandaged up, some limping and on canes, arms in slings, that sort of thing, and there was this big guy sitting on the next bar stool, bullshitting about the Chosin. He was getting off some of the worst crap I ever heard and I called him on it, and he and I got into it. I'm six-five and he was pretty big and we were about to go. Brennan grabbed me. We were already absent without leave, and I was about to punch an enlisted man. Which officers just don't do. "You'll spend the rest of the war in the brig," Dick reminded me. "And with your arm, you can't fight anyway." A badly shot-up Brennan had his own problems, but on something like this, he cut keenly to the core and issued sound judgments. Joe Owen must have listened.

The "big guy, the enlisted man," turned out of course to be Hector Cafferata, and after an exchange of both insults and compliments, no blows struck, an armistice was negotiated and Joe and the future Medal of Honor laureate swiftly became the closest of friends. Hey, they'd both fought at the Chosin.

Early in 2006 Hector reentered my consciousness through a couple of letters from Fort Myers, Florida. A retired Marine colonel from New York, a Xavier High School grad named Robert J. Stolarik, a neighbor of and something of a Cafferata fan who had read about Hector in an earlier one of my books, decided to bring me up to date on the great man, actually sending me at his expense a paperback edition of the book for me to inscribe for Hector. He cited Cafferata's Medal of Honor commendation, and I went back to read the official, barebones Marine record, volume 3, *U.S. Marine Operations in Korea*, page 181. Here's what it said about Hector's role in that night battle of Fox Company and the Chinese atop Toktong Pass in North Korea:

"Fighting with small arms and grenades also raged on the hillside to the left, where the Chinese attempted to drive a wedge between the 2nd and 3rd platoons, repeated assaults were hurled back with grievous losses to the Reds, and they apparently threw in fresh units in their bid for a critical penetration. That they failed was due largely to the valor of three Marines who made a determined stand at the vital junction: PFC Robert F. Benson, Private Hector A. Cafferata of the 2nd platoon, and PFC Gerald J. Smith, a fire-team leader of the 3rd. These men, assisted by the members of Smith's team, are credited with annihilating two enemy platoons."

Other accounts described how Hector fired so often and so fast that his hands blistered and smoke was rising from the scorched wooden stock of his weapon. One of his fellow Marines, having been blinded early in the fight, reloaded weapons by feel and handed them to Cafferata to do the firing for both of them. In his book *Medal of Honor,* Peter Collier adds some detail. Following the worst of the nightlong fight, Hector "tried to retrieve his boots and parka from his sleeping bag but was hit in the arm and leg. He was evacuated and hospitalized for eighteen months. Later he learned that American officers had counted approximately a hundred Chinese dead around the ditch where he had fought that night, but had decided not to put the figure into their report because they thought that no one would believe it.

"In 1952," Collier wrote, "back home [from the hospital] in New Jersey, Cafferata was informed by telegram that he had been awarded the Medal of Honor and was to go to Washington to receive it. When he replied that he'd prefer to have it mailed to him, he was contacted by a Marine officer who barked at him, 'You will get down here so that President Truman can personally give this Medal of Honor to you!'"

In the end, Hector went to D.C.

If you have ever been in a close-range fight like his with grenades and small arms against the Chinese, you have a good idea what it's all about. And if you throw in the mountainous terrain, the isolation, the cold and the snow and the night, and that these were three kids just out of their teens, well, just think about it.

Which is why I wrote back to Colonel Stolarik that I'd be delighted to sign a book for Hector, but I felt that he rated at least a hardcover copy, so I signed one and sent it off to Stolarik for hand delivery. According to the colonel, he'd been trying to get Hector to participate in a golf outing and Marine Corps birthday celebration on November 10, but Hector declined, saying he "had conflicts. He had been invited to attend the dedication of the new Marine Corps Museum at Quantico on the birthday and he also has a hunting trip to the Dakotas about the same time and I think the hunting might win out." So it sounds as if Hector's new hips are working after all. Old Marines worry about shit like that, like their precious spit shines.

I know, because when I asked Hector to tell me about the presidential award of the medal, he responded with energy. "President Truman pinned it on, the little shrimp, and was standing on the toes of my shoes when he did. Ruined the damned spit shine."

There would be one more letter from Colonel Stolarik and a local newspaper story. In April 2006 Cape Coral, Florida, named its elementary school after Hector A. Cafferata Jr., "the only living man in southwest Florida to have a school named after him." They worked up a ceremony and a history lesson, but a few things were lacking, according to Hector. There was no drum and bugle corps, no playing of Taps, no rifle shots fired in salute. Worse still, the affair would take place after three P.M. when most of the children were already aboard school buses and headed home, and not there to enjoy the festivities, such as they were. The local *News-Press* quoted Hector precisely on the matter.

"Without all the kids there, why are we having it? I feel like a horse's ass. I have never seen such a mess."

You'd think someone scuffed up his "damned spit shine" all over again.

27

A young lieutenant hits the beach "sprayed with his sergeant's brains."

By LATE 2006 THERE WAS SO MUCH MAIL (NEVER MIND THE PHONE calls) coming in from that story in *Leatherneck* magazine about my working on this book, I was running out of entire chapters for each Marine. The newspaper clippings had a wonderfully dated look to them, the lacquered yellowing of faded newsprint, of time past; the letters were wonderfully terse, often biting, occasionally eloquent, packed with incident and event, sometimes thrilling when you heard again the names of famous battles fought. Here is a sampling.

John C. Chapin wrote from Manchester, Vermont. He was recruited on the campus of Yale by a Marine officer, joined as a PFC, was sent to OCS, commissioned a second lieutenant in December 1942. "February '44, first wave at Roi-Namur, K Co., 3rd Battalion, 24th Marines. Reaction to hostile fire, tense, not afraid, because of intensive training. I knew my men and my job. Head blown off my platoon sergeant 100 yards from shore so I hit beach sprayed with his brains. Charged by Jap with bayonet, blew up pillbox with Bangalore torpedo. Hit on right cheek. June '44 to Saipan. Company shattered by artillery barrage. Fought there for three weeks through cane fields and jungle. Hit in side."

I read up briefly on the fight (January 31–February 2, 1944) to flesh out Chapin's spare account. Roi and Namur were two small linked islands in the Kwajalen Atoll, the Japanese air base from which the Marines of Wake Island were attacked in the early weeks of World War II. The U.S. Army took Kwajalen itself while the 23rd and 24th Marines assaulted the two islands, Chapin's 24th having "a tougher time," according to the history. In the joint operation in three days, 3,500 Japanese were killed, along with 313 Marine dead and 502 wounded, including Lieutenant Chapin. His first but not last Purple Heart.

His letter concludes: "Why I fought? (1) Everyone I knew enlisted. (2) USMC mystique. I knew the proud traditions. (3) Endless hard training prepared me. I knew I was going to beach assaults and combat. (4) Pride in men I trained. I could not let them down. So I led them. Semper Fi, John Chapin." He was keeping it pretty simple, I concluded, still visualizing his sergeant's brains "sprayed" all over the young platoon leader in a landing craft heading for a hostile beach, the youngster hired off the campus at New Haven.

Murl Bright, another multiple Purple Heart Marine, wrote his letter on 2nd Marine Division Assn stationery from Caldwell, Idaho.

"For starters, enlisted May 1939, asked for and received my discharge December 7, 1945. Sailed with the 2nd Marine Brigade in December 1941 for the Pacific, landed in American Samoa January '42 to build a defense. After August 7, 1942, prepared to join the battle for Guadalcanal. Arrived last of October/first of November. Wounded on Guadalcanal. Going through hospital system joined my company in 2nd Mar Div in New Zealand. We landed at Tarawa and fought the last two days on the island and was shot four hours before the end of that battle."

Tarawa was one of the bloodiest though briefest of all Pacific Marine assaults. In three days that November of '43, 941 Marines died and 2,072 were wounded. Out of 2,619 Japanese defenders, only 17 survived, all of them wounded. The operation was largely felt by the Marines involved to have been a bloody screwup. Since the topographic charts and maps were nonexistent or faulty, the landing craft ran aground on coral from six hundred to a thousand yards out, forcing the fully armed and burdened Marines to wade in through deep water laced with machine-gun fire. On the chaotic beach, littered with smashed gear, dead bodies (all Marines), and wounded men, still being heavily shelled, then Colonel David Shoup, though wounded himself, organized the survivors and mounted attack after attack, earning Shoup a Medal of Honor. (He was for a brief few months my CO at Quantico and later became Marine commandant).

Shoup's radioed message from the beach to his commanding officer aboard ship is a model of brevity. And of positive thinking: "Casualties many; percentage of dead not known; combat efficiency; we are winning."

Sort of reminds you of Marshal Foch in 1914: "My center is giving way, my right is retreating, situation excellent. I am attacking."

Bright concluded his story. "I returned through hospital to U.S. and never returned to combat. My service record is available. Not a day in the Brig. Sick bay time only for wounds. No VD time to make up at end of enlistment—those were the rules at the time. I drew my clothing allowance in cash when we were switched to free clothes. I also drew the maximum allowable for annual leave not used up on discharge. My Marine duty formed my opinions about the greatness of the USMC."

I was impressed with the admirable precision of Murl's account of his service but found it too brief (had Colonel Shoup or Marshal Foch inspired that in him?), so I phoned Idaho to get more details on Tarawa and to ask what he did after the war. Bright started his account where so many Marine assaults on hostile beaches began, getting into the boats.

"We unloaded from the transport into a landing craft the first morning, ready to go but in reserve, waiting until called at the edge of the reef. Then one big Japanese eight-inch shell came real close to our own transport so they pulled us back, almost out of sight of the shore, even the treetops, just the plume of smoke rising, so we circled all day, all night. Two squads plus HQ and attached units, 30 men in all, standing up, no room to sit down. We took a whiz over the side. I had a typical good Navy breakfast and wasn't hungry so I left the C-rations alone and didn't eat anything. Finally we headed in to the lagoon for Red Beach 2. I was platoon sergeant in Able Company, 1st Battalion, 8th Marines. A damn good battalion commander, Major Lawrence C. Hayes, a damn good company commander, Howard Gunther. This was the second day and I said, Jesus Christ, they're still fighting. It should have been over by now.

"The ramp went down and I stepped into the water, just over my waist at first, maybe 600 yards from the seawall [the shore]. I had good corporal squad leaders, all good experienced people, most of whom fought on Guadalcanal, all of them courageous, no guys farting around. We headed in to the beach. Don't let anyone tell you a man can run on coral. You can't run across coral. One minute it's ankle deep then you're in a hole up to your middle. Your field shoes are filled with water, your pockets, your pack. I never did like a carbine—it had no stopping power—and wanted to get an M-1 rifle. I cut open my pack, pulled out a fountain pen and notebook, threw away the pack, the map case, the gas mask, the carbine, kept my tin hat and a canteen.

"There were machine guns onshore raking our line of men left to right, right to left. Every time I saw the bullets splashing toward me I dove under water. On the beach I grabbed an ammo belt and a rifle from a dead Marine. Dead bodies all over the place. There was a sunken Jap freighter. They had concrete pilings and barbed wire, by the second day all of it tangled up. Still in the water I had a big Marine I was counting on to carry the explosive charges, but I lost him." Dead? I asked. "No," said Murl, "they fished him out and after the war he became a customs agent in New York."

More from Murl Bright on Tarawa: "There were about 35 of us from Able Company (usually 240 men) left, not enough men to form up proper [four-man] fire teams, and the lieutenant, Mark Tomlinson, paired us two by two. He was a sergeant on the Canal who got a field commission. A hell of a good leader who could find his way around a jungle and the men would follow him. He said, 'Hey, guys, let's go kill some Japs,' and we took off. Our best scout was shot right away, ran right into a machine gun. They blew him right past me. Tomlinson got killed there, too. They ask what makes 'em fight. Training or what? I think it's because the Marine Corps recruits people who want to fight, and they put responsibility on them from private up. Men like the lieutenant.

"I was resting with my back against a concrete piling and felt like I was the safest man on the island. I could see about two dozen people from our company still moving. But when we moved just before dark the second day we were ashore, I usually held my rifle at high port, but my left arm was tired and I carried it low. There in front of me I saw two white teeth. Then above them, a mustache, then a gun barrel. He shot the rifle right out of my hand, spinning me around, the rifle bolt going through the back of my hand."

That was the end of Bright's combat on Tarawa. Couldn't use that hand. Four hours later the fight was all over. Tarawa was taken.

Murl Bright said he'd be eighty-eight in February of '07, feels pretty good, even having been wounded twice in two of the worst of the Pacific battles, the Canal and Tarawa. He said he'd been a mail carrier in a rural area for thirty-eight years, had three kids, two sons nearby in Idaho and a daughter in Ohio. He retired from the post office in 1990, an American who delivered the mail literally and in war.

George E. Krug reported in from Buffalo Grove, Illinois.

"Mr. Brady. Here is my perspective on the Marines under hostile fire. I am a Marine combat veteran of the Korean War, duty with Fox/2/5 from March '52 to March '53. All I can remember about my first action is that I reacted first and was scared afterward. What motivates a Marine to fight is a very hard question to answer. Let me relate to you something about the members of my squad, second squad, first platoon, Fox Company.

"August 1952 Fox Co. manned a section of the Jamestown Line known to the grunts as the MLR [main line of resistance], located on the west side of the Samichon Valley. The area was called the Hook because of the odd shape of the trench line. Fox not only defended the MLR but was responsible for several combat outposts, one named Irene the other Warsaw, with the British Commonwealth Division on our right flank. Fox was on line for the month and we were relieved by the 7th Marines and went into reserve and the fill-ins went back to their regular outfits. We had casualties I believe were heavy.

"The skipper Captain Gately made me squad leader and had me promoted to corporal. At the reserve area I had twelve fresh-off-the-boat Marines assigned to my squad and we had three weeks training before we returned to the line. The twelve new squad members were a cross section of the United States. My three BAR men were farmers from the Midwest, Jones a rancher from S.D., Houseman a dairy farmer from MN, Kron a wheat farmer from ND. The riflemen were Curtis James, a fish farmer from ND, King a farmer from FL. Goff a geologist from NM ["he was a nutty son of a gun," King told me later], Deverow a cowboy from Montana, Roundhouse a Navajo farmer from NM, Gomez from LA, Golden, Karlsted a farmer from MN, Evans and Ledden. I don't recall where Evans came from or much about Ledden's background."

He needn't apologize. I was continually astonished by these men's memories after so many years. Krug continues:

"The one thing we all had in common was, with the exception of three, we were all drafted. The Marine Corps chose us. We had casualties and lost some of these men. I stayed with the squad the next six months until rotated home. Captain Kurth called me to the CP. My orders for rotation came through. But first Fox was going to give me a going-away party. He told me to get my men ready for extra patrols because we were going to assault a Chinese outpost called Detroit on 23 February. In this action King lost a leg, Goff a hand; Jones, King and Gomez were wounded but returned to duty. Our platoon leader was killed but I don't remember his name as he wasn't with us long.

"Two weeks after Detroit I left for the States. Captain Kurth asked me to stay behind for a month and he would get me sergeant's stripes. I declined and regretted it for many years. Fox Co. and the rest of 2/5 went on to Reno and Vegas [other outpost fights] where they took a good pounding.

"Why did these men fight? The answer is simple. We were ordinary people molded into Marines. The same can be said of those who served in the army. We all had the proper upbringings of common folk, when you have a task to do, you work hard, give it your best and get the job done. We came from different backgrounds; however, we became a team, moving and fighting as if we had known each other all of our lives. All of us have bonded for life and still keep in touch by phone, letters, and visits. If anyone of the second squad needs help you can be sure the rest of the squad would be there. All of those I have kept in touch with have been successful in the life endeavors they chose.

"Not one of them is bitter about giving up two years of their life to 'Serve Their Country.' "

Corporal Krug signs off, "hope it helps. Sincerely." When I called him to check on a few facts and spellings, he told me that right after Korea he thought about re-upping in the Marines but was "struck by a wonderful disease, matrimony." Now he's seventy-six, has six kids, is still working in the building trade as a licensed architectural hardware consultant and construction documents guy. And he put his wife, Marianne, on the phone to swear to all of the above.

Which the charming Marianne promptly and happily did.

George Peto, soon to be eighty-five and still frisky, wrote from Columbus, Ohio. "My service dates from August 5, 1941, to November 1945. I joined the 1st Mar Div in Australia right after the Guadalcanal campaign and left it at Okinawa when the war ended. My rank was Sergeant, forward observer for 81-mm Mortars, 3rd Battalion, 1st Marines. The obvious answer [to "why we fight?"] is 'for your country,' patriotism, and all that crap.

"But the last thing a Marine in a firefight thinks of is home. He is trying to survive. Number one, he worries about his fellow Marine to his right and left. Without them his chance of surviving is small, so you definitely fight for your buddies. A Marine fights hard due to his indoctrination and love for the Corps and his own self-respect. The greatest fear you have is to let your fellow Marines down. Speaking only for myself, competition with your peers was a great motivation. Friendly competition whether in a liberty port or battlefield was a lot like a ballgame. Everyone wants to be the best.

"On my fourth and last campaign, Okinawa, I lost a close friend I'd been with three and a half years. It was May 3, 1945, and for the last forty-nine days of WWII I was driven by pure hatred, and the real-ization I could get killed. The glory part of war was gone. I fought for revenge. To this day an old photo of a Japanese soldier brings back the hatred. I will carry my feelings to the grave.

"Duty in the Fleet Marine Force was not for the faint of heart. The food was bad, the training tough and continuous, rain and shine, disci-pline was harsh. I got thirty days on bread and water for two weeks AWOL. Given the same circumstances, I would do it again today. But in defense of the punishment, it was necessary to maintain discipline. You can't make a good fighting man by coddling him. The harsher the treatment the more the troops will bond with each other and after it's over, they will boast they had it rougher than any outfit. The Corps says it will make you into a Marine. My version is the Marine Corps attracts certain types of individuals who like to be tested.

"I hope these ramblings of a member of 'the Old Breed' help you in your book. Semper Fi. George."

And this longer but well-crafted letter from New Port Richey, Florida, from Walter E. Kuhle, a Marine staff sergeant:

"Having been raised in a small town in Florida in the 1930s, I was familiar with guns, hunting dove and quail from age eight with my grandfather and his pointer dogs. There was little income then and we mostly hunted for what we ate. In 1936 my family headed north to visit my grandparent in New York via an Arlington Cemetery sightsee-ing tour. At the unknown soldiers' tomb a sentry was pacing back and forth. My mother said the sentry was a Marine. I'm sure she didn't re-ally know, but from that day in 1936 when I was seven, I knew I had to be a Marine."

At seventeen, in 1945, Walter tried to enlist but had an eye prob-lem. He found an optometrist, had some work done, and on February 18, 1946, the Corps relented and he was shipped off to boot camp. "At Port Royal, South Carolina, a cattle truck waited to take us to Parris Island. There was an old man in uniform with stripes up and down his sleeves, the chevrons meeting the hash marks. Our drill instructor later told us this was Lou Diamond [the legendary old Marine mortarman of World War I, still on active duty]. I've bragged about that for the past sixty years," Kuhle wrote.

He spent a year and a half aboard ship as a seagoing Marine "and saw Japan, China, Hawaii, Philippines, Guam, Saipan, and the Panama Canal Zone. In Shanghai in 1947, Kuhle writes, "We went to the race track down Bubblingwell Road and on the way back to the docks we were way-laid by red communist students. During the riot my buddy was hit with a cobble stone to the thigh and I was blindsided by a wall-eyed chink with a board. Knocked out my two front teeth. I feel like I got even with him in North Korea three years later. I pray I killed him up there.

"In Panama at Colón on a floating dock I spotted a five or six foot gator next to us. I grabbed a sailor on a lark and pulled him in with me on top of the gator. It scared the gator and the sailor. The gator went one way, the sailor was back on the raft so fast, he almost didn't get wet." Since as a boy Walter had a pet alligator and knew how to handle them, he picked up the nickname "Gator."

"I took a discharge and tried college, but couldn't stand all those pimply-faced kids playing grab ass and walking out of step and in need of a haircut. I deserted an education for a life of adventure, and reenlisted. I spent most of my 1949 training aboard troop-carrying subs, recon commanded by Captain Kenney Houghton, the best man and Marine I ever met. We practiced landing in rubber boats, even helped John Wayne make *Sands of Iwo Jima* while stationed at Camp Pendleton. Shirley Temple was there with her husband, John Agar. Those two ignored us but Wayne liked Marines and he engaged us.

"When the Korean War started most of us helped form the 3rd Battalion 1st Marines led by Colonel Chesty Puller. In Japan he made us get rid of the Coke machine or whatever else had to do with pogey and geedunks bait [candy and sweets and the like] and had two GI cans half-filled with ice, can openers on strings hanging down the side. We were told the beer was rationed. Yeah, two cases of beer per man per day [ha ha!]. Around 5 PM Chesty would come walking down the company street with his swagger stick and an aide asking us how we were doing. You would follow this man anywhere. I became an ammo carrier for a heavy machine gun. We trained at Otsu, Japan, for ten days and I made my peace with God and wrote my mother to be sure to receive the $10,000 should I die. I was sure I would, so I was thoroughly at ease with it.

"Japanese prostitutes told us we were going to Inchon because they knew ladders were being made and Inchon had a seawall. What a secret! Upon disembarking my LST, there was the ladder. I lit a cigarette and took a chew of tobacco and about halfway to the seawall, I was surprised that we were still alive, so I lit my last cigarette. The cox'n started firing his .50 caliber at a North Korean gunboat, so I got high enough to fire at it, too. Our staff sergeant made me get down but it was sure amusing seeing how scared some of the men looked. For the next three days I made a few hits, fired my carbine not by aiming but the same way I fired my shotgun hunting as a kid, with no sights. On the third or fourth day from Inchon we took heavy fire from a 120 mortar on what was later called 'Shrapnel Hill.' We were told later that 30 men were killed and wounded. That was the only day I ever had any fear whatsoever in the war. Mortars were coming in all around my foxhole and I couldn't shoot back or do anything about it.

"Overlooking the Han River, Item and George Companies had found a brewery and started rolling barrels down to us where we were dug in. It couldn't get any better than this. I was made gunner and we were told we'd jump off and attack Seoul at 8 A.M. Instead, we went at 10 P.M. that night, most of us half drunk with diarrhea from the green beer. On the north bank of the Han we went straight up the main drag toward the city center and took quite a few casualties. In the middle of the boulevard a corpsman was working over a Marine shot in the head. He was trying to stuff his brains back into the hole. Another Marine was standing there watching them when he too was shot, and fell over the corpsman. I guess it was too much for him; he took off. I later saw him in a house behind my gun position that night, sobbing. He had cracked.

"The North Korean who did the shooting was in a small house up an embankment from the boulevard. He was hoeing in a little garden and when he spotted enemy he would go back inside and shoot from a window. The next time he came out to do some hoeing, I shot him.

"We were told we would attack that night. About ten P.M. we

heard tanks thinking it was our amtracks and tanks. Instead it was T-34 North Korean tanks (bigger than ours). At the road block Major Edwin Simmons was our weapons company commander. That night we called for our tanks to come up and help but they responded they don't fight at night because it's against Marine tactics [and you wonder why Marine infantrymen hate tankers?]. All we had was a 75-mm recoilless rifle and heavy machine guns. The 75 was fired when the first T-34 came in range and it bounced off the tank. The back blast knocked some glass windows out of a house and my lieutenant, Lt. Savage, got glass in his ass. On his way out on a stretcher the tip of his nose got shot off. Major Simmons called in artillery and walked the shells up and down the boulevard. One of the T-34 fired a round that cut his radioman in half. That night I fired 37 cans of ammo. The armor-piercing ammo went through the side of the tanks' cannon into the bore. All the heavies kept the tanks buttoned up. One shell fired at my gun hit below me into the embankment. Its impact raised me up but it didn't explode. I couldn't remember the last time I had so much fun. The adrenalin was flowing and the heavy [machine gun] made you feel like no one could touch you—the power and excitement of it all. Artillery was smoking, their bores almost burned out. Colonel Puller, it was said, told Major Simmons he better have a good reason for all the artillery. He must have; he [Ed Simmons, a wonderful man and author, I know—JB] became a general." And would die in May 2007.

Following the tough Seoul fight, Kuhle's outfit was crossing the Han River on an army pontoon bridge, heading north, when an American army unit in crisp new khakis, having been shunted aside to allow the Marines to cross first, mocked the Marines, pretending to have movie cameras and yelling insults. "It was obvious they had not yet seen combat. In every second or third pontoon were two soldiers with a light machine gun guarding it. I took my K-Bar, unscrewed the bottom of a hand grenade, dumped the powder out, pulled the pin and threw it into the pontoon next to the soldiers. They dove into the river and the grenade gave a little pop, which was the fuse. That sobered them clowns up."

Next stop for gunner Kuhle and his mates, Hagaru-ri, North Korea, up against the famed Chosin Reservoir.

"When the Chinese attacked they first hit our perimeter at the end of the air strip and to my right flank where HQ Company bandsmen, engineers, etc. were firing as much ammunition as a battleship under attack. So here come the Chinese along my front heading east around our perimeter. There were two farmhouses 200 yards to my left front. I set them on fire with my tracers and the Chinese between me and the houses were silhouetted perfectly. I used a free gun, no traversing or elevating mechanism. The Chinese were going down. They were firing mortars at us, landing beside my hole or behind it. Bullets were buzzing by my head, down behind the gun, sounding like bees, that's how close they were, one through the side of my parka hood. My tracers gave our position away but they didn't hit us. It was 40 below [exaggeration?— JB] and snowed all night. The next day I saw many mounds, the snow covering the bodies. During the firefight I saw what they call 'your life flashing before your eyes,' usually just before you die. I don't believe it because my adrenaline was flowing so fast sweat was flowing down my back. In 40-below weather it was all adrenaline and I loved it. We knocked out three mortars and four machine guns that night, and until daylight, it was small arms fire. This firefight was won by us because we were on level ground and had grazing fire. To our rear the air strip was overrun and the Chinks were ransacking HQ Company. Now we had our rear to worry about."

When the Division pulled out and their march to the sea began, Kuhle thought his shin was cracked but didn't like the idea of getting into a truck with the other wounded since it made such a good target for the Chinese. The machine gun was wrecked. "I said to hell with this. I still had my .45 pistol and sleeping bag and started walking south, pain or no pain. There was a gallon can of peanut butter and guys scrounged from that. At Koto-ri just before dark and near the air strip was a pile of dead, frozen Marines, stacked and frozen solid. I left them and not far away found a tent, thinking it was a warm-up tent. There stood Chesty Puller and a gunnery sergeant in the British Marines. I started to leave and he offered me a cot, said his driver wouldn't use it tonight. I checked my bandaged leg and he offered to call a corpsman. I said no thanks and I could see he was proud of that; he didn't have sissies. He and the sergeant had a shot of whisky and we all slept." Apparently Kuhle wasn't offered any.

After the Marine evacuation, Kuhle's feet and hands were black with frostbite and he was sent to a hospital in Kobe, Japan. "They cut off one and a half joints of my right index finger (his trigger finger, I guess); my shinbone had a hairline fracture, my hands and face peeled. I was sent to Otsu Rest Camp for R&R and reassignment. My foxhole buddy Dick Weider was there also with frostbite."

The boys may have been frozen and were now hobbled, but this didn't inhibit their mischief. Waiting for a Japanese trolley to Kyoto, with the conductor mysteriously gone missing, the two Marines and a middle-aged Japanese woman got on board. Still, no conductor. Weider, for some reason, knew how to start up a trolley. "He switched the rear pulley to a live wire and we took off. Behind us was a Japanese policeman in a charcoal-burning taxi [a scene worthy of the Keystone Kops?]. The lady was scared stiff [of the crazy Marines or what?]. The cop never caught us, and we left a shocked lady and cop angry as hell."

His buddy Weider was later given a Section 8 discharge for schizophrenia. "His brains got scrambled when his machine gun squad was overrun near the air strip at Hagaru-ri. We shook hands, said goodbye, and we never heard or saw each other again."

Which is how things go in wars. Kuhle said he was "discharged October 1952 only because I passed the Border Patrol exam. If I failed I would have stayed in the Corps. I had gone from PFC to Staff Sergeant in one year." With a wife and four children, and needing money, he left law enforcement after thirteen years and went into audiology, manufacturing and fitting hearing aids. These days seventy-eight-year-old Walter lives in what he calls "God's waiting room," otherwise known as Florida, has emphysema, which requires sleeping with oxygen, rates a 90 percent VA disability because of his hands, feet, and hearing loss. When I thanked Kuhle for his letter, all of which he assured me is true, he apologized for his slight speech impairment. "I had all my front teeth knocked out in Shanghai when I was seagoing," he explained, and began to spin one more yarn.

There he was in Florida, an old soldier hooked up to oxygen, recalling a turbulent and raucous youth as a Marine, and all I could think of was the Irish drinking song about "the wild colonial boy." And see Walt Kuhle hunched behind his heavy gun pumping out rounds at the Chinese coming at him through the snow, illuminated by the burning farmhouses, and then on a broken leg lurching southeast with ten thousand other Marines on the long, hard mountain road to safety and the sea.

I said his account of a barroom fight in a Shanghai gin mill would be a swell story, but when he started telling it, I begged his understanding and said it would have to await another book at another time. It was the day after Christmas of '06 and Gator Kuhle didn't argue the point, but exchanged holiday greetings and wished me well. I still get the occasional letter from the old machine gunner, signed with, "Happiness is a belt-fed weapon."

28

Joe Owen was too tall and skinny for the paratroops.
So the Marines took him.

I MENTIONED JOE OWEN BEFORE AS THE OFFICER WHO ONCE NEARLY slugged the immortal Hector Cafferata. Imagine that bout manqué, two giant and brutally damaged Marines, one of them soon to be sporting the Medal of Honor, who'd both fought the Chinese at the Chosin Reservoir, duking it out in a New York gin mill in slings and bandages, and hospital robes while over the hill from St. Alban's Naval Hospital. But the Joe I know had his own story, had written his own book (*Colder than Hell*), and at my request would generously share his *pensées* and adventures with me.

Remember that Owen is an educated, cultivated, gentle, quiet-spoken, and evidently prosperous man, a graduate of Colgate University who lives with his wife, Dorothy, in Skaneateles, New York, wintering in chic Naples, Florida. I treasure a brief letter from Joe that long predated this book. He'd written about his Marines, "those beautiful men that we were both blessed to lead into places scarier than hell. Crazy bastards they were, yours, mine," Joe wrote. "Doc Toppel with his own Chinese prisoner that he kept as his batman until the

Skipper made us turn him in. Bifulk and Perkins, my Katzenjammer twins, 'rassling' under Chinese fire over a can of pineapple . . ."

Joe went on to catalogue an entire roster of colorful and joyous warriors, wonderful men at war. Like many of us young officers, he'd fallen in love, not with war but with the men who fight it. If a mere British subaltern, equivalent to our shavetails, rated having an enlisted servant, a "batman," why couldn't Owen's "Doc Toppel"? Why couldn't his Katzenjammer Kids rassle? This tendency to "overidentification" was something we all had to resist in order to command effectively. If Jones was your most capable point man, then you sent him out on the dangerous point whether he had a kid or a gray-haired old mother waiting at home. The platoon, all forty Marines, deserved having the best point man out there in front. You had to send Jones, and not some lesser scout without kids. Owen knew this, we all did, but it was never an easy decision.

Later, in 2006, his long memo to me began, "When you ask, 'why do Marines fight as we do?' I go back to WHY we became Marines. We joined to fight." That punchy response was pure Owen. He doesn't tap-dance around a question. And then, in a typed half-dozen pages he sketched out this extraordinary and self-effacing account of an American boy in two wars.

Joe's yarn opened in 1943 during the lower depths of World War II (so far, the empire of Japan seemed to be pitching a no-hitter) at Syracuse University in upstate New York.

"WWII was on everybody's mind and I wanted to enlist, wanted to fight, up-front fighting, persuaded, excited by the pro-US media. My dad wouldn't sign enlistment papers. Volunteered for the draft and tried signing up with the Army paratroopers. They wouldn't have me, too tall, too skinny. The [Marine] Corps had Para-Marines, so the Army recruiter sent me across the hall and the Marines guaranteed jump school after boot camp. 'First, you got to be tough enough to get through boot camp!' Reported aboard Parris Island 19 Mar '43. Eighteen years old, 6'4" (then) and 165 pounds, height came sooner than dexterity. A pure klutz, but tough from paper routes through hostile neighborhoods and fighting my way up the caddy lines, and second-string football/basketball in high school (Christian Brothers, very tough!).

"Platoon 232 fell in, according to height. I was the first boot in the forward rank, where I was natural target for Platoon Sergeant Sutton, Drill Instructor. Tall as I, 200 pounds, lean and mean, back from Guadalcanal, a deep Alabama accent, yelling that we were the saddest bunch of shitbirds ever seen. He saw little chance that he could make Marines of us, so his duty to the Corps was to make our training unbearable, so difficult that we would beg to get out. He approached me, first shitbird, first rank, jabbed my chest with his swagger stick and I almost lost my balance. 'Ya'll think you are a Marine, Shitbird?' 'Not yet,' I told him. He pounded the top of my pith helmet with the swagger stick, screaming in my face. 'SIR! I am SIR! You address everybody as SIR! Except other shitbirds. You got that, Shitbird?'

" 'Yes, sir!' But I vowed to show this sonofabitch that nothing, especially him, would stop me from becoming a Marine. The abuse continued but I was not singled out. Platoon 232 as judged by Sutton was composed solely of hopeless shitbirds. The eternal drill field, infinite physical drill under arms, midnight musters and nighttime conditioning, scrubbing heads with a toothbrush. . . . Sutton wanted us out of his Marine Corps. Very few dropped out. All of us shitbirds had joined the Corps because we wanted to fight and Marines offered the surest way to battle. So we endured the insane discipline and we each wanted to show that sonofabitch that nobody could stop us from being Marines.

"Maybe four weeks in, we ran the bayonet course. Clumsy oafs the first time. Next time up, though, I'll show the sonofabitch. Parry, thrust, butt stroke, side step, advance. Just like basketball drill from high school, perfect run! Sutton yelled at me to run it again, and he told the platoon to watch. 'If this sorry-ass shitbird can do it, all of you can do it.' Another good run, and the swagger stick tapped my pith helmet. Like a pat on the back. From Platoon Sergeant Sutton! A few days later he ordered me to take a detail to the mess hall for sweep and swab duty. Shaking, nervous, I called, 'Attention!' Damn! They snapped to. Just like the DIs demanded. Right face, forward march . . . they did it! Shitbirds they were, but I knew now that I could lead Marines. A gangling shitbird myself, I had the power of Platoon Sergeant Sutton behind me, and the entire Marine Corps backing him up. On the range, I fired expert, as did far more of us than the average platoon. We were a damned good platoon. The last days we spent on the drill field, polishing up for the graduation parade. Sutton remained his grim self, but no longer called us shitbirds.

"When the parade was over and the reviewing officer dismissed us as MARINES, Platoon Sergeant Sutton came down the ranks. He grabbed my arm, shook my hand, looked me in the eye, and said, 'Well done, Marine.' The accolade, 'Marine,' was the greatest in my life. Since that moment, I am a United States Marine, and it's engraved on my heart that I will always be one of 'the finest ever seen.'"

Joe Owen had bulked up at Parris Island to 180 pounds, but by then they'd disbanded the Para-Marines. Why? During one practice jump in the Pacific, pilot error dropped an entire planeload of Marines into the ocean on an ebbing tide that swept the heavily laden men out to sea off an atoll, and most of them drowned. Which understandably dampened enthusiasm for paratroops in the Corps. Owen was packed off to Camp Lejeune and Field Telephone School under a Corporal Bill Gately, late also of Guadalcanal, and a man who would retire as colonel. Like DI Sutton, Gately was lean, mean, and tough, double-timing the troops everywhere. But never calling them shitbird. "He told me I had it in me to be a good Marine," says Joe, adding, "Inspiration!" At Lejeune, with the Japanese waiting in the wings, the boys "ran, ran, ran, pulling commo carts, stringing wire through the boondocks, topping the tall pines with climbing spikes. Learned the basics, too. Weapons, knife fighting, map reading, scouting and patrolling and reconnaissance, all the tools of the combat wireman's trade." Combat. There we have it. That's where they were headed. Except that Joe graduated high on the list, was promoted to PFC and was transferred to radar school. He was too smart, the shitbird, and was going to miss out on his dreams of war.

"There I was, an unhappy misfit. I wanted to get into a combat outfit and did not relate well to electrons. Made corporal though and was finally shipped out to the Pacific [only his Pacific turned out to be peaceful Hawaii]." Here's a kid who wants to go out and shoot Japanese and they kept sending him back to the classroom. He went to a forward observer's squad, B Battery, 5th Gun Battalion, 5th Amphibious. Trouble was, "The squad was eight misfits, all former NCOs busted down to private, mostly drunk & disorderly. Four were Sioux, used as talkers, great Marines except for the Island gin. As a boot corporal straight from stateside, I got a surly reception." But he was still pretty damned big and smarter than they were. "Gave them right face, double time, forward march. Thank you, Corporal Gately. There were some rough times with my eight misfits, but these people were Marines by choice, and wanted to avoid piss & punk brig time. The Marine Corps give authority with the stripes. We trained in the lava fields of the Big Island, worst, most miserable terrain ever seen, humping the equipment to high elevation observation posts the lieutenants chose. We became a good squad, especially the Sioux in the field. On rare liberties to a coastal village, we caroused together, and my Sioux did relatively little ruin. Together, we stole an ammo truck full of beer from an army warehouse. That brought close brotherhood, and we were admired for throwing a beer bust for the parched Battery."

But there was new trouble ahead for happy, beer-dispensing, Kemo Sabe squad leader Owen. The battalion commander wanted to send him to Officer Candidate School. More classroom? Joe wanted to go to Leyte with the Sioux, with MacArthur, with his squad, beat up on the damned Japanese, but a silver-tongued senior officer "told me I was a fortunate young man . . . rare opportunity . . . and sent me stateside where I spent the rest of the war as a college Marine, V-12 program. War ended, I was still a corporal, decided to finish college on the G.I. Bill. Graduated Colgate, '48, and accepted regular commission [in the Corps]. Had married in '46, and already two kids, poverty on a second lieutenant's pay.

"Quantico, Basic School, nine months, physically more rigorous than Parris Island, but we were much fitter now. Intellectually, we opened the 'Book of War,' studied *The Ways of the World,* and history, especially USMC, emphasis on combat. Our instructors, mostly platoon and company commanders who had fixed bayonets against the Japanese. Role models, fiercely proud, they glorified the Marines they led across the beach, and up the ridges. It was pervasive pride. You had to be one hell of an officer to deserve to lead Marines like these. Basic School and 2nd Marine Division, learning the trade from experienced officers and salty NCOs who demonstrated that Marines were 'the finest ever seen.' Role models, seasoned, savvy, proud. They cited proud history, Mameluke saber, Montezuma and the blood-red stripe on our trousers, Samar, Dan Daly in Cuba and WWI. And there were those who remembered Belleau Wood, Nicaragua and Haiti, North China, Pacific island battles. They were devoted to the Corps and they made us believers."

It was peacetime and for Owen and his platoon, there were amphibious assaults, not on hostile beaches but safely, on Crete and Malta, brutal hikes across the hills of Sicily. Wondrous liberties at Cannes, Lisbon, Athens, Algiers. "I was thoroughly in love with the Corps," said Joe, "troubled only by Dorothy's uncomfortable life as a second lieutenant's wife. But I was very experienced by now, a confident and motivated lieutenant, when the Korea War exploded.

"Although I had as yet no combat to back me up." Nor had he heard the last of Marines as shitbirds. It was in 1950, north of Seoul, Korea, that Joe would lead men for the first time under fire and he and his shitbirds would be blooded.

"My troops in B/1/7 [Baker Company, 1st Battalion, 7th Marines] were Platoon Sergeant Sutton's shitbirds reborn. Mostly suddenly recalled reservists with little experience beyond falling-in and manual of arms. No boot camp. I ignored the niceties of close-order drill, Customs & Courtesies, Marine Corps lore, and kept them running the hills of [Camp] Pendleton, weapons, tactics. In 1/7, under the eye of Ray Davis [then a lieutenant colonel, a future general and Medal of Honor recipient], the intensity and severity of training was extreme. Get them ready to fight before first combat. North of Seoul or lambs to the wolves? In a few week's time.

"Now the doubts. Am I Marine enough to lead men on brutal Tarawa, through the woods of Belleau? First casualty, gut shot, Marine screaming agony, guts pouring, fear paralyzed me. Breaking free was like a physical struggle. Now the Corps depends on me. Turn fear into action (as taught by officers and NCOs who had done so). Let the troops know you're there. LEADING. Yell like hell, move them forward. Fog of war, first time, hell blowing up around us, but the troops stayed with me. Made it to a rice paddy, nice safe rice paddy. And the second paralysis of fear. My head and binoculars over the paddy, the kid next to me head-shot. He goes down dead, I go down terrified. Seconds pass. Skipper on the walkie-talkie, machine gun ten o'clock, voice calm. Again, fear into action. Head over the edge, carbine up for aiming stake, range, fire, adjust, fire for effect. Enemy still pelting the dike, and rounds zinging close, but now too busy for fear."

Clearly, Owen had thought this letter through before sending it. He wasn't talking off the top of his head.

"Fear is basic to combat. You must not let it take hold. My worst fear came while waiting to attack. I moved around, rechecked the troops, grab-ass talk. Promise extra fruit rations if they don't fuck up. Stupid stuff, but they know you'll be up front with them. We're especially scared before attacks. We always lose men in the attack."

At this point Joe inserts in his narrative the comments from another book by Lieutenant Colonel Joseph Hedrick, *One Out of Line,* describing the young Joe Owen in this first firefight when Hedrick was a forward air control team sergeant: "I remember before starting up Turkey Hill observing Lieutenant Joe Owen joshing good naturedly with his men. I knew he was a good officer from my limited observation and from what I heard from his men. At any rate, here was the lieutenant [Owen], smiling, joking, and seemingly 100 per cent confident we would accomplish what we all knew was likely to be a difficult task."

And all the time, despite Hedrick's favorable account of his first firefight, Joe was scared and talking to keep his nerve up.

Now Owen resumes, writing about a later fight in the snows of North Korea: "The word comes, Move out! You're moving or firing or directing fire and action trumps fear. Exhilarating, the men moving with me, following orders under deadly fire. Fire and movement. Kill the bastards! You were invincible . . . as I was when I got hit! The irony, Baker's last hill and I'm the last of Baker's original seven officers to go down. Then a corporal took over the assault. All sergeants casualties, but the attack went on until we had the Gook position, top of the hill. Leadership takes over, top to bottom."

That was Joe's description of the firefight against the Chinese at the Chosin in which he was wounded. In his book, *Colder than Hell,* he ends the story with these few modest lines: "My wounds were treated in U.S. Naval Hospitals for seventeen months until May 1952. I was unable to regain full use of my right arm and was disability-retired from the Marine Corps as a first lieutenant. Dorothy and I had four more children. Mike became a neurosurgeon and Dinny is a writer."

There was a postscript to his typed account. I include it here. "Jim, I've rambled this far without the word 'courage.' To me, that's sublimation of fear. The apparent absence of fear, the will to fight. Chew een Lee was most courageous of us . . . didn't seem to know fear. But he did . . . he's human. Joe Kurcaba would never go down . . . not even crouch under heaviest fire. 'If I go down, might never get up.' Which happened as we stood together and he took a round in his forehead, and I put him down and he never got up."

So why do Marines fight like that? Pride? Joe's version: "'Finest ever seen.' Leaders' creed, 'Take care of your men and they'll take care of you.' Tough discipline, tough training, leavened with genuine concern/love for the troops. I could be a tough officer when needed . . . but not horseshit . . . and I get calls today from my men; we're family and I'm proud I led them. Marine tradition can have palpable effect when you're under fire. Once we were stopped cold by very heavy fire across a field of snow. There came a memory of the attack at Belleau Wood [1918]. Col. Thomason wrote, 'The platoons assailed now by a fury of small arms narrowed their eyes and inclined their bodies forward, like men in a heavy rain, and went on.' Those Marines in a wheatfield, and now my Marines in a snowfield, fury of small arms, they went on! Those bastards did it, we would do it. BARs on full automatic bear into the rocks, rifles forward with me. BARs cease fire, grenades into the rocks, gooks dead or gone.

"Leadership. Colonel Litzenberg, not a stranger to the squads on the line, Lt. Col. Davis, familiar presence during firefights, Captain Wilcox, Lt. Kurcaba always there or close by when the walkie-talkies didn't work and they were within runners' range. None showed fear, good example to the lieutenants and the troops. And the troops need to see the lieutenants and NCOs. We made ourselves visible when a fight was going on. We're fighters. That's why we became Marines. We wear the emblem with pride and become worthy of it. Our Hymn is about fighting. 'First to fight, every clime and place, where we could take a gun.' We're all front line fighters. Take a cannon cocker [artilleryman], an office pinky, an MP, put him in a fire team and he already knows how to fight Marine Corps style. Talk to the kids in Iraq today. They admire us, honor us, but they know they're the finest Marines ever to meet enemy fire. God bless them for that."

Joe and I were scheduled to lunch with magazine publisher John Ledes (another aging Marine lieutenant) at Ledes's Yale Club last summer. Ledes, smashed up in a plane crash into the Truckee River en route to Korea, Owen, Dusty Rhodes, Dick Brennan, and a few other damaged officers had either known each other at Quantico or met at St. Alban's Naval Hospital, and Ledes's ground-floor apartment in Manhattan on posh East End Avenue swiftly became their command post when off base and not undergoing physical therapy. The joint was a twenty-four-hour cocktail party always full of young women, models, actresses, girls on the magazines, Russian nobles and émigré princes of Ledes's acquaintance, with Ledes (himself an attorney and a Greek related to the Fox movie studio people) the pied piper. Owen, I believe it was, acquired some classy silk and fashioned matching slings for himself and all the boys with wounded arms, and they cut quite a swath through Manhattan society in the 1951–53 era (I joined in their revels in the fall of '52 when I belatedly got home from the wars) roistering about in their dashing Marine forest green uniforms, chests full of ribbons, and their colorful slings. "The lads would sing and the boys would shout and the ladies, they would all turn out, as Johnny came marching home again, hoorah, hoorah." Billingsley at the Stork Club took them in, and "21's" Bob Kriendler, a Marine colonel himself, and Toots Shor's, and P. J. Clarke's. But you know some of those stories because I've written them before.

I was looking forward to seeing Owen again. He was being flown down from Skaneateles in a private plane piloted by his son the neurosurgeon, but at the last minute Joe had to cancel. His wife Dorothy was suffering from dementia and her usual nurse was out sick and Joe couldn't be away from Dorothy. She'd always been there for him and the kids, their six children and fourteen grandchildren, and now she was the one in need. Duty called; Lieutenant Owen, as he always did, answered the call. And Ledes and I lunched alone and drank a Yale Club toast, as we often did, to Joe Owen, to absent friends.

29

Some Marines handle war better than peace.

THERE ARE MARINES WHO THRIVE AND PROSPER ON BATTLE. A DIS-
cernible, dangerous enemy brings out the best in such men. While the
safety, predictability, and boredom of garrison duty here at home, especially in a time of peace and shorn of even the looming tension of a
war yet to come, tends to get them into trouble.

Take staff sergeant John J. Walters, USMC (retired) of Decatur, Indiana, who died of brain and lung cancer on September 7, 1990, but had
served more than honorably in World War II and in Korea and later on
a 1958 tour in Lebanon, where Marines also, though briefly, saw combat, but who while stationed at Camp Upshur at Quantico, Virginia,
went over the hill to go to the assistance of his wife, who had taken ill,
and of their infant and two-year-old, and was subsequently court-
martialed and lost two stripes of rank. Years later, his widow was still
waging a small, annoying, quite possibly fruitless, but undeniably gallant campaign on Sergeant Walters's behalf. In the noble cause of a
Marine who fought well and then screwed up.

In late summer of 2006 I received a letter dated July 26 from the widow, Doreen (Walters) Frecker of Decatur. Here is some of what she wrote.

"We married February 23, 1950. I am from Manchester, England, and served more than four years in the Royal Navy. John was on a two-year goodwill tour and I was stationed at Chatham Naval Barracks near London when his ship [the USS *Columbus*] came into port near Gravesend. We met in a pub. We all went there as there was music and dancing and for a few hours we could forget the war."

And this is a woman who knows a little about war. Once again, from her letter to me: "My dad served in WWI with the Lancastershire Fusiliers. He was at the battle of the Somme and at Ypres. He was mustard-gassed and died at age fifty-nine years, having lost a lung. My dad told us kids about a Christmas Day when they stopped the war and the Germans and the British declared a truce, and played football. I was there all through WWII. My city of Manchester was bombed over and over and we spent many hours in air raid shelters. We [children] were evacuated too but it didn't last because the Germans bombed where we were sent. I was fourteen years old when England declared war in 1939. Before the U.S. came into the war we were on our own and if it weren't for the English Channel we might have been overrun by the Germans. When the Japanese bombed Pearl Harbor the American military sent some planes over and they saved our bacon. God bless America! And British women over the age of seventeen had to serve their country, either in the military or on the land or in munitions factories. My oldest brother served ten years in the RAF, another brother went in the merchant navy."

Then she got to the point of her story about Sergeant John Walters. "He was born and raised in Decatur, Indiana, where today his nephew is mayor and has been for many years. John was a farm boy while I was a city gal.

"John served with the 3rd Battalion 7th Marines and was at the Chosin Reservoir November/December of 1950. He told me about the frozen C rations and the 30 below zero. John earned his staff sergeant's stripes in Korea and he was a machine gunner. I remember him telling me he fired the machine gun so much it got too hot to handle. His nickname was 'Pappy' Walters and I was Mrs. 'Pappy' Walters.

John had served in WWII in the Pacific and was a lot older than his men. Once one of his men, a youngster, fell asleep while on duty. John crawled to the foxhole and held a knife at the young Marine's throat and whispered . . . 'You are dead, as are some of your comrades.' I don't believe he ever fell asleep on watch again.

"John wrote of the fourteen miles they had to walk from the Reservoir to Hagaru, he said they were the dirtiest, smelliest bunch of Marines you ever saw, some of the men had to have their uniforms cut off them. John told of the thousands of Red Chinese coming over the mountain tops and some of them wore tennis shoes. He told me he walked on the bodies of dead Marines and he never got over it. He smoked about three packs of Camels a day and had a drinking problem late in his life. When he returned he was a changed man. He had post-traumatic stress disorder and was hard to live with and I had to commit him to hospitals. He returned from Korea in September of 1951. Then it was Lebanon, then the Bay of Pigs when John F. Kennedy said no troops would be involved . . . oh, but the Marines were there aboard darkened ships waiting for orders to go ashore. John felt badly when they left without helping the people left on the beaches."

The Walters had three kids, two boys about two years apart, and a girl seven years later. Alan was the first born, but it was when Bryan was born that trouble began for the couple.

Doreen fell ill, was unable to handle both the newborn and the two-year-old, was hospitalized, then sent home and told to stay in bed. Alerted by neighbors that she was in difficulty, and not being able to afford an auto, Sergeant Walters hitched a ride in from Camp Upshur to the main base at Quantico and requested emergency leave from a second lieutenant duty officer, was turned down, and Walters went AWOL to be at his wife's side. There is no indication that the second lieutenant attempted to assist, or referred Sergeant Walters's problems to higher authority or, if there was one, to a chaplain. No one apparently thought of calling the Red Cross or anyone else. The court-martial followed. Walters lost two stripes and hope of future promotions.

Despite his father's unhappy experience, the eldest son Alan joined the Marine Corps at seventeen, and at eighteen was badly wounded in Vietnam, lost a leg and an arm, and died some years later, "filled with shrapnel," his mother says. Bryan joined the army and was killed in an accident. Sergeant Walters served out his time, and then he died, and Doreen Walters has been trying ever since to get the court-martial set aside. Sixteen years after Walters's death she was still pestering people, including the president, in a vain effort to restore her late Marine husband's good name. On July 3, 2006, a White House letter was sent her by Darren K. Hipp, acting director of presidential correspondence. It was very brief.

"Dear Mrs. Frecker.

"On behalf of President George W. Bush, thank you for your letter.

"The White House is sending your inquiry to the Department of Defense. This agency had the expertise to address your concerns. They will respond directly to you, as promptly as possible.

"The President sends his best wishes."

Doreen Frecker as of yet has heard nothing more. She sent a copy of that White House letter to me along with a 1975 Department of the Navy list of Sergeant Walters's thirteen military decorations, some of them with stars for duplicated awards. A good combat Marine who'd done well in battle had fallen afoul of peacetime, a stateside garrison billet, and the stress and expense of family illnesses and concerns, within a structure that seems not to have been of much help to the Walters family. She said she wrote personally to me as a Marine and as an author who'd written books about Marines.

"When I read your books I cried, so much of where John was in Korea and what he and the others endured, that any of them made it back was a miracle. Your books when I read them took me back in time."

In that appeal to me, she demanded, "How dare the big-shots bust a man of John's caliber? He was a damn good Marine and they took away his pride. John's name needs to be cleared of all charges. He didn't go AWOL to get drunk. He came home to a very sick wife and two babies. What would you have done under the same circumstances?

"I hope I get a reply from you. Don't tell me it's been too long. Baloney. If someone wants it done it can be done."

I wrote to an angry widow, Doreen Frecker, to say I wasn't a politician or a Marine anymore but if she agreed, I would write about Staff

Sergeant John "Pappy" Walters in a book. "Who knows, maybe someone in power will read his story and do something." If she didn't want
her privacy invaded, I would understand, and forget the whole thing. It
was up to her. I'm not at all sure this was of much comfort. I wish I'd
been able to do more. But you've got to admire a dame who hangs in
there for her guy, even after he's gone.

A couple of weeks later she wrote back, agreeing that I write Pappy
Walters's story. "I would feel honored if you wrote about my late husband. If John had lived we would have been married 57 years February
23rd. I never regretted coming here to marry John. I would do it all
over again if I could. He earned 20 medals and served his country well.
It is nice some people do care."

The man fought against the Chinese at the reservoir in Weapons
Company, 3rd Battalion, 7th Marines, at the reservoir, was one of "the
Chosin Few." Later on, he screwed up, a man and a Marine trying to
help out a struggling, troubled family. And all those years later, a loving and faithful woman who lost two sons, one of them a combat Marine, and was still tending the flame. Maybe, as Arthur Miller once
wrote of his salesman, attention must be paid.

Let me know if anything happens when her story is published.

30

Chuck Curley took a buddy's body home from Korea to Olean, NY.

Machine gunner Charles W. Curley is very specific about what drew him to the Marines. And to combat.

Chuck, a West Coast kid enrolled at Pepperdine College, quit school to join the Marines in 1950, but, after his fighting was over, ended up in upstate Olean, New York, because it was to that small city he accompanied another Korean War Marine pal cross-country to deliver his corpse to the kid's family. Marines used to do that, traveling by train with the dead Marine in the baggage car, the escorting Marine riding coach as a sort of honor guard. It was an old-fashioned gesture but the families seemed to be comforted by it and welcomed the escorting Marine warmly. Which was what happened to Chuck Curley. He saw to his official chores, looked around Olean, liked what he saw, met a girl named Janice, got a local job, married Janice, and settled down. He's still there, in smalltown upstate New York, still with Janice, more than half a century later.

This is what Chuck wrote to me about why he joined the Marines.

"Here are some thoughts as to why I joined the Marines and why I believe Marines are much better fighters than other outfits. Maybe it's

because they 'brain-washed' me in Boot Camp, but I still believe in my
fellow Marines because of Boot Camp [he always capitalizes it that
way in his letters, as if recruit training were the Deity] and combat.

"As a 10-12 year old boy during World War II, I and many of my
friends used to listen to the radio about all the fighting that was going on
and often asked each other what it would be like to be in combat, charging up a hill with machine guns firing at you and never get hit. To this
day I still don't know how one managed to get to the top of a hill without getting one's guts splattered all over the ground—truly amazing.

"We would go to the movies and see pictures like *Gung Ho, Back
to Bataan, Destination Tokyo, Wake Island, Guadalcanal Diary,
Pride of the Marines,* and we would envision ourselves as part of those
men doing that. In a sense, we were dreamers. High school sports gave
us the opportunity to work/play with other guys in a team effort situation for meeting a common goal."

That line from Chuck suggests earlier lines about "wars being won
on the playing fields of Eton."

Chuck went on. "As a teenager I always enjoyed reading about the
exploits of the Marines, how they fought on Wake Island, Guadalcanal, Tarawa, Eniwetok, Guam, Saipan, Roi-Namur, Iwo and Okinawa, and I envisioned myself being part of that elite group of men
who make history. When the Korean War broke out on June 25, 1950,
I already had one year of college at Pepperdine. I told my dad I would
join the Marines so I could get the GI Bill for education—as I believed
the government would provide the GI Bill for us as they did for WWII
veterans.

"Probably the most important transformation of a young eighteen-
year-old civilian into a 'lean Marine fighting machine' comes from
foundations instilled into us recruits during our Boot Camp and then
'honed to a sharper edge' during combat training. The key points are
always Discipline, Discipline, Discipline, and following orders, and
Team Work, Team Work, Team Work, often repeated—with the emphasis on 'There is no such word in Marine language as "I can't." Or,
"I quit." '

"So when one goes into combat it is almost 'routine' as to what to
do, how to do it, always with the emphasis on Team Work, Team

Work, Discipline, Discipline, Discipline as it was instilled into each of us during our Boot Camp days.

"I was a machine gunner. We in machine guns always thought that if one can survive Boot Camp, he certainly can survive combat—and learn to be scared AFTER the firefight. We were always training, even when we were on line or in a rest area after several days of fighting. When we were on line our officers and sergeants made us do gun school on the machine gun—take it apart, put in together, name the parts, go over the functioning process. When we came off line to a rest area for several days the officers always put us on a training schedule for eight hours during the day, which included gun school, booby traps, map reading, first aid, fire-team tactics, supporting fire to help the assault squad, how to take out a pillbox, and many other things."

All that training, repetitive, often exhausting stuff, I remind you and remind myself, was what combat Marines did between, and supposedly resting up from, firefights.

More from Curley: "We also sent out patrols behind our own lines to make certain no enemy infiltrated behind out front line troops. We also placed 'listening posts' several hundred yards from our camping site in various directions to provide security as we stayed in the rest area. Because of this, many of us preferred to be on line rather than in a rest area. We often thought we got more rest when we were on line than when we were in reserve.

"But it all comes back to Boot Camp training—where Discipline and Team Work are Supreme and there is no tolerance for excuses. Speaking for myself, I always felt that combat was much easier than Boot Camp. I also thought that I was performing something that would be remembered in history and that I was part of a team of people who were writing history and helping others to be free."

The stationery on which Chuck Curley wrote to me as "Dear Lieutenant," still using my rank fifty years later, carries at the top a small replica of a Purple Heart, which he was awarded, and the words, "The Military Order of the Purple Heart." Stuff like that, properly addressing an officer, having earned that Purple Heart, still mean something to the machine gunners of our youth, the old-school, old-fashioned guys, men like the Chuck Curleys of Olean.

31

*An old man remembers Belleau Wood and those
who died there.*

Men like Curley with their passionately held fixations about boot camp and training, men who served long before Curley's time, my time, arouse memories of the immortal Dan Daly and his cry, famous within the Marine Corps, "Come on, you sons of bitches. Do you want to live forever?"

Daly became famous in 1918. There were other Marines you never heard of, fighting there in France that June day at the bloody wheat field of Belleau Wood (an entire book, *Into the Wheat,* was written about the fight). I came across a newspaper account of one of the survivors of Belleau Wood some years ago, a young fellow named Maynard Dunham who was ninety-eight years old when the Associated Press sent a reporter to talk with him on a Memorial Day in Sabula, Iowa, and got Dunham to tell his story.

Here was the 1993 AP story as it ran in New York's *Daily News* and other papers:

"When the color guard passes by and the bugler blows Taps today, Maynard Dunham will be thinking of battles fought in France 76 years ago. 'I get sentimental. I cry,' said the 98-year old ex-Marine. Dunham,

among the shrinking number of surviving World War I veterans, still
drives (an '85 Oldsmobile), dates, and climbs the 15 steps to his tidy
apartment where he's lived alone for 16 years.

"From 1917 to 1919 Dunham served in the 84th Company of the
3rd Battalion of the 6th Regiment Marines. His battalion was among
some 10,000 troops who fought the Germans for twenty days in the
Battle of Belleau Wood near Paris and in other campaigns in France.
Dunham said they gave the Germans all they could handle and earned
the nickname *die Teufelhunde*—devil dogs [Marine historical sources
question the accuracy of the nickname and its spelling, but that's Dunham's story.—JB]

" 'Belleau Wood was a very significant battle,' said Dan Crawford
of the Marine Historical Center in Washington, D.C. 'It was the first
major offensive action of the war for the Marines.'

"Dunham remembers the battle well. 'It was hell,' he said. 'Young
folks like we were, weren't automatic killers. But Belleau Wood was
the first time; that's when we knew we were going to have to kill
people—and we did. It went on and on and on.' A bullet grazed his
scalp and shrapnel broke his right arm. At age 35, his hearing started
fading, residual damage from a shell that exploded near his trench. He
won the Purple Heart and Medal of Valor and the French Croix de
Guerre, awards he keeps with his dog tags and other mementos in an
old wooden box.

"Dates, places and faces are at his fingertips. 'Look at that picture,'
Dunham said. It shows 161 grim-faced young men of the 84th Company, all clutching rifles in the German village of Herbach. 'We had
that taken while waiting for the Armistice to be signed. I'm the only
living person from all those guys. I look at that picture and sometimes
I just cry.

"May 30, the traditional Memorial Day, has always been special to
Dunham. That's the day he arrived at Parris Island, S.C., boot camp;
the day his unit was ordered to Belleau Wood; the day that Jacqueline,
first of his five children, was born. He now has 23 grandchildren and
43 great-grandchildren."

So ends the AP dispatch about Maynard Dunham's Memorial Day.
A personal note: My own May 30 memories date back to childhood

parades in the 1930s starting at the Bill Brown Post of the American Legion in Sheepshead Bay, Brooklyn, where veterans marched, most of them from World War I and still incredibly young, but including our skinny old neighborhood carpenter, Mr. Ryan, in his sailor suit, from the Spanish-American War. We children would cheer the veterans as they marched, probably not yet understanding just why, and then were given ice cream and got into a movie free at the Sheldon Theatre, known locally as "The Itch."

Those were my first Memorial Days. Then, in Korea in 1951, there was a splendid Memorial Day firefight with the Chinese, and eleven years later, Memorial Day of 1962, when my second daughter, Susan, was born in Neuilly-sur-Seine, France, not all that far from where a young Marine called Dunham fought the Germans forty-four years earlier.

The generations follow, one on the other, and as you talk to and remember the old soldiers, you conclude this isn't such an old country after all.

Certainly, the Marine Corps and France count the generations. They remember Belleau Wood. Each year on the anniversary of the battle there is a little ceremony at which there is a French speaker and an American Marine as the honored guest. Several years ago it was the turn of Jim Jones, the commandant of the Corps who later became the first Marine to head NATO, a job from which he stepped down after four years in December 2006 and returned to the States. But while he was there, General Jones was one of those who spoke at Belleau Wood, who remembered those who had died in a French wheat field in 1918. All such speeches are more or less eloquent and moving. But that of General Jones was special. Son of an American businessman whose company kept him in France for years, young Jim grew up in France, attended French schools, played basketball on a French team (he was and is six-five), and according to him, "I spoke English with a French accent and when I came home as a teenager, other schoolboys teased me about my accent."

In the recent year when it was General James Jones's turn to say a few words, and perhaps for the first time ever for an American, he spoke entirely in French, unaccented and pure, the language of his own childhood. Needless to say, the chauvinistic French who so love their tongue and remember that in two wars Americans came to fight on their turf, went more than slightly gaga, cheering francophone Jim Jones to the blue French skies.

32

The Jesuits taught Pierce Power Latin;
Hill 749 taught him the rest.

By September 1942, when the country had been at war for nine months, even the Society of Jesus had been swept up in the excitement.

I was thirteen years old and along with another 149 Catholic boys had just entered Regis High School on 84th Street off Park Avenue in Manhattan, an all-scholarship Jesuit prep school of such rigorous academic standards that on the very first day the boys were gathered and warned, by one of the priests, "Before Graduation Day four years from now, half of you will have dropped out or been expelled for failure to maintain grades. Continued poor work merits dismissal." Talk about your warm, welcoming gestures.

And these incoming freshmen were in a small way the elect. We were all smart kids, having taken the first 150 places in a fiercely competitive written exam given the previous spring to 1,200 boys. Each of us had been the top boy or one of the top boys in his elementary school in New York City, the northern suburbs, New Jersey, Long Island, and even nearby Connecticut. Yet the stern disciplinarian who issued this dour welcoming speech was as good as his word. About half of us were kicked out before June 1946 had come around.

For all that, it was a swell school. Pierce Power and I were among the boys in that entering class, and we found ourselves in a Regis that, because of the war, was starting in small but meaningful ways to modernize, to change. As freshmen, we would still be studying Latin two hours a day, five days a week, then for one hour a day through our next three years. As sophomores we would add to Latin another foreign language, French, Spanish, or German. But suddenly Greek was no longer required in third year.

No Greek? Was the Society of Jesus, known familiarly by some as "God's Marine Corps," going soft? Chemistry and, I believe, physics were substituted for Greek in the third-year curriculum, a Jesuitical bow to modernity and a world war, and basketball coach and phys ed teacher Don Kennedy, a gruff drill instructor sort with a pitted face and a heart of gold, began to include parade ground drill instruction in the daily gym class, Hup two three four, hup two . . . and lots of about-faces, which I never did get quite right. I was pretty good at standing at attention, however. None of the Jesuits were being drafted, of course, but senior boys, some of them just turned eighteen, were busily investigating the possibilities of various officer candidate programs. A math teacher, Mr. Purcell, vanished mysteriously, only to turn up four months later rigged out in the natty blue of a naval officer's uniform and white cap. And in freshman Latin, even the thirteen- and fourteen-year-olds were mobilizing, playing closer heed to the strategic aspects of *Caesar's Gallic War* which we had begun to read in the original. You know, *"Gallia est omnis divisa in partes tres . . ."*

Pierce Power, a tall, good-looking, and naturally athletic kid from Flushing who would eventually make the varsity baseball team, survived Regis. Though he admits all these years later, "I was close plenty of times to having my ass kicked out." I didn't make it. And the day a chill and distant Jesuit named Father Charles Taylor coldly informed me I had just been flunked out of Regis High School in the spring of sophomore year may well have been the unhappiest moment of my young life since my mother and father split when I was nine. Now I was fifteen. And crushed.

Pierce and I met again at Manhattan College, classmates once more, joined the Marine Corps Reserve together, graduated from college and were commissioned together, and on January 2, 1951, drove south in my rattling old '39 Buick convertible to report in for active duty at the Basic School, Quantico, Virginia. (Remember the split windshield ragtop in *Casablanca* that Bogie drove through Paris with Ingrid Bergman at his side? That was the car.) I remember we stopped overnight to see the Power cousins in Silver Spring, Maryland, flirted with the girls, played basketball against some local boys, and then went to the war. We were still just kids ourselves, you understand. Pierce got to Korea first, was in some bad fighting, and shortly after I went over we met during a brief period of reserve area duty and were able to talk. He looked worn and tired. Not at all the Pierce I knew, now older, sadder, changed. He'd been wounded (on his birthday) in the assault on Hill 749 in September that took a thousand Marine casualties in four days. But except for saying it had been bad, Pierce didn't go into much detail. He just wasn't the same guy. He was rotated home after that, and I stayed in Korea until midsummer.

We didn't see each other again until a year later, back in the States, when we met by chance at a basketball game Manhattan played at Hofstra University. And after that we resumed a closer friendship. We had come from the same place and had both visited a variety of private hell. So last December ('06) I called Pierce about this book. What could he tell me about his war? What would he want to tell me?

"I sailed over out of San Diego in May of 1951. We landed in Japan and had a day's liberty and then we took a little ship to Korea. On the way a first lieutenant grabbed me. He was a personnel officer and he needed a little help sorting out the guys. No enlisted men; we were all officers. I tried to tell him who was who, and after he sorted through all the papers I guess he wanted to do me a favor for helping him out, he said, 'And where do you want to go?' I said I wanted to go to the infantry. He said, 'Nah, you don't want to go infantry." I said, That's the only thing I know. He said, 'We'll send you to artillery.' I don't know anything about cannons. 'You'll learn on the job,' he assured me. In the end, when we got to Korea, they sent us all to the infantry anyway."

Had he gone right up to the front or did they ease into it gradually?

"I went right away to the 1st Marines as a rifle platoon leader, 2nd battalion, Dog Company. They were engaged at the time. In fact, to report in I had to crawl on my belly to get there. My platoon sergeant was Bill Reed [or Reid?]. I said to him, Listen, I'm just out of the Basic School. I don't know anything, so help me out. He said, 'Hell, in two weeks you'll know as much as we do.' And it worked out okay. Wilburt 'Big Foot' S. Brown was our colonel. After I was there for a while someone said, 'We've got some Chinese trapped in a cave and we're going to burn them up with a flamethrower. You want to come?' I said sure. So the guy aimed his flamethrower and fired it into the cave and everything was burning and guys came running out, some of them on fire, and Marines began to shoot.

"I said, Hey, they're surrendering. Why'd you shoot them? One guy said, 'Lieutenant, they were trying to kill us last week; we were trying to kill them yesterday. And what the hell are we going to do with prisoners up here anyway? We're short of men. There's nobody to guard them.'

"I don't know if you want to put that in the book," Pierce said. "You know, 'Marines kill babies.' Headlines like that."

I told him I'd think about it but would probably put it in the book. He'd made his point but didn't argue.

Pierce went on. "We fought Chinese most of the time. In my humble opinion the Chinese didn't give a shit. They couldn't care less about being in Korea. They were all drafted. The North Koreans were a lot tougher, better soldiers. It made sense; it was their country."

I asked him to tell me about the fight against the North Koreans for Hill 749. "It was September. We [the 1st Marine Regiment] were in reserve. The 7th Marines were attacking. It was supposed to be a relatively small operation. But something happened up there and the 1st Marines were ordered up. We passed through the 7th Marines in the night. It was my birthday. I remember one of the corpsmen fell and broke his leg. He was the happiest guy in the world; he had the million-dollar wound. He wouldn't have to go up the hill."

Were 7th Marine casualties coming down the hill at the same time? Were you stumbling over them?

"No," said Pierce, "but it was pitch-black. I couldn't see anyone. We just kept going uphill. Everyone was firing, but you couldn't see where. I got hit on the way up. With what, I don't know. But it must have been shrapnel. My face was bleeding and I had a cut arm and something in my back." But you kept going. "Yeah, there was nothing else to do. Nobody there to evacuate me. I had a sergeant, I think his name was Beamon. Big guy, maybe six feet, same as me, but 190 pounds. I was maybe 135 then. He got hit and he came over to lean on me. 'I think I'm going to faint, Lieutenant,' and I'm thinking I'm going to faint with this guy's weight on me. I think later they credited our 1st Marines for getting to the top [of the Hill 749 ridgeline] first. All I know, it was still night, and when I got up there I didn't see anyone up there before us. My platoon was spread out all over the hill in the dark. I relied on my three squad leaders to handle them. On top of the hill we dug in and set up a hasty defense in case the North Koreans counterattacked. I helped Beamon and we stumbled down to find a corpsman and I got rid of him. He got patched up and the next day he came back and apologized. I think he was embarrassed." I stopped Pierce then. Did he ever think of turning himself in to the corpsman and getting out of there on the famous million-dollar wound? After all, he'd been hit in three places.

Pierce said, "I didn't even think of it." Then he laughed. "Maybe I wasn't that smart."

Power got his Purple Heart and was written up for a Bronze Star but they bargained that down to a letter of commendation with a combat V for valor, as they often did. "When I read the citation," he told me, "I said, Jeez, did I do that?" His platoon, as best he can remember, suffered 50 percent casualties. After the fight for 749 platoon sergeant Bill Reed took him aside. "He would talk to me privately about a man he didn't like. And now he said, 'We gotta get rid of so-and-so. The guy never came up the hill.' And we did get rid of him that day."

Power stayed up on the line with the infantry for a time. Not many firefights, mostly patrols. "I'd been fighting in the infantry almost six months and it was my turn to be rotated to something else. They asked if I wanted to be assistant operations officer, and I said, No, I want to go as far back as I could, and they sent me back to motor transport.

"On March 17 I left Korea. I was assigned to teach at the Basic School in Quantico, not doing much, and in September of 1952 I put

in a letter asking to be released early because I'd been accepted at
Fordham Law School and I wanted to get started. 'You'll never hear
from them,' someone warned me. But by return mail, practically the
very next day, I got a response that I could get out and wishing me luck
at law school. They never even asked for documentation from Fordham
or anything. Word got around Quantico and guys were putting in letters all over the place, saying they wanted to start law school, divinity
school, medical school, veterinary school, anything to get out."

He earned his law degree, passed the bar exam, joined a Long Island law firm, eventually becoming its senior partner, got married, had
kids, and now splits his time between a house in Cutchogue, New York,
and a place in Florida at Tierra Verde. Plays a lot of golf, both places.
Good golfer, good guy, wickedly funny sense of humor. And one of the
first Marines to stand atop Hill 749, where a thousand Marines went
down.

"Call me once in a while," Pierce Power finished up. "But after three
in the afternoon. Mornings I'm playing golf."

33

Frank Kiss won the Silver Star atop a tank on his "last raid."

Frank R. Kiss of Westbury, Long Island, was badly wounded on February 23, 1953, and awarded the Silver Star for heroism during a Marine raid by infantry and tanks on a Chinese position called "the Boot," in the last year of the Korean War. He responded to my question about what made Marines fight by sending me copies of six or seven pages from a book called *The Final Crucible*, written by Lee Ballenger, pages that describe what Frank Kiss prefers to call "my last raid." Ballenger's words were liberally annotated in ink by Kiss, who corrected or elaborated on Ballenger's account where it applied to tanker Kiss, himself. I happen to like readers who angrily (or otherwise) scribble marginal notes on the pages of books they feel are worth reading. And commenting on. And so I phoned Frank Kiss at his Westbury home on a recent Sunday morning after church.

The citation for Frank's Silver Star reads in part: "While transporting wounded Marines from a forward area to an aid station in the rear, Corporal Kiss voluntarily remained on the exposed part of the tank to insure the safety of the casualties. When an estimated two squads of enemy infantry ambushed the tank, he voluntarily prostrated himself over the bodies of the wounded while passing through the ambush in an effort to shield the casualties from the enemy fire. Although painfully wounded, he steadfastly remained in his position to protect his comrades."

Frank Kiss grew up in Queens Village, New York, and dropped out of high school at age eighteen. The Korean War was on, and he opted to join the Marine Corps. "After I got out of Parris Island [boot camp] they sent me to tracked vehicle school. They were reactivating the 3rd Marine Division and I was out on the West Coast. At one point my commanding general was Chesty Puller." Ever actually meet the legendary Chesty? "Several times. But I never looked him in the eye." That wasn't a lack of respect, Frank made clear, just that Puller was too short. Oh, ha ha ha, I responded, getting into the spirit of the moment. Kiss earned a tanker's 1800 MOS, but when they were shipping Marine replacements out to Korea he realized tank crewmen were being left behind in favor of infantrymen (the division was losing more foot soldiers than tankers, apparently). Frank Kiss wangled himself a transfer to an 0300 infantry MOS, and was included on the next replacement roster. His cleverness got him to Korea, but when he arrived and they looked at his service record book and saw the former MOS, he was assigned to a tank company after all.

Kiss had been in Korea for about three months when, on February 23, 1953, while the truce talks wore on at the Panmunjom conference site and the war raged all around, rifle company units of the 7th Marines, supported by fourteen tanks, including one in which Frank Kiss was a loader, feeding ammo into the main gun, and by a recon company platoon, jumped off against the Boot, about 2,000 yards in front of the Marines' MLR. The fighting was fierce, with the Chinese sending fresh troops into the fight to reinforce their positions, and at least one tank hitting a mine and being disabled early, and as night fell there was hand-to-hand fighting, including bayonets, something relatively rare in what we called the outpost war.

Ballenger wrote about the tank in which Kiss rode. "A tank evacuating wounded Marines from Hill 90 to the stream-bed had to fight its way back as Chinese troops ambushed it with hand grenades and small arms, which were ineffective against steel but dangerous to men

exposed outside the tank. Six wounded Marines were riding on the
tank. The assistant driver [who was actually the loader, Frank Kiss],
also exposed while holding one of the wounded, was hit. The tank
commander took a BAR from a wounded man [Kiss testifies it was really a Thompson submachine gun] and accounted for five enemy casualties. Illumination flares, exploding overhead, were most useful."

Was that really how it was? I asked Kiss.

"We couldn't get back to the line, and these guys, the half dozen casualties, were from a squad that was attacking with us. Some of them
were dying. We got them up on the rear deck of the tank and I rode out
there with them." "Why?" I asked. Why would a man whose job was
inside the tank feeding ammo to the guns, decide to ride outside under
small-arms fire? Kiss gave a logical answer, trying to explain the situation to someone who knew nothing about tanks. "I had to be out there
because otherwise some of those bodies might roll onto the mufflers,
mounted outside on the rear, and get burned. I was just taking care of
them. They were all wounded, and in the cold they were freezing and
getting stiff. At least one of them died up there."

And as the citation noted, did he fling himself on top of the bodies
to protect the wounded? "I was just taking care of them," Frank said
with what I thought was considerable modesty. As for the bodies
rolling up against the mufflers and burning, Lee Ballenger corroborates
that in another passage.

For intelligence purposes, Ballenger wrote, "Five Chinese bodies
were loaded on the back of a [different] tank and transported to the
MLR. . . . unfortunately, the Marines neglected to relieve the bodies of
ammunition. En route, one of the bodies lying near a muffler caught
fire and ignited the soldier's supply of hand grenades and ammunition.
This in turn ignited the other bodies and they all began to burn and explode. On returning to the MLR the tankers unceremoniously stopped
and dumped the grisly mess on the ground. So much for intelligence
efforts."

Meanwhile, Corporal Kiss was the target of enemy fire as he
crouched up there with the six Marines, living, wounded, and dead. "I
was hit first by small arms, the left ankle, a compound fracture of both
the tibia and the femur, then I was hit in the knee and the thigh. Next

a grenade exploded and fragments hit me. One went into my mouth. And we never would have gotten out except that we headed for the peace corridor [leading to and from the truce talks site at Panmunjom, a place I knew from my own fights in '52] and from there they took us to the rear in Weasels [troop-carrying vehicles]."

The Marines never got to their objective, the Boot, and so the mission was secured (shut down) just before midnight. Official count: 96 Chinese killed and 123 wounded, 5 Marines killed and 22 wounded. Just another day at the office in the outpost war.

Frank was evacuated to the hospital ship *Consolation,* standing off Inchon. He had been in Korea only ninety-two days. From the hospital ship he was shipped back to the States. "I wanted to stay in [the Corps] and go back to Korea, but they said my ankle was in too bad shape. I still wear braces on both legs today [fifty-four years after the raid]. So I went to work for my father, as a bartender. But I couldn't stand up for long periods. Then a friend tipped me off to a job as a wood finisher. I could do some of that sitting down. I got married and bought a house, the same house we live in today. I only had to put ten dollars down, if you can believe it. Today, it must be worth four [$400,000]. We have four kids. Good kids.

"Oh, yeah, one other thing. I'm a state officer for the DAV [Disabled American Veterans] and I do volunteer work at Northport VA Hospital." Any guys there yet from Iraq or Afghanistan? I asked. "No, they're still in military or naval hospitals because they're still in the service. But we'll get some of them, as soon as they become vets."

All those years have gone by since that fight against the Chinese in which he was wounded, and he's still suffering from his wounds. But the guy never bitched, not once. Instead, Kiss is working to ease the way of other, worse-off old soldiers. His citation got it right, I guess. "By his outstanding courage, daring initiative and indomitable fortitude in the face of extreme peril, Corporal Kiss served to inspire all who observed him and upheld the highest traditions of the United States Naval Service."

He actually sounded pretty cheerful swapping yarns, and we talked for a bit about how grand the late fall weather of '06 had been on Long Island, where Frank Kiss and I, a couple of aging gyrenes, both live.

34

Why Joint Chiefs Chairman Peter Pace joined the Marines.

WHEN GENERAL PETER PACE BECAME THE FIRST MARINE EVER TO be named chairman of the Joint Chiefs of Staff, I went down to Washington to follow him around D.C. for a morning and then drive over to Virginia for an interview at his Pentagon office. He would not actually take over as chairman until the end of the month, when Richard Myers of the air force stepped down, but Pace graciously allowed me to do the interview a few weeks early so that even with my long lead time, I could get the piece into print in *Parade* magazine the week of his formal installation.

Pace, known jocularly (though not to his face) as either "Peter Perfect," or "Perfect Pete," for his smooth, trim, drill-field manner and style, is a kid from Brooklyn whose father immigrated from Italy and whose own son is a Marine captain studying for his MBA at the University of Chicago. When we spoke, Pace was fifty-nine years old, a lean six-footer who takes thirty- to forty-mile bike rides to keep fit, and looked ten years younger than his age, and he got into the interview by first thanking me for my own service, and then said, "Call me Pete." I swiftly confessed that never having served on active duty as anything more than a first lieutenant, I had a good deal of trouble addressing four-star Marine generals by their first names, but after we got over that hurdle, the conversation went well.

This was 2005, Iraq was going badly, Afghanistan was conquered but uneasy, and Katrina had just blown through the Gulf Coast to devastating effect, with the entire nation, obviously including the military, anxious and considering ways to be of assistance. We discussed all those things for the interview and then I got to the general himself. How did Pace end up a Marine? And where did he do his fighting? I was aware he'd been a Naval Academy midshipman at an institution where most of the graduates enter the navy as ensigns and only a smaller number the Marine Corps as second lieutenants. Peter Pace must have made a choice at some point. When, and why?

"I was a squad leader for new plebes coming in. I enjoyed that. I thought I would have more opportunities like that for hands-on leadership [in the Marines]. And my older brother had become a Marine. So in my fourth year [when such career choices and preferences are made] I walked over to the Marine desk and signed on." That was 1967, and Vietnam was bad and apparently getting worse. Lieutenant Pace went through the Basic School at Quantico, Virginia, graduated in '68, and was promptly shipped out to Southeast Asia. In Vietnam he was a rifle platoon leader, was promoted to captain three years later, and his climb up the ladder of command had begun. Then we spoke about combat, about fighting as Marines.

When Pace was nominated chairman of the Joint Chiefs, President George W. Bush called his life an "American dream." He then said, "It tells you something about Pete Pace's devotion to his troops that under the glass on his desk at the Pentagon he keeps a photo of Lance Corporal Guido Farinaro, the first Marine he lost in combat in Vietnam."

True story? I asked. The general got up and walked to his desk. "I'm in temporary quarters here until confirmed, but I keep the photo in the top drawer of this desk until I get my own." Sure enough, he had the picture of a long-dead young Marine in the borrowed desk and showed it to me. During his Senate confirmation hearings he'd been grilled by several senators as to whether there were parallels between Vietnam and Iraq. I asked that same question again.

"I use my experiences from Vietnam today. They help focus me and help focus the people I'm talking to about how Iraq is going to play out on the ground. As a rifle platoon leader, as you and I both were in the Marines, we know that ground combat doesn't change that much. If we sat down with a rifle platoon leader from Fallujah, there would be shared experiences. But I remember the lessons of Vietnam."

Good officers in all armies always want more—more men, more guns, more ammo, more air. I asked this old rifle platoon leader, now the biggest of the big brass, do we have enough troops in Iraq? Said General Pace (and this was September of '05), "I believe we have sufficient numbers now. We do need more security—not more American forces, but more responsible Iraqi army and police forces. If we knew that two or three years from now we would still need these things, then that would impact my thinking about the level of sustainable active forces."

I asked how we would know the Iraq war was over and we could "bring the boys home."

Pace said, "There won't be a VE Day or a VJ Day," referring to the days on which the Germans and the Japanese gave up in World War II. "An end to the war in Iraq does not mean the end to the war on terror. It will be going on for a long time."

Why had no earlier Marine general ever become chairman of the Joint Chiefs? Did they mistrust Marines, think we were wild men and crazy? Pace grinned at that, perhaps recalling Smedley Butler. "Well, I'm sure there was some of that, and often with good reason. But I think there have now been enough Marines on the Joint Chiefs that they realize we're not all wild men but can work with others."

And can the chairman still be at heart a Marine? Can he still think as a Marine even in the rarefied atmosphere of the Joint Chiefs? Said Pace, "You never stop being a Marine. Though, when the chief says, 'Okay, this is how we do it,' we all get on board." And does he work for the president or the secretary? Or both? "The definition is that I am the principal military adviser to the president, to the secretary of defense and to the National Security Council. In a normal week, there are two or three NSC meetings that I go to with the secretary of defense. The secretary and I also have some private time with the president."

I returned to the basic question of motivation, why for example he had stayed a Marine when surely there were big bucks offers out there from the private sector to a man with his background?

Peter Pace had a ready answer. "Every Christmas I've sat down with a yellow pad and listed 'reasons to stay,' and 'reasons to go,' discussing the list with Lynne [his wife, whom he met while still an Annapolis midshipman]. But I always end up with the same bottom line on the 'stay' list. 'You still owe more than you can pay.'"

The big question about Pace that I heard asked by other Marines was, Would he stand up to Defense Secretary Don Rumsfeld or, as General Myers did, cave in and play yes-man? At this writing (shortly before Rumsfeld was sacked) the jury was still out, but in the fall of last year (2006) Bob Woodward's latest book, *State of Denial,* seemed critical of the Marine, quoting General Jim Jones, a former commandant now commanding NATO, as asking fellow Marine Pace if he really wanted to take on a job which Rumsfeld had stripped of any real power. "You should not be the parrot on the secretary's shoulder," Woodward quoted Jones as telling General Pace. But when I met and interviewed Peter Pace, he had already accepted the chairmanship while being all Marine, still very much his own man. And only weeks into the job he had actually stepped forward to contradict the defense secretary on the rules of engagement, the matter of what Marines would do if they witnessed Iraqis cops beating up civilians. Rumsfeld had just said the men were instructed to report the incident. Sorry, sir, said Peter Pace, but American Marines were instructed to try to halt the damned beating, not just report it.

I believe a thrill went through those of us who knew Pace at all when he corrected his boss. That's the Peter Pace we wanted to have as chairman of the Joint Chiefs; not Bob Woodward's or Don Rumsfeld's or anyone's parrot. We didn't want Maureen Dowd in *The New York Times* calling Pace a yes-man. We wanted a Marine. And everything most of us knew about Pace shouted, "Marine!" Which version of Pace as chairman would prove the more accurate?

I saw him again a few days before the November '06 midterm elections that would repudiate a failed policy of a disastrous war and doom Rumsfeld. It was the usual Marine Corps birthday black-tie gala in

Manhattan, where so many of the movers and shakers in broadcasting and publishing, on Broadway and Madison Avenue and Wall Street, turn out to have been Marines earlier in life. Tom Brokaw presided, Police Commissioner Ray Kelly would be honored as a "Marine for Life," Edward Cardinal Egan was in attendance, the Marine Drum and Bugle Corps played, and General Pace had come up from Washington to make the customary remarks.

He began by asking us to join him in thanking all those Americans in uniform, "regardless of your individual feelings about this war." Which I guess was about as far as a serving officer of his rank could go without being insubordinate. But when Pace got into the guts of his brief speech, he spoke not of policy or strategy but of combat, of being a young officer under fire, of the price men pay in war. He admitted that as an Annapolis plebe and four years later as a lieutenant at the Basic School, he still "didn't get it" when Marines celebrated their Corps' birthday with pomp and circumstance, the somewhat corny ritual cutting of the cake with a Mameluke sword, the oldest and youngest Marines in the room taking in turn their ceremonial slice. It was, Pace said, not until Vietnam, "when out of 258 of us, 155 were killed or wounded, that I got it! I never again wondered why we gather, why cut a cake and remember. The names are engraved in my heart, starting with Lance Corporal Guido Farinaro, the first Marine I lost in combat." He then rattled off other names, name after name, of "men all killed on the orders of Second Lieutenant Peter Pace. I can never repay them. I tried. I promised myself that when I came back, I would try."

I was seated that evening at a table that included Pace and Brokaw and publisher Gerry Byrne and others, some of them women, and it was hardly a matter to be chatted about over a glass and a meal. But I remember thinking that, no matter the differences in station or vocation or style of life, in our relative influence or ages, we all are close who have been young Marines. And that if you have ever been a rifle platoon leader of Marines in combat, you are that for life. Whatever else happens, whatever you become or wherever you go, whether you are a four-star general or a baggy-pants journalist, you have been shaped forever.

And when the vote was cast and Rumsfeld cashiered, less than a week later, I pondered General Pace's remarks about the debt he owed and could never repay to the men he'd sent in harm's way, some to their deaths. Did others in the government, from the president and his secretary of defense on down, also understand those responsibilities, ever pause to consider such matters? Or must you have once been a Marine platoon leader or its combat equivalent in the other services during a shooting war to appreciate that burden?

It's a question Peter Pace may be able to answer. I can't.

In the end, with the Bush administration under fire for mismanagement of the war, Pace turned out to be too closely associated with the failed Rumsfeld policies to survive. Robert Gates came in as secretary of defence, wanted his own man as chairman, and Pete was told he would not be nominated for the usual second two-year term. Cool as ever, general Pace told pals, other senior Marines such as retired general Les Palm, he disagreed with the Gates decision but accepted it. After all, his appointment had been "political," so too the decision to replace him in the fall of 2007.

35

*Gonzalo Garza worked in the fields, became
a Marine, and earned a Ph.D.*

TEXANS ARE RARELY ACCUSED OF UNDERSTATEMENT. SO I WAS NOT
surprised when I received in the mail Gonzalo Garza's autobiography
(published in 2005) to see the book's title, *A Texas Legend: Pasó por
aquí*. Gonzalo was born in Texas of Mexican parents, served as a
United States Marine in World War II and in Korea, where as platoon
sergeant of a rifle outfit he was awarded the Bronze Star in fighting
against the Chinese, returned to Texas, married, had five children, finished college, and ended up earning a Ph.D. His father at age six was
sent into the Mexican hills to tend sheep, a little shepherd boy right out
of the Bible story, while an uncle, Federico Villareal, was a brigadier
general in the Mexican army during one or more of their numerous
revolutions, and knew Pancho Villa. Whether old Federico was also an
amigo of Zapata, I am not reliably informed.

Garza's book, and his story, begins not with memories of Mexico
but with a shout of slightly ironic elation for his adopted country.

"America! Oh, America! The land of milk and honey, the land of
opportunity where money grew on trees, the magnet that enticed my
parents to leave their beloved Mexico. My parents' roots, embedded in

the infertile grounds of the small, obscure, Villa del Carmen, near Monterrey, Nuevo León, Mexico, were pulled up for America!"

The father of the family went first, armed with a legal work certificate to take employment in the States, where, it turned out, the "money [was] not growing on trees," as a farm laborer, with his wife and their growing family coming along later, all of them relying on the same dog-eared original working papers to give them legal cover, the tacit assumption being they were now all legal residents of the States. In 1927 Gonzalo was born and he soon joined the other, older brothers and sisters and both parents in the fields as a farm laborer. All went well until 1933, when the Garza family was living—so much for the land of milk and honey—in one end of an abandoned bowling alley (a family of moonshiners occupied the other half of the defunct alleys) and armed men came to the door, waving guns and badges, shouting, "Where are the wetbacks?" Mama Garza dived into an old trunk and produced the famous papers, which, of course, hardly sufficed. But once it was demonstrated the Garzas weren't in the illegal distillery trade and that seven of their kids were Texas-born (including young Gonzalo), the Immigration boys sat down without being invited, happily ate the family's lunch of tortillas and frijoles before they left, and the crisis passed. The Garzas, alas, fasted until supper.

"These days they're a little more understanding," Garza wryly assured me of the Immigration officials. When he and I spoke last Thanksgiving, I asked why he'd joined the Marines. World War II was on and Gonzalo first applied at age sixteen. The Marines told him to come back when he was seventeen, which he did. Despite parental objection, he was taken, a boy so young that during boot camp he came down with a case of the mumps and graduated two weeks later than his class. Feeling pretty proud of himself as a newly minted private first class, and in his own mind, ready for combat. As he wrote later, "They had prepared us to fight and to do a job very few people are required to do. We were in good shape physically, mentally and emotionally. The Marines brain-washed us to perform unusually difficult tasks that required much skill. We were trained to kill the enemy and to survive in extremely difficult situations. We had to be ready because we were at war and it was kill or be killed." This was what the drill instructors preached, and how seventeen-year-old Marine boots were supposed to feel.

But why the Marines? There was no familial link to the Corps. To Pancho Villa, perhaps. But not the Marines. An older brother had been drafted into the army. Why not follow his lead?

Here's what Dr. Garza said from his home in George, Texas, where he'd been playing horseshoes with some of the other old geezers: "My brother wanted to go Marine, too, but because he was drafted, they didn't give him a choice, and he ended up in the army. For me, I wanted the Marine Corps from the start. I was ready to go. So I enlisted. As one of my fire-team leaders in Korea, Corporal Fred Frankville said, when I asked him while we were out on a night outpost, 'What are you doing here?' Sometimes he'd say, 'If it wasn't for the pay, I'd quit.' Other times he'd say, 'Two reels of *Iwo Jima* with John Wayne and two Marine Reserve meetings and here I am.' "

During the so-called Big War Garza was sent to Hawaii for training, where he ate so much pineapple he never wanted to see a pineapple again. Next he shipped out for the attack on Saipan and Tinian, the two Japanese-held islands strategically important to us as potential air bases for the bombing campaign against the Japanese home islands. As a member of the 4th Marine Division he was in a few firefights on Tinian, but his worst scare came when he and another Marine were asleep under a shelter half. Garza was aroused by a mysterious sound and movement inside the tent and slashed out with his knife at what he thought was a Japanese infiltrator but turned out to be a local goat. Garza survived without injury, but the goat died. Once Tinian, the smaller of the two islands, was mopped up Gonzalo was transferred to the 2nd Mar Div ("I still don't understand why," he confesses now) and again served in a rifle company. He took part in flushing out wandering Japanese soldiers still holding out in the hills after the main forces were defeated. More firefights. When the Japanese surrendered and the war ended, he was sent to the home islands with the occupying forces and became handy with the language and found himself thinking about the Japanese people as people and not, as he had thought previously, as "the Little Yellow Bastards the propaganda films and cartoons showed us."

Back from Japan and in Texas, Gonzalo was working a part-time job and was within two semesters of his college bachelor's degree when the trumpet again sounded. The Korean War began in June 1950 and as a member of the Reserves, Garza was called up for active duty. Was he ticked off? "No, but my parents were. My father couldn't understand why, having fought in one war, I now had to go to another." On October 2, 1950, he was back in a Marine uniform, soon to be sailing in harm's way again. Arriving in Korea on his twenty-fourth birthday, January 10, 1951, Garza was sent up as a replacement for the badly shot-up Dog Company of the 2nd Battalion, 7th Marine Regiment, the company in which I would later serve, also as a replacement. Because of his rank and experience Garza was made platoon guide (the third ranking position in a Marine rifle platoon after the platoon leader and platoon sergeant). As February began the 1st Marine Division was on the move north, attacking the North Koreans and, increasingly, the Chinese Communist regulars. The weather was lousy, cold and rainy, the men's uniforms and the near-useless shoepacs soaked through by the rain and then, as temperatures fell, frozen by the cold. It was during this period, after fording a fast-flowing and rather deep stream, that the young Sergeant Gonzalo would suffer frostbite damage which, decades later, was still working its mischief on a middle-aged man's damaged tissue. As he notes, "To this day I still suffer what I call 'the agony of the feet.' "

No one I know, soldier or Marine, who fought through a Korean winter will ever forget the cold. Garza remembers. "We used to say that the only thing between Korea and the North Pole was a barbed-wire fence. That stream ran at the base of a hill which showed 880 meters on the map. I remember that because someone said that was the highest point in South Korea, which was as mountainous but not as high as North Korea. While climbing this mountain, darkness overtook us, the temperature dropped to below zero, and the wind blew in gale force. We sat all night on the top of that mountain while our wet shoes and uniforms froze on us."

Then came one of those defining moments of a combat soldier's career. And his life. Gonzalo describes it this way.

"We began our march northward when, on March 1, 1951, we

encountered automatic weapons and small-arms fire from the North
Korean Army. We defended a position on a very steep mountain when
they attacked us. I had a young Marine who constantly refused to
wear his helmet. I kept after him over and over again and he responded
positively, but the next moment his helmet was off. We were hit quite
hard as we moved forward when we approached the top of a hill [in a
counterattack]. Several of my men were wounded and I knew this
young man [the kid who hated helmets] had been hit. He was the point
man with the lead squad and was somewhere in front of our platoon
behind some rocks. I didn't know exactly where he lay, as several big
rocks stood ahead of us. I went down a path toward where I thought he
was and found him.

"The North Koreans had shot him in the head and he was deliri-
ous. And he had his helmet on. He also had three or four enemy rifles
with him on his back. Why he had them, I don't know. Souvenir hunting? Who knows? Blood covered his face. I picked him up but the rifles
were cumbersome so I tossed them away and carried him. I was five-
nine but only 129 pounds, but I got him up. A lot of fire was coming in
and he was giving me a hard time. He was shouting, 'I gotta take a
shit! You don't understand. I gotta take a shit!' I got him down behind
some rocks but he's yelling. And he gave me a time and they were
shooting at us. Finally I got him quiet. The men later told me they
could see the bullets hitting dirt right behind my feet. They told me
that if I'd stopped for an instant, I'd have been hit. He was still deliri-
ous and I had to get on top of him to keep him down for nearly two
hours until the enemy was neutralized."

But why had Gonzalo gone down that path into the rocks looking
for a self-destructive kid without a tin hat? What made Garza do that?
I asked. He reacted as if the question were absurd, that it answered itself. "Because he was one of my men," Gonzalo replied. "I was the
platoon guide and he was one of my men."

The platoon leader, Lieutenant Dick Humphreys, wrote up Gonzalo Garza for a Bronze Star with combat V, which he was awarded
later. The citation said, in part, "He fearlessly and with complete disregard for his own personal safety made his way forward through heavy
enemy fire to reach him, and then courageously stood guard over him

until friendly fire had sufficiently neutralized the enemy fire to permit him to carry his comrade to safety."

If that was Gonzalo's best day, worse were to come.

"April 5, 1951, we crossed the 38th Parallel (still going north toward China) and that was a very bad and a very sad day for Dog Company. We lost four men from my platoon, including [navy corpsman] De Wert. Our platoon leader was a very courageous and gung ho lieutenant by the name of Richard Humphreys. We used to call him 'John Wayne Humphreys.' He always gave you the feeling that he was in control and you need not worry about the enemy's force."

As the day began, Garza remembered, "We stopped for the night and dug foxholes. Dog Company was in reserve and Easy and Fox Companies were to attack on two ridges meeting together at the top, two ridges that reminded me of a chicken wishbone. As Easy Co. and Fox Co. went up the two ridges they got pinned down from enemy fire and could not advance. The Koreans gave those two companies heavy rifle and machine gun fire. Dog Co. was in reserve, hoping those two companies could capture the objective. When this didn't happen, Dog. Co. was called upon. We used to say Dog was always called to the rescue. 'Don't be Easy, let's be Foxy, let Dog do it.' Lt. Humphrey's third platoon went up one of those ridges. We were hit pretty hard. Jack Larson, one of my squad leaders, had the point and his squad was hit hard. Our platoon suffered four dead and plenty of wounded. The dead were Richard (Bull) Durham, Anthony J. Falatach, Richard De Wert, and Donald D. Sly. Wounded on that day were Keith Ester, Warren Gerweek, John (Hokie) Hokanson, Frank Perry and others who were evacuated, among them Mike Gubanbik, George Crawford, Jr., and John Pendleton."

Here was an old sergeant experiencing his second American war, and yet half a century later, recounting a small fight on a chickenshit wishbone of a hill you and I never heard of, he still had the names of the dead and wounded, as a good platoon guide should. He even catalogued details to flesh out the casualty rolls and turn mere names into actual eighteen- or nineteen-year-old American boys. "Anthony Falatach had just been notified a few days before that his wife had a baby girl. Donald Sly had just requested leave to attend his father's funeral.

After De Wert got killed another Marine got shot in the arm and I gave him medical aid. Jack Larson remembers that I let the man see where the round entered but not where it went out the other (and presumably messier) side. I don't remember the name of this Marine but Warren Gerweek remembered an ammo carrier being hit in the arm."

It is astonishing what old soldiers retain and in what exquisite detail. As for De Wert, he was a corpsman from Taunton, Massachusetts, who once, while sharing a foxhole with Garza on a cold night, gave the young Texan his own field jacket. "I'm from Massachusets, Sergeant. I'm used to it. You Texas boys aren't." On April 5, 1951, De Wert was shot three or four different times while tending to Dog Co. wounded, but kept going.

A fourth or fifth enemy bullet killed De Wert. He was awarded the Medal of Honor. The navy named a guided missile frigate after him, and the town of Taunton renamed a hospital and a street. While in Texas a seventy-four-year-old sergeant turned Ph.D. remembers the Massachusetts kid who gave him a coat against the cold.

After the war Gonzalo again returned to Texas, fell in love with and married Dolores Scott, finished college, taught, earned his doctorate in education (curriculum and instruction) from the University of Texas at Austin, was superintendent or associate superintendent for several different school districts, was passed over at age sixty-four for the superintendent's job in Austin itself, sued on grounds of age discrimination, ended up with an "interim" title, shook hands with everyone, and walked off into the sunset of retirement. Except that his golden years sound pretty appealing, such as leaving with his wife just after we spoke for a ten-day pre-Christmas Caribbean cruise. And, of course, playing "killer" horseshoes with the lads. One of whom, Fred Schmallerger, writes to inform me, "There is a very big high school in Austin named after this Marine."

Viva, Garza!

36

*"I was 'Dirty Harry' of the Marine Corps,"
said Bill Phillips.*

Not every Marine turns out to be a poster boy for the Corps. Which does not mean he isn't a pretty good Marine; only that they're not going to give him much ink.

Former first lieutenant William R. Phillips was calling from his hometown in rural north-central Pennsylvania, where he lives with his wife, Peggy, talking about the Marine Corps of the Vietnam era. Not a very happy time for America, for the Marines, or for Lieutenant Phillips himself. We spoke in December 2006, a few weeks before Christmas, and Bill Phillips was telling me they were expecting a mixture of rain and wet snow, and how to spell his last name, "two *l*'s, just like Route 66." We talked about his often turbulent nine years in the Corps, an honor graduate at boot camp, his marksmanship as a shooter aiming to compete in the Nationals, about being reprimanded for duking it out with a smart-ass enlisted man attacking his duty officer, and especially about his bitter, "angry" experience of Vietnam combat.

A mutual friend in Pennsylvania, writer J. David Truby, had put us in touch. "You ought to talk with this guy Phillips. A Vietnam guy. He got into some sort of trouble, so I don't know if he'll want to talk. But

he was a Marine officer who fought." And when I first told Bill Phillips
what questions I'd be asking, what information I wanted, he listened
but grew cautious, a little cagy. Sure, he said, he'd talk with me. And
candidly. But he'd like me to show him what I'd written before publication. No, I couldn't do that. I'd written other books and in this one
I'd already interviewed several dozen other Marines and hadn't cut any
deals with any of them to check my copy. That wasn't how I worked,
submitting copy for anyone's approval except that of my editor. Phillips
was entitled to ask, but I was also entitled to turn him down. I suggested he think about it and call me back if and when.

"Okay," Phillips said when he phoned a few days later. And we began to talk on the record.

"I was 'Dirty Harry' of the Marine Corps," he said bluntly. "I did
very well as an enlisted man but didn't do well as an officer. I was thirteen months in Vietnam and was angry every day I was there." But why
was Phillips a Marine at all?

"One of the guys I looked up to in my hometown went into the
Marine Corps. And when I was about ten my father took me to see
Sands of Iwo Jima. I think it was maybe the only movie he ever took
me to. He had been too young for World War I and when World War II
began he was forty-one years old with three children, so he was never
in the service. But he drove trucks carrying C rations from the Chef
Boyardee plant in Pennsylvania to the docks in Brooklyn to be shipped
overseas. In Vietnam every time I had C rations I thought about Chef
Boyardee. I guess I always wanted to be a Marine, and when I was seventeen, one week out of high school, I joined up, June 18, 1958, and
off I went to Parris Island. I did well, and halfway through they pulled
me aside and asked if I wanted to go to [the Naval Academy at] Annapolis. In the middle of boot camp they ask, 'Do you want to do four
more years of this shit?' So I said no. But I graduated with honors and
they assigned me to a naval science/education program. It was [Admi-
ral Hyman] Rickover's baby. What I really wanted to do was to fly, but
my eyes weren't good enough for pilot."

Despite his eyesight, the Marines were sufficiently impressed by
young Phillips's potential to send him to Penn State University and the
USMC Platoon Leaders Class, and after being commissioned he entered

the Basic School at Quantico where all new officers are trained, and where he had a first run-in with authority. "My dad was dying and I asked for four or five days leave to go home and I was told, no way. So I said, 'If I don't get leave, then I'm going over the hill.' They really pissed me off, and I walked away out of the office and was charged with insubordination. Later, three of us were given radar navigation flight orders but told to go home for three or four weeks before reporting in. Which made no sense to me. I couldn't get four days off at home to see my father dying but I got four weeks at home to kill time."

He ended up at Cherry Point in a fighter squadron without any flight training. "This is like brain surgery self-taught," he concluded. More screwups. A flight surgeon said, "You'll thank me some day for this, but I'm washing you out. You have a sinus condition so bad and you ever lose cabin pressure, your head is going to explode."

But the kid could shoot. No eyesight problems there. And isn't the Marine Corps about shooting people? "They sent me to the rifle matches and I shot pistol and rifle. I went to small-arms training and then was assigned to motor transport school [his father's trucker genes?] and in January 1965 it was off to Okinawa and the 3rd Mar Div. Things soon began to get hot in Vietnam. In March the 1st Marines went in to secure the airfield at Da Nang. I was in nuclear/chemical warfare school then, but I followed them two weeks later. And I was angry every day I was in Vietnam."

Why?

Bill Phillips didn't hesitate. "In 1965 we were prohibited from issuing live ammo until we were under fire. Vietnam was a mess. So we issued ammo anyway. The ARVN [Army of Vietnam] was responsible for perimeter security. And in July '65 there was a penetration, a breakthrough at the airport, so we were sent in as the first airport provisional defense battalion since Wake Island. [Author] Phil Caputo was there then, executive officer of Bravo 1/3. I was running convoys up from the beach and we were repeating the same shit as the French. We had M-14s and rigged ring-mounted .50-caliber machine guns on the first truck in the convoy. The trucks were all eleven or twelve years old and they needed servicing, spare parts. We had two drivers per truck, the A driver and the B driver. There was no place to circle the wagons,

just one-lane roads through the boondocks. We went into Da Nang gas
stations to steal parts for our trucks. It was weird, weird. But the VC
weren't very smart. They attacked us where we were strongest and
chose the one night we were double-forced."

But with conditions that bad and disorganized, how did a young
officer keep his command functioning, keep the men motivated?

"We had a full battalion-sized outfit, elements of the 3rd and 9th
Motor Transport Battalions combined, all run by second lieutenants.
There was no security. I was a very junior first lieutenant and the operations officer by then and I give all credit to the troopers, from the low-
est private to the second lieutenants. And we had some excellent,
excellent sergeants. One gunny had been wounded in the Pearl Harbor
attack and again in Korea. He kept saying, 'And I don't want a third
one.' Gunnies run the damned Marine Corps anyway. At the Basic
School I said that so much they called me 'Gunny.' The truckers were
worked so hard one of them fell asleep at the wheel and backed into an
airplane. I was running around with coffee trying to keep them awake.
They say at that stage of the war, motor transport running convoys
had more casualties than any other outfit. I had a lieutenant colonel
who was a drunk. A real jerk. Let's not mention his name."

Any drug problems then, or did that come later? "We had more
problems with race than drugs." Which races? I asked. "Black and
white. We had had a mini race riot on Okinawa. I had been a sergeant
and was commissioned as a mustang, so they knew I wouldn't take any
shit. I called some people in and laid my .45 on the table and told them
to shape up. We held a shakedown [of the troops and their gear] and
you can't believe the number of civil weapons that turned up."

While all this was going on, Phillips said somewhat mysteriously,
"And I did a little work I can't talk about for the State Department. After my thirteen months in Vietnam were up I was debriefed for three
days because of that crap I'd done for State. Then I was ordered back to
Quantico for a season with the rifle team. I was hoping to go to the Nationals. A good thing at Quantico was that some of the best boys back
from Vietnam were assigned to schools troops at the base [schools
troops help train the young officers in field problems, acting as "the enemy"] because in '67 they expected [antiwar] violence and Molotov

cocktails. We rigged up chicken wire over the trucks against the Molo-
tovs and we and the schools troops of Quantico were organized out of
fear Congress might be attacked. The Marines at 8th and I [Marine
headquarters barracks in downtown Washington] would respond to and
protect the president and the vice president and the White House. We
[from Quantico] would take care of Congress.

"Finally, on June 8 of '67, I got out. I'd had enough. I resigned my
commission but I needed my own local congressman to get it accepted." Why was that? "A letter of reprimand I got during an airborne exercise in the Philippines, a fiasco, flying people in where half
the planes broke down. They didn't crash. They just didn't fly very
well. I busted up an air force enlisted man when he took a swing at a
young AF duty officer. He was a smart-ass who swung a haymaker at
the OD and I dislocated his shoulder, and off I went in handcuffs. And
got a letter of reprimand from the base commander."

Bill Phillips wrote a book, not about his adventures, or even about
the Marine Corps, but about a nasty little Vietnam battle which the Institute of Naval Proceedings thought sufficiently interesting to publish
in 1997 with a foreword by General William Westmoreland, the top
commander in Vietnam, and which St. Martin's Press (my own publisher, coincidentally) later put out in paperback, *Night of the Silver
Stars*. It's a nonfiction account of the Battle of Lang Vei, a fight too
small to have attracted much notice, involving only two dozen Green
Berets, one of them Phillips's first cousin, Dan, but the only battle of
that war in which regular North Vietnamese Army troops used armor
against Americans. Of the twenty-four U.S. Army troops defending
Lang Vei, one earned the Medal of Honor and nineteen others the Silver Star. It is that fight by the U.S. Army and not, interestingly, a battle
by Marines, that drew Bill Phillips's attention, his time, and several
years of his life.

And where did he work and what else did he do after his colorful,
if not entirely successful Marine Corps career? I asked.

"I went home, worked ten months in a bank, then taught school for
about two years, not certified, and when my wife got pregnant and the
$5,400 a year I was making wasn't enough, I went back into banking.
Worked at that and became a bank examiner and then for seventeen and

a half years I was treasurer of Bucknell University." He also served as secretary of the investment committee of the university's board of trustees. And for his shooting abilities Phillips holds a Life Master classification with the National Rifle Assocation.

Any residual hard feelings about the Corps?

"I think my morale was shot when I was turned down for pilot training. Everything stemmed from that." He paused, and then got off his apologia pro vita sua, and surely best line:

"I was 'Dirty Harry' of the Marine Corps," Bill Phillips admitted, not without a cocky pride, I thought. An intelligent, educated man, but something of a ballbuster in an organization as structured as the Corps. Though not evidently in civilian life, considering his prestigious job at a fine university. When I thanked him for putting up with my questions, he said he was sorry we'd begun on an uneasy footing, and signed off with a hearty, "God bless you for asking."

Maybe Bill Phillips was simply waiting all these years for someone to ask.

37

Before he was a Marine, Jack Vohs joined the army.
And the navy.

L<small>AST</small> S<small>EPTEMBER</small> (2006) I <small>ATTENDED A REUNION OF OLD</small> D<small>OG</small> Company Marines at San Diego, and for the first time in half a century spent some time with Jack Vohs over lunch and Pacifico beers on the veranda of the Catamaran Resort Hotel where I was staying on the beach at Mission Bay. As the waterskiers sped by and onshore the joggers and in-line skaters and bikers passed, Vohs brought me up to date. He's a small, neat man (did he really play varsity football for famed coach "Pappy" Waldorf at Cal?) with a crisp haircut and well-cut clothes and obviously had been quite successful in business for a long time.

Vohs lives up in the Bay Area east of San Francisco at Walnut Creek, and looked so trim and in shape, no old gyrene gut hanging over his belt, that I asked if he were a runner. "Used to be but not any more." Why not? "I have a pacemaker now, had one for years, but every four or five years you have to keep getting them replaced." Why? I inquired, not having one, and feeling rather left out. "The batteries run down," Vohs explained as if he were calmly discussing a change of engine oil. But he wasn't retired, at least not fully. "I still keep a half dozen accounts," at the company, Bancroft Bag, Inc., where he's worked for years, selling industrial, heavy-duty paper bags to the manufacturers of charcoal chips and similar bagged merchandise. Over the Pacificos, I told him about this book, and he said, politely feigning enormous enthusiasm, "That's interesting. You know, before I was a Marine. I was in the army. And the navy . . ."

Well, of course, that was a story I had to hear, so I asked Jack to set it down on paper. A few months later his letter arrived, dated November 27, 2006, and starting with an apology:

"This is probably more than you wanted but I didn't know how else to show how I was actually in the Army, Navy and Marines." I told Vohs to relax, it sounded as if it might be a small American saga worth telling.

Here's the story. "I was born in LaSalle, Illinois, February 9, 1927, then moved to Idaho Falls, Idaho, when I was nine months old. On December 7, 1940, when I was thirteen and in seventh grade, my mother, grandmother, brother, and I moved to Berkeley, California. My parents were separated and my dad was a physical ed instructor with Matson Lines and was at sea most of the time. When I was a junior at Berkeley High in 1944 [he played varsity football as offensive halfback and defensive back], I decided I wanted to become a Marine pilot. The war was on and we knew that we had to enlist in the preferred branch of the service or be drafted and have no choice. I applied for the V-program which was Naval (including Marine) Air. I was advised I would be able to take the test for entry into the program. I received my draft notice in February of 1945 [on his eighteenth birthday]. I met with the draft board and showed them my letter of acceptance into the V-5 program and was told I could disregard the draft notice. Some time later I was advised by the navy there had been an error regarding my age, so I was no longer eligible for the program.

"The draft board had been notified of this by the navy and I was ordered into the service immediately. I reported to the board and was given a physical exam during which I was asked, 'Which do you prefer, Army, Navy or Marines? I replied, 'Marines,' but the exam showed a heart murmur so I was scheduled for a re-examination [an EKG] a month later. I took the exam and was classified 1-A, was asked the choice of service question again and of course said, 'Marines.' I was to be the contingent leader of a busload of some fifty inductees going to Camp Beale, California, a kind of processing station. We arrived at the camp, were issued Army uniforms, boots, wooden rifles, etc and spent three or four days drilling while waiting for assignment to basic training destinations. By about the sixth day the choice of service question came up again and since I was issued an Army uniform [pro tem, Vohs assumed] and couldn't imagine why the question was even being asked again, answered in jest, 'Navy.' Eight of the 200 of us were told we had been assigned to the Navy, were to return home, report back to the draft board where arrangements would be made for transportation to San Diego for boot camp."

So the kid now had been briefly in the army and was heading for a career in the navy when all he really wanted was to be a Marine. Jack's report continued.

"The war ended while I was in boot camp. I graduated and was assigned to the Occupation fleet in Japan, took the train to Treasure Island, boarded the light cruiser *Biloxi,* and made Tokyo in sixteen days, five of those days in the 'great typhoon' of 1945. Most of the 500 in our draft were terribly seasick, the ship rolling and tossing so badly it was impossible to set up the mess hall or cook so we were issued C rations. It was also impossible to sleep in bunks so most of us spent our off-duty time in the radar nest, to be away from the vomit and the stench." In Japan, Jack was assigned to a heavy cruiser, USS *Baltimore,* commanded by Admiral Forrestal and flagship of the Naval Occupation forces. "Very interesting duty being in Japan so soon after [VJ Day]. We in the Navy were more of a military presence than anything else. The Army and Marines onshore did sort of police duty, some of which was protecting the Japanese from angry Americans still sore about the war. I was there about six months and we were able to take walking tours of both Hiroshima and Nagasaki."

When Vohs got home, he enrolled at the University of California at Berkeley, near his home, and went out for football (as a defensive back), "along with another 500 guys," and had three concussions in the first four weeks of practice, one sufficiently severe that he spent five days in the hospital and was told he'd never play football again. But he did. And played "in 1949 and 1950, two of our three Rose Bowl years. I was on the squad but never actually played in the Rose Bowl."

In Vohs's junior year a former Cal football coach, Frank Wickhorst, who'd been fired after a losing season (two wins, seven losses) and a student petition against him, had become personnel director for Henry J. Kaiser Industries. He asked Jack if he wanted a labor relations job after graduation. Vohs, grateful but somewhat embarrassed, thanked the old coach, then confessed, "I signed the petition that got you fired, sir." Coach Wickhorst soothed the boy, assuring Vohs, "You were only one of 16,000." Jack began taking labor relations courses, was formally offered a Kaiser job, but had to turn it down when Korea came along.

Also at Cal, one of Jack's teammates, a Marine captain now in the reserves, had persuaded Vohs to join the Treasure Island USMC Reserve unit to play baseball and hoops with the unit team. Since Jack was still in the Navy Reserve, the Marine Reserves listed him as a corpsman to make it sound legal, and make Jack eligible to play ball. The team won enough games to qualify for the tournament, but when a Marine Colonel learned of the dubious paper shuffling that made navy reservist Vohs a Marine reservist, and fearing the unit's team would have to forfeit games, he cracked down. Vohs says, "I had to resign from the Navy, enlist in the Marine Reserve, and that made it legal." But with four games left in the season, the Korean War began, the tournament was canceled, and all of the reservists, including brand-new Marine corporal Jack Vohs, were called to active duty.

"Since I had only about four months until I got my degree, I was deferred until I graduated. Football was also messed up when I got orders to report to duty, after having started on defense in the spring 1950 final [intrasquad] game. I didn't enroll for the fall semester, and when I got that deferment, two days before our first game, I scrambled to get the classes I needed for graduation and asked permission of our new coach 'Pappy' Waldorf to get back on the team, but it was all too late to get enough playing time to make the squad. In the mail, however, came a letter asking if I desired a commission in the Marine Corps since I was going in as corporal. I was interested and filled in the forms and called Coach Wickhorst about why I couldn't take the

Kaiser job. He was a captain in the Navy Reserve and understood, and said he would be more than happy to write a letter for me. I'm sure it got me into the program."

So now, thanks to the old coach whom he once helped get sacked, Vohs was officially on the way to becoming a Marine officer after having served in both the army and the navy.

"I was ordered to report to that first OCC [officer candidate class] at Parris Island on 18 April 1951, and took a job with Pacific Electric and Gas Company digging ditches to get in shape for Parris Island. My brother made sure to bring several young sorority girls by to show them what a wonderful job my degree had earned for me. But boarding a train at Berkeley headed for South Carolina I remember how happy I was that I was finally going to be a Marine.

"I graduated from OCC and received my commission 29 June 1951, was assigned to [Quantico], graduated in the top five of our class, and requested FECOM, FECOM, FECOM as my first three choices, FECOM as you know meaning Far East Command. I arrived in Korea in early February '52 and I really wanted a rifle platoon but was given the machine-gun platoon [somewhat infra dig, he and I might both remark] in Dog Co. of the 7th Marines, and bunkered with Mack Allen when he had the second platoon. My dreams were fulfilled when Mack was made adjutant and I got his platoon."

I was by then battalion intelligence officer after having commanded the third platoon of Dog Company and been company exec, and when I first got to know Vohs. Who, despite having been in two wars and served in the army, navy, and now the Marines, was about to fight for the first time.

"You know most of the rest of the story," he wrote. "Combat showed me a lot about myself, gave me a tremendous amount of confidence, and made me more of a man. I think I became pretty good at what I did. During stressful times, I was able to become detached, see the situation, and make good decisions. It was somewhat like today's pro football that, as you gain experience, everything slows down. You see what's happening and can react in the correct way. I always tried to show the men that I was calm, confident, and knew what I was doing. Our training really prepared us for these situations. I always thought it was easier for the platoon leader, or for any leader, to show calmness under fire because the leader is responsible for the people reporting to him, and is concerned about their welfare and making the right decisions (very little time to worry about oneself!). I always felt sorry for the last man in the fire team because he had less to keep him distracted."

We all had our own theories about combat and how and why we functioned reasonably well under fire, and mine may differ from Jack's idea about "detachment." But he ended up with an official letter of commendation and a Bronze Star, both with combat Vs. So he must have been doing something right before coming home in November 1952, in, as he says, "good physical health and good mental health. I have great respect for my Marine training and I still have a great love for the Corps and for those I served with."

That commendation and the Bronze Star, how did he earn those? "We were fighting in the outposts near Panmunjom and the truce zone when one of my squads went out looking for prisoners, and one of my kids, my favorite squad leader, stepped on a mine. So I went out with a squad and corpsman to get him. I just took my chances and told the others to follow in my footsteps, and ran like hell through the mine field tripping only one wire. The wounded squad leader's leg was shattered just above his boot and I had to cut it off."

"Wait a minute, Vohs. Why would you do that? What was your corpsman doing?" I demanded.

"He got sick, couldn't do it. All that blood, I guess. So I said I'd do it if he told me what to do. He gave me the surgical scissors and it was just tendons and stuff to cut, the bone was shattered. Then when I was trying to give him the morphine, I was screwing up and the thing wouldn't work. So I got the corpsman to give me another needle, and my squad leader said to me, 'For God's sake, Dr. Kildare, can't you even give me a shot?' And I did. On the way back I used the surgical scissors to cut the trip wires, sweating it out, trying to remember what they taught us at Quantico about trip wires, and we got him back, he lived, and did very well. Became a big deal in Texas."

So that was his letter of commendation. What could Jack tell me about the Bronze Star?

"The Army was calling the shots and word came down to send out a daytime patrol with cigarettes and surrender leaflets to leave for the Chinese. I complained, but they told me, 'Listen. It's an order. Came down from division.' So I said okay and sent out one of my squads and they were ambushed, taking machine-gun and mortar fire. There were people in the neutral zone [between the Panmunjom truce talks site and the front line] dressed like farmers but they were lined up on a ridge-line firing at us. We already [had] one dead and several wounded and I went out with a squad to extricate them. We drove the Koreans [he thinks the "farmers" were North Koreans and not Chinese] off the ridge. We had no radio and one kid's shoulder was shattered and the corpsman said he was going to die if we couldn't get him to a chopper. I tried to get the FO [the artillery forward observer] to call in some covering fire, even into the truce zone as if 'by mistake,' to help us out. I got the kid on my shoulder and into the truce zone behind a little hill. But there was a seven-foot wire fence and I couldn't get over it with him. So I took his gear and hustled back to the outpost for help, but by the time we got back to him, he was dead."

Could Jack read me the citation?

"It used to be in a closet but Charlotte said, 'You're going to lose that.' So I put it somewhere safe where it wouldn't get lost, and now I can't find it. Can't remember where it is."

After the war Jack and Charlotte got married, in 1953, and had five kids. He sold furniture for a year for a manufacturer in Kentucky and then went to work for the second biggest paper manufacturer, Crown Zellerbach. "That was a great company and they put me into a nine-month training course. It was later on that I got into the bag business with Bancroft." The day before we spoke, he'd gone to the big football game, Cal versus Stanford at Berkeley, and Cal won, so Jack was in a good mood. I asked him a few more questions. This is how he wound up: "I find now that I am very close to eighty, my experiences in the Marine Corps are still, except for family, of course, the most important part of my life."

What more needs to be said by a guy who sells paper bags for a living, and who served this country in two wars and three services, sports a pacemaker, and played on the Cal varsity under the immortal Pappy Waldorf?

38

A machine gunner they all called "Hollywood"

DURING THAT SAME DOG COMPANY ALUMNI GATHERING IN SAN Diego, some of the men weren't looking all that frisky anymore. I was shaking hands with a few who might be answering their last roll call. More than a few walkers were being shuffled around the hotel's banquet room and a wheelchair or two rolled through where we were gathered for dinner.

A fellow I didn't recognize called me over. "I remember you the day you came up Hill 749 to join Dog Company," he said. "Yeah, so do I," and that was no kidding. You never forget the day you went to war. "You got off a chopper," the fellow said complacently.

I wasn't having any of that. "The hell I did. Mack Allen and I were replacements and we climbed the damn hill shepherded by a couple of men returning to duty from the hospital after the fighting. I remember how they told us right out to stay in their footsteps in the snow climbing up because there were mines. I'll never forget that climb." This old boy nodded. "Could've sworn you got off a chopper. But anyway, I was standing there with so-and-so and he said to me, looking at you, 'How we gonna keep this kid alive?'"

We both grinned uneasily. Even all these years later it was discom-
forting to realize just how helpless and even childish I must have
seemed to these hardened veterans I had just arrived to command. So I
said something vague, like, I was wondering about that myself at the
time, and then another old Dog Company Marine came up, a big guy,
and in shape, with a close-cropped head and a competent air. He didn't
look vintage 1950, not a bit of it. All his clothes, casual as they were,
seemed to fit and to coordinate. An off-shade pastel, a muted tan, more
off-orange than khaki, tailored trousers, pleated and sleek, with a
matching blouse, everything well cut. Back home, I suspected, people
worked for this guy. They did what he suggested they ought to do. I
said this to myself, though I didn't recognize him. "Yes?" I said aloud.

"You put me in your damned book," he said, pointing a big, useful
thumb toward his chest. "I'm Hollywood. Remember?"

I did then, of course. But Hollywood was sufficiently menacing
that whatever he asked, I probably would have said yes. His square
name was Bob Knight and he was from somewhere in Michigan, belonged to the local Marine Corps League, and you didn't want to fuck
with this guy. I was seventy-seven years old and he couldn't have been
much less, but being an enlisted man he was probably a few years
younger and in shape. No taller than I, but barrel-chested and solid,
unkillable. Oh, was this bastard in shape! He was a Dog Company machine gunner and a good one. He explained his nickname had been
tacked on by other Marines, considering him something of a "lens
louse." Because they all claimed the minute a camera came out, there
was Hollywood, posing for the camera.

"I'm Fitzgerald's buddy," he reminded me. "From Flint." Sergeant
Fitzgerald had been my best squad leader. Hollywood and Fitz had
fought together on Hill 749, taking it from the North Koreans, damn
them, in a fight that chewed up two regiments of Marines, the 1st and
our 7th, and in four days killed 90 Marines and left 800 wounded, just
in one lousy firefight for one goddamned hill they didn't even bother to
give a nickname, just its height in meters. It was part of the same ridgeline as Bloody Ridge and Heartbreak Ridge, but it just rated a number.
That fight happened before I got there. And when I joined Dog Company you know who took us, me and Mack Allen, up the hill to report

in to the captain, to Captain Chafee? Dog Company enlisted men, guys who'd been shot up attacking 749 and now they were coming back from the naval hospitals in Japan and here were college kids like me they were escorting, replacements checking in as their new officers. You think they were pissed? You're probably right. And around the time that I showed up, Hollywood Bob Knight was being rotated home after eleven months of combat. We may have passed on the hill but we never met. Not until now, all those years later, at a reunion in Dago would I find that out. So I said:

"Hello there, Hollywood. Boy, you look pretty good, kid." And he did.

After the war he worked for GM as a floor inspector, re-upped in the Marine Reserve, and graduated from Michigan State where he earned a master's in education. Did he play football for Biggie Munn? He had the size. "I taught for twenty-nine years and coached football and wrestling. Today I coach football and basketball at Grand Blanc and that helps me stay fit. And I'm out there with the Marine Corps League, pulling honor guard duty for Marine funerals. I do a lot of that." So I asked Hollywood his address and wrote to him later, asking if he could write about his time in the Marines and in combat. On December first of '06, a Friday morning in East Hampton, the Weather Channel was reporting on a big snowstorm slamming into the Midwest, closing airports, shutting down schools, and generally screwing up travel, so I thought that might be a good time to phone a snowbound Knight, knowing he couldn't escape, and harass him a bit about why he hadn't produced a few hundred well-chosen words for me. Dammit, the book was waiting. Hollywood sounded slightly ashamed of himself.

"The snow's coming but hasn't gotten here yet," Hollywood said, "but I'm having a hell of a time writing this thing. I talked to Fitzgerald the other day after you called and we half promised to have lunch. I've done three pages and gotten from Pusan to Operation Killer and that's about all." So I told him to send the three pages and we'd take it from there. He was agreeable but did argue with me on one thing. I'd told Hollywood how pleasantly surprised I'd been that combat veterans spoke so freely to me about their feelings since we were forever being told men were reluctant to discuss their wars.

He thought for a moment and then Hollywood Bob Knight said, "They won't talk about combat to most people. Only to a guy who understood, who was there himself." Then, the week before Christmas, Hollywood's story arrived. Four single-spaced typed pages instead of three.

"I was eleven when the Japanese attacked Pearl Harbor and my stepmother's brother enlisted in the Marine Corps. Needless to say, because of him and newspaper headlines about Marines in the South Pacific, I asked my father to sign for me to join the Marines. Of course he refused, claiming I would first have to finish school. My argument was that I could get my education in the Marines. Still he refused [the boy was eleven, for God's sake!—JB]. After each birthday I would ask him to let me join and I would get the same answer. When the war ended in 1945 I relented until my seventeenth birthday and I enlisted in the USMCR [Reserve] for three years.

"About the time my enlistment was over, the North Koreans attacked. My reserve unit was activated but I was discharged. I didn't want to be left behind so I enlisted in the regulars on July 25 and went to Recruit Depot San Diego for boot training and on completion was sent to Infantry Training Regiment at Camp Pendleton for basic infantry training. While there we heard the war was going so well, the police action would soon be over and U.S. forces would be sent home before Thanksgiving. I was thwarted again and disappointed. Then the Chinese crossed the Yalu River and attacked and I was elated. I was going to make it."

A normal person would rejoice that the war was ending. But we're talking Marines here. All that good war news had sent poor Bob Knight into depression. Thank God for the Chinese intervention! They hadn't yet run out of wars.

"After ITR we flew to Korea by commercial air essentially to fill the ranks of the 1st Mar. Div. that had fought their way out of the trap at the [Chosin] Reservoir. The draft reached Japan December 8, 1950, and we pulled liberty and waited. We were finally shipped to Korea on a ferryboat to the port of Pusan where we boarded open six-by-six's in the cold of winter and motored to the 'bean patch' in Masan where the division was bivouacked. It was Christmas Day. We off-loaded and fell in formation in front of a company CP where there was an NCO reading off our names and assigning us to different platoons. He called my name and assigned me to machine guns. I answered up with, 'I don't want to go into machine guns. I want to be a rifleman.' He let me know he didn't care what I wanted, 'You're going into guns.' I replied, 'I'm not giving up my rifle.' His answer, 'Well, that's okay with me.' So I became a gunner.

"I'd been assigned to Tom Cassis's section of guns and when you first become a gunner your job in a machine-gun squad is an ammo carrier. I was told to carry two cans of ammo that weighed ten pounds each, which I could swear weighed fifty when you were on the move, my M-1 rifle, ammo for my rifle, and my pack. I very soon traded in my beloved rifle for a carbine, the Table of Organization (TO) weapon for ammo carriers. It still didn't seem any lighter. We trained with guns there in the 'bean patch' until we knew how to set up our guns and go into action and give support to Marines in the assault. There in the bean patch I came down with a gastrointestinal disorder. Late one night I was in a nice warm cozy mountain sleeping bag in my long johns when my stomach began to ache and churn. I held off as long as I could and then I crawled out of the bag and slipped on my boondockers and headed for the four-hole latrine down the hill. I got to the edge of the rice paddy and jumped down and when I landed, it happened. I defecated into my long johns and into my boondockers. I took off my bottoms and wiped myself off, threw them away, and walked back bare-assed to the squad tent in the cold.

"We broke camp in January and moved to the Pohang-Andong area to clear the area of North Korean guerrillas. We set our tents up and proceeded to make it as comfortable as possible. We managed to confiscate peanut butter and jelly, eggs, ham, and loaves of bread. We converted our oil stove into a decent grill and even managed to frequent a local brothel."

But the sweet life of girls and grilled peanut butter was not to last.

"We soon got orders to saddle up and move out to chase some guerrillas. We climbed the hills which never seemed to go down but only up. No matter how much training and climbing the hills in Pendleton you did, it didn't compare with the actual experience of climbing the hills in

Korea with two cans of ammo. I lagged my squad and nearly ended at the tail end of the company in column. The front of the column made contact with the guerrillas. There was a small skirmish and my section of guns was involved. The word was passed back to bring up some ammo to the gun. I ran, trotted, and stumbled over open ground for what seemed like miles, so tired I didn't care if I got hit or not. I finally reached the gun, tossed the cans of ammo down to the assistant gunner [who feeds the belt to the gunner] and literally fell prostrate on my back, not worrying about cover or concealment. On this day I saw my first Marine KIA. He had been zipped up in his sleeping bag for a permanent sleep, waiting for someone, anyone, to carry him back down the mountain. I never did find out who he was."

The kid had wanted to be a Marine since he was eleven, and now he had at last caught up to his war, and wasn't sure he was enjoying it that much.

"The guerrillas were on the run and we were to pursue them. We continued into the night thinking we had them trapped on a hill. We dropped our packs at the bottom of the hill preparing the assault, and were told the packs would be brought up to us when we secured the objective. We never saw our packs again. Fortunately there was one bright Marine who knew too well how things got snafu-ed and kept his GI blanket, green wool, USMC. Several of us tried to stay warm under it that night. We were not there long when we were told to move out. We were chasing the guerrillas again. Told to be quiet, in case of an ambush. What a laugh. After hiking all day and through the night you had a company of tired Marines. The company would 'take ten' and before you knew it practically everyone was snoring, so much for quiet and stealth. I stumbled, fell, and rammed my shinbone on a rock and tried not to cry out in pain. We made it through the night and on the way back we came upon the 11th Marines [the artillery regiment] and my old friend Carlson.

"He was an unhappy Marine because he was a cannon cocker and wanted desperately to be a grunt. We visited and joked a lot and decided to write a letter to the *San Francisco Call Bulletin*. We complained we never got any letters from home. We would answer mail call and come away empty-handed. Within a few weeks I was getting bags of mail, passing out letters to my buddies and keeping letters of prime interest to me [with pictures of the best-looking girls?]. In Operation Ripper Carlson was clobbered by a mortar round while operating as a forward observer. So he finally got to be a grunt. I saw him when four Marines were carrying him downhill in a poncho, his chest full of shrapnel. He was shipped home but later died of a cerebral hemorrhage before I was rotated home."

Hollywood wouldn't have much leisure to mourn Carlson's wounds. Or poor Carlson himself.

"In February we jumped off and I was soon in my first serious firefight. Fox and Easy Companies were in the initial assault and we [Dog Company] were in reserve. They sustained casualties and needed reinforcements. Dog was committed to pass through them and take the objective. We attacked up the hill. It was steep and the slope had very loose dirt. You took one step forward and slid back two. In training you are conditioned to keep a decent interval between the man in front of you so you don't bunch up and take multiple casualties from mortars or arty. I was following my training and every time the man in front stopped, so did I. It was in one of those delays when an automatic weapon from the left flank started shooting. A Marine in front of me caught it and a Marine was shot in the leg behind me. Geysers of dirt were spewing all around me. That was when I decided it was time for me to get to the top of the hill and not worry about the space between men. I can honestly say I was not scared, but you might say I was concerned about my safety. I reached the top and was lying prone under a pine when I heard rounds whizzing through and cutting branches above my head and limbs falling on me. It was time to vacate the area for better cover. I looked around and saw a crag and decided to seek cover there. I wasn't there very long when word came down to move out. We were going to set up a hasty defense for the night as dusk was rapidly falling.

"While moving into our positions for the night I saw a Marine who had been killed lying faceup with his arms outstretched resembling a cross. His right leg was bent at a ninety-degree angle at the knee and under his straight left leg. His rifle lay a few feet away from the outstretched right hand. As I remember, he looked very peaceful. As we moved through the area I will never forget the sight of another dead Marine. It reminded me of the documentaries about World War II when men who were killed were being pulled to safety, dragged by their leg or arm over the ground, their head bouncing like a rubber ball. That was a scene of the Marines I will never forget.

"We set up a hasty defense for the night as we were not able to secure our objective before nightfall. Another Marine we called Chicago because he was from Cicero, Illinois, and I were tasked to go back down the hill and get more ammo for our gun. By the time we arrived it was dark. The squad leader told us to find a place and dig in for the night. We were both too tired to dig a fighting hole, so we just scraped off an area level enough to spread our sleeping bags. That night we received, what seemed to me, several hours of incoming mortar. We lost two machine gunners with a direct hit on their position and the company sustained other casualties. At daybreak the word came down to saddle up and renew the assault. While getting ready to move out I spotted the tail fins of two dud mortar rounds within three feet of our sleeping bags. Chicago and I moved very gingerly after that.

"We assaulted our objective that morning with very little resistance and secured the hill. We captured a North Korean officer, or I should say he walked into our lines and gave himself up. Word came down to move along the ridgeline into a valley where a regiment of 'Doggies [U.S. Army troops]' had been ambushed and slaughtered. Moving through the area we saw the dead soldiers being loaded into six-bys like cordwood. Dead Koreans were lying all over the place and we actually saw where the tankers had driven their tanks and pinned them against big boulders. It looked like they gave them a hell of a fight before they were overpowered. We gave the place the name Massacre Valley.

"We were involved in many more firefights and I remember some of them more vividly than others. The Spring Offensive in April when I thought we were going to buy the farm. The Chinese had broken through the ROK (our side) lines and attempted to surround us. It was the first time as machine gunners that we ever gave up our guns to the company jeep so we could, very smartly, 'mogate' to the rear. ["Run like hell," I assume that meant.]

Hollywood Knight didn't write about the bloody fight for Hill 749 that took so many Marine casualties. On 749 he was a squad leader and lost a couple of machine gunners to enemy fire. Maybe Hollywood doesn't want to remember that. Or maybe he was just running out of steam. But he ended his report with this note.

"You asked what feelings I had going into combat. Quite honestly when you are ordered to jump off in the attack and the word comes down to 'saddle up, we're moving out,' butterflies start flying around in your stomach. You wonder is this the day you get yours. You always have the company clown and as you are going to the line of departure, someone is making jokes and taking your mind off the task at hand. Once you cross the line of departure, you forget about everything except getting the job done and securing the objective. Once that is done setting up a defensive posture gave me a sense of relief, even though there was a distinct possibility of a counterattack.

"Give me a call anytime. Semper Fi, Robert L. a.k.a. " 'Hollywood.' "

I phoned once more to ask a few personal, follow-up questions, including whether he remembered the date he left Korea. "Yes," he said, "November 27, 1951, same day you arrived in the replacement draft, Lieutenant. We never met that day but that was when we passed into and out of Dog Company." The precision of memory of these guys over half a century remains astonishing to me until I reflect that, for many of us, the war we fought had been the single most significant event of our lives.

Knight and his wife, Barbara, (they have a grown son going on fifty) met, literally and coincidentally, in Hollywood, California, were then stationed for a time in Hawaii where he made the 3rd Marine Division football team, and actually got himself court-martialed. "Some trouble I was in," he remarked airily, and without going into detail, and for which he apparently was forgiven. He took his discharge at Treasure Island in 1954 and went home to Flint, going back into the Marine Reserves.

Hollywood was the fighter I never was, but we shared the secret handshake, Dog Company Marines who once passed long ago on a North Korean hillside in the bleak November.

39

"Wild Hoss" Callan was saving his combat pay to help keep the ranch going.

I'VE WRITTEN BEFORE ABOUT JIM "WILD HOSS" CALLAN AND how guilty I felt and still feel about getting him into trouble, so they shipped him out to the division the spring of 1951. We met at Quantico in January of that year when we were assigned to the same platoon at the Basic School. He and his dad owned a working ranch in New Mexico that for drought and other reasons seemed ever to be trembling on the brink of bankruptcy and Wild Hoss spoke freely of how he was saving all his Marine pay and wasn't going to draw down any money in Korea, where he couldn't spend it anyway, so that his old dad would have a few bucks to tide him over until the weather changed or the market for beef went up or some other economic miracle occurred. Which made Wild Hoss just about the only one of us at Basic School who confessed he was going to war for the money.

He was a wonderful, laughing, broad-shouldered fellow from Texas A&M who had been in the Corps briefly toward the end of the big war, a fine-looking boy, lean but strong with blond hair and a flat mouth with a good smile, and crinkly, narrow eyes, slitted down almost as if he'd been out on the range too long staring into that low southwestern sun at dawn and sunset looking for dogies, and had developed a perpetual squint, watching for Commanche raiders or maybe rustlers out to steal the Callan family cattle. We got along pretty well for a cowboy and a city kid but it was as an English major that I made Callan read the book that quite possibly got him an early ticket to the war.

I was reading this B. Traven paperback, *The Treasure of the Sierra Madre,* which had become a John Huston movie with Bogie and old man Walter Huston, a swell flick and an even better novel, and when I'd finished it I grabbed Wild Hoss. "Here, read this. It's all about your part of the world, Mexico, the Wild West, gold and bandidos, and it's a great book." Wild Hoss would not have taken my opinion seriously on, say, the Civil War or ranching, but he respected the literary conceits of English majors and he shoved the paperback into his pocket and took it to classroom lectures so if they were dull, he could get through them without falling asleep by whipping out the old paperback and surreptitiously reading a chapter or two.

They caught him. He was called up onstage by the officer lecturing, who took the novel with its lurid multicolored cover art and held it up, inquiring sarcastically if it were the latest manual on small unit tactics. Callan was ordered to report himself to his platoon leader. To me, after class, Jim Callan apologized for losing my book. "Hell with it. I'll get another one." He got the usual black mark on his record and early orders to "duty beyond the seas," which in time of war always meant combat. The odd thing; I felt worse about Callan's punishment than he did. I was sore as hell about what happened to Callan because of me and my stupid paperback. He was thrilled. Wild Hoss really wanted Korea, the 1st Mar Div, and most of all he wanted to command a Marine rifle platoon in a fight. He was delighted when his orders were cut for Korea, as the boys delicately put it, "happy as a pig in shit." And off he went to the war. A dozen of us stayed behind at Quantico as platoon leaders and instructors but Callan and most of our pals flew west to advanced infantry training at Camp Pendleton and then to the division in Korea. In San Francisco his bunch checked into the St. Francis Hotel where, over drinks I'm sure, someone had the bright idea of chartering a private plane to fly to Reno and spend a last night in the States, dicing, gaming, and wenching at the tables.

Prudently saving his money for the ranch, Callan passed on the flight. As did Doug Bradlee, off to Palo Alto with a few others to spend the evening at Jim Brananman's family home. Dick Brennan had friends in town. But John Ledes and Dusty Rhodes and Carlton Rand and his wife, Edie, and a few others went gambling. They never got there. The chartered plane ran into a late-season snow over the mountains heading toward Reno and crashed into the Truckee River, killing Carly Rand, an heir to the Rand McNally fortune and a recent Harvard graduate, breaking his wife's back, badly injuring Ledes, and banging up Rhodes, who made his way to a riverfront tavern to call for help. Seeing this big, shambling fellow, soaked and bloody, lurching into his place, the proprietor, understandably alarmed, cursed out Dusty, shouting, "I told you drunken Marines to stay out of here!"

Callan and Brennan and Bradlee and the others didn't even have time to mourn Carly Rand or say goodbye to Ledes and Dusty. They flew out the next morning, replacements going to the war. Wild Hoss, the westerner, the rancher's son, the fellow saving up to pay off his daddy's debts, and Bradlee, the Bostonian of good family, of St. Mark's and Harvard, the rangy redhead who played varsity tackle and wanted to teach schoolboys, both got to the division and what they wanted, to command rifle platoons of the 1st Mar Div on the offensive, going up against the Chinese regulars on the Korean ridgelines.

Back in Quantico in June of '51, we got the word. Wild Hoss Callan was dead. Killed by a Chinese mortar shell leading his rifle platoon against a ridgeline. No other details. And it would be long after his death that I learned much more about Jim Callan.

Years later, I received a letter from his sister, Gloria Callan Toombs.

"Dear Mr. Brady, For forty-nine years I have looked at pictures and war stories and TV pictures to see if I would ever see or hear anything about my brother. In the *Parade* [magazine] today there is my brother's name mentioned: Wild Horse [her spelling] Callan of New Mexico. I was in shock and can only have this thought, someone besides those of us who adored him, remembered Korea.

"Wild Horse was really James Callan III from Menard, Texas, a descendent of Texas pioneers and of the Republic of Texas. He graduated after World War II ended from Texas A&M University and moved

with all my family to a new ranch in New Mexico. We were newcom-
ers there, having been in Texas since before the Civil War, indeed during the days when Texas was a nation.

"Our lives, after the shock and incredulity of his death, were forever changed. There were my parents, Mr. and Mrs. James Callan Jr.,
and my brother and sister left besides me. Months later, about the time
you arrived in Korea [I had written about all this in *Parade*], our
brother's body returned, flag-draped, and the tears have been flowing
ever since. His grave is in the Callan family plot in Menard, Texas.
Only the simple GI stone marks his grave: 'Lt. James Callan III, USMC
July 9, 1925–June 14, 1951, Korea.'

"This is all that's left. He was twenty-five years old. My mother is
next to him; then my father and grandmother, all with the same head-
stones. There is a marble Catholic cross in the center of the plot that
says 'Callan.' "

My magazine piece had cautioned against the country's casually
going off to wars in places like Bosnia and Kosovo [Afghanistan and
Iraq were yet to come in the sweet by and by] without due contempla-
tion and sober consideration of the cost in American lives, the cost to
families like the Callans. Mrs. Toombs wound up:

"We shouldn't fight not to win. Even now. We shouldn't put up with
defending our Constitution and our Bill of Rights with any thought but
to win. Thanks for remembering my brother and the other martyrs. I
wonder if any of them knew Jimmie. And how can I find out more . . ."

I told her I didn't know any more. I'd written all I knew. By the
time I got to Korea, Wild Hoss was dead five months, that wonderful
boy with the enduring grin and the squinty cowboy eyes. The son of
Texas pioneers who wanted to command a rifle platoon in battle and
would be saving up his combat pay to help his daddy pay off the ranch.

40

Harvard footballer Doug Bradlee hoped in war to "find God."

In the summer following our sophomore years at college, Douglas H. T. Bradlee and I met in the Platoon Leaders Class at Quantico, Virginia. Two more disparate young college boys, or aspiring Marine officers, could not have been imagined. I was what I was, Doug was a big, six-four, rawboned redhead with a broken nose who played tackle on the Harvard varsity and came from an old Boston family I assumed was prominent and probably wealthy. (Ben Bradlee of later *Washington Post* and Watergate fame was a first cousin.)

Because the Marine Corps assorted people alphabetically, Doug and I would draw bunks side by side that summer and the next, and then later when called to active duty and assigned to the Basic School. When we shook hands for the first time that opening PLC summer, I asked the usual question about where he went to school. Meaning college, of course. St. Mark's, he said, mentioning the famous and exclusive New England prep where he'd starred in football and ice hockey and been a decidedly big man on campus, and I, rather gauche, certainly naïve and not very polished, said, oh, but so did I, citing the little Catholic parochial school of St. Mark's I'd attended for eight years in Brooklyn. Harvard, as I recall, didn't come up until someone else, a third party, mentioned it. Bradlee was too decent to put me ill at ease by delineating the chasm between my St. Mark's and his. And Doug was too self-assured, and too real, to have to name-drop about Harvard or anything else.

We became close friends. The summer when war broke out I was loading and unloading trucks for a living at the St. John's Freight Terminal on the rough-and-tumble West Side of Manhattan close to the Hudson River, where whores screwed stevedores and other longshoremen on the floors of empty trucks. That job paid the bills while I tried to find a newspaper reporter's job, finally settling on a copywriting gig in the ad department of Macy's, while Doug did what he'd hoped to do after graduation, teaching and helping coach football at a boys' school in Colorado. And now in January of '51, while other Marines fought and died in Korea, Bradlee and I and several hundred others began a Basic School course that presumably would fit us to take command of Marines in battle.

I enjoyed it that Bradlee, typical of him, arrived at Quantico in an antique sedan so old the floor up front had rotted or rusted away, and he'd done a jury-rigged job of patchwork using wooden four by fours bolted together to provide a flooring under the driver and front-seat passenger. He'd spent his Harvard summers pulling lobster traps off Boston's North Shore, working hand in hand with career professional fishermen and admiring, he told me, their simple yet rewarding quality of life, its plain and rugged style. You had the feeling with Doug that if the prep school job hadn't worked out, he might have been quite content with his Harvard degree to become a commercial fisherman, and a good one.

He was a big guy and tough, but soft-spoken, and laughed easily, not at his own jokes, which he wasn't very good at telling, but at the japes and jests of others, the usual class clowns and cutups in any young male society. They found in Bradlee a receptive audience, who grinned on cue and broke up over the silliest of comedic routines. And he had stamina. Not all the footballers had that. They were strong, but their strength came in short spurts. On a lengthy field problem in the damp Virginia heat of early spring along the Potomac, football stars often keeled over after a few hours, their bulk and weight a weakness. Not Bradlee. Or me. I, too, held up, not due to strength but because I wasn't packing much weight and had very little mass. I think it was one reason Doug enjoyed having me around.

One of the strange things about Korea was how the best men, the educated elite from the top schools, gravitated to the Marine Corps. How different from Vietnam, when deferments were routinely solicited and sought by the upper classes, and just as routinely granted, and it was generally the blue-collar kids and the blacks who fought. Different, too, from Iraq and Afghanistan, when the sons of the rich and powerful stayed home and, without conscription, had no reason not to. Korea, well, Korea was just . . . different. I was a lower-middle-class kid who, when I looked around at our Quantico ranks, saw half the Harvard football team and scholar athletes and even intellectuals from Princeton (Allen Dulles's boy), the University of Michigan, Yale (Dick Bowers, the rangy tailback), from Stanford (Bob Phelps the footballer and, a year later, decathlon champion and football star Bob Mathias), from Texas and VMI and Brown and RPI and Illinois (Rose Bowler Joe Buscemi), and Dartmouth. There must have been some Notre Dame men (their first Heisman Trophy star Angelo Bertelli had been a Marine office in the Big War); I just never met any.

The Harvards I knew, Bradlee saw to that, wanting a kid from Sheepshead Bay to know his friends. Phil Isenberg, who would be the Harvard captain that following year, a tough linebacker who would become a famous surgeon, and whose daughter and her roommate would be murdered in Manhattan by some whacko years on. And Heinie Dunker, who also played on the Harvard line, a big, slow but affable guy who'd not been the brightest bulb shining in Harvard Yard. And others, footballers all.

Football was Bradlee's sport. At Quantico it would become his problem. The commanding general then was Randolph McCall Pate, who would eventually become twenty-first commandant of the Marine Corps. Pate was a big jock, and the base football team at Quantico was his pride and joy. Wars came, wars went, but Quantico football endured. And now they had a chance to get an authentic NFL quarterback, Eddie LeBaron of the Washington Redskins (you know, "Hail to

the Redskins / Hail to the Chiefs" and all that), a second lieutenant in
the Marine Corps Reserve headed to the Basic School, conveniently
just in time to prepare for the fall 1951 football season. Marines were
fighting in Korea, up to their ass in Chinese regulars, but football was
important. So they called in Doug Bradlee. They needed some big line-
men who knew what they were doing to play with Le Baron, and
Bradlee had played varsity ball at tackle for two or three years. They
called him in and a colonel turned on the charm. Bradlee said he was
looking forward to a command in Korea.

But surely Doug would want to do his part for the Corps, and the
Quantico eleven, and if he would just agree to stay around for the
football season and play a full schedule, why then he could have his
pick of assignments in Korea or anywhere else.

Bradlee played football in college, he said. But he joined the Marine Corps to serve as a rifle platoon leader. That's why he'd joined the
Marines. Not to play football.

The colonel said there were plenty of potential rifle platoon leaders;
there weren't that many big tackles. Didn't Bradlee owe Quantico
something?

Doug wasn't a stubborn man ordinarily, but on this he dug in.

Damned fool! Doug could have ridden out a cushy additional year
here in Virginia and by that time, the war might be over. General Pate,
after all, knew what was best, didn't he? When we graduated Doug
was one of the first of us to be shipped out to the division. General Pate
saw to that, yes, indeed, sir.

Considering all that happened, I was pleased, much later, when a
respected USMC historian wrote of the man as commandant that "Pate
gained a reputation for being languid, detached, and too fond of travel
and for absenting himself from Washington. . . . most of his World
War II service was on staff duty . . . as a logistician." There are few
things a Marine can be called worse than that. I was also cheered to
learn that "he was not a well man and died within a year and a half of
his retirement."

The entire Marine Corps wasn't as superficial as General Pate, or
as stupid, and I, on the other hand, instead of being sent to the fight,
stayed behind, for much-needed seasoning as a platoon leader in an

incoming class of newly minted second lieutenants, so that in effect an immature kid like me would have gone through the course the equivalent of twice, and then I, too, was dispatched to the division as a replacement platoon leader. And Doug? Well, there were letters. To his dad Malcolm Bradlee, to Harvard friends, to fondly recalled faculty and classmates at Saint Mark and fellow Marines at Quantico to be passed around to the others. Good letters. He wrote well. For a football player, I reminded him sarcastically, while conceding grudgingly that, well, maybe a little of Harvard had rubbed off after all.

Some letters were posted home from his trans-Pacific flight to the division and the war. Others from Korea after he went into action. Typical was this one: "I keep thinking of *Kon-Tiki* as we fly along . . . the ocean is very blue. Sometimes we fly over white cloud banks that extend for miles and miles to the horizon. I feel content and very appreciative of the sunshine and good company, the little things which mean so much." This from a young man going to war.

In an earlier family letter he wrote, "As I once said, try not to be overly upset by my present situation. I have felt during the last seven years or more that I might have been cut out for things away from the beach and country club—not away from business into school teaching but really away. I didn't figure on its being in this form, but this might be a good foundation.

"I look to the world of the spirit and the world of human relationships as the most important thing. No peace treaty, no international government, is any good at all without the spirit underneath it. I look to the principles of a Christian life, not stopping at a 'gentlemanly' Christian life but working toward a saintly one.

"I hope one day to find and work toward God." And I never even knew what religion this boy was, some sort of Protestant, I suppose.

In Korea, it was June, and he described the fighting, described his men, talked eloquently about Korea, war torn and in places desolate and devastated, but also seeing its spare beauty: "The country is very rugged, almost unbelievably so. We are dug in for the evening around the bottom of a ravine for a change. Stream about a hundred yards away, babbling over stones, cold and clear. Washed myself and clothes and feel wonderful. Yesterday my platoon was sent up to seize a ridge.

We really pushed hard and found the Chinks had stopped on a ridge 600 to 800 yards away. Small arms and machine gun fire came sporadically but we didn't pay much attention and they gave up in disgust. Marines are far and away best fighters in Korea but tired out. I've lost five men in the last three days through prostration and exhaustion.

"The spirit of the Corps never ceases to amaze me. Walking to our assembly area yesterday it rained all the way. Much singing, horseplay, laughter, even though pretty miserable actually. Spirits kept high and we were rewarded by a beautiful day when we arrived.

"Have impressions of Korean civilians, farmers, as they watch Marines move onto their farms and set up camp. They can only look and hope for the best. No language bridge, no talk exchanged, except extra rations usually find their way to them. Many houses burn because of thatched roofs. On ridges at night I can see two or three burning in valleys below. Usual procedure is to set up in a line around a bowl of terrain. Each platoon tied in with one on each side. Firing holes are on the front slope, sleeping holes on the reverse side."

Along with such tactical remarks, and with a natural eye which suggested Doug might one day become a considerable writer, Bradlee noted in wonderment that "there are mockingbirds here exactly the same as in Colorado."

Trifling, casual remarks like that made you think about war from another aspect entirely. In other letters Doug continued to pass on tips about the fighting to us rear echelon "warriors" stuck back in Virginia, not being wise-ass about it or putting on airs as a quotes seasoned veteran unquotes. He also took time, and considerable care, especially in earlier writing to family, to strike a more philosophical, even spiritual tone, such as this, scribbled in the plane en route from California to the war:

"Frisco was fun. I went to Palo Alto for the night with Jim Brananman. His father runs a combination filling station and garage. They have an old not very Californian-looking white clapboard house with a home-made barbecue fireplace in the back yard, plus garage so filled with junk it warmed my heart to the core.

"Had a very interesting talk with Champion as the evening wore on. He's the man who has three children, two Purple Hearts, and fought through the almost entire last war. He was a lieutenant on Iwo and Okinawa after coming up through the ranks. Very quiet, mild, slim guy who was a refrigerator repair man in Muskegon, Michigan. He considering moving and I told him about my liking for old-timers in New England, the rather reduced but satisfactory scale of living for lobstermen. He likes to work with his hands, too."

That was Bradlee, the rich Harvard boy who liked working with his hands, loved the spare life of lobstermen and junk-filled garages. Those were the men that year we were sending to the war, a refrigerator repairman who had already been wounded twice in an earlier war and had left his children home, the son who had also fought before, of a gas station man with a garage full of junk, and the Harvard star a year out of college who'd never seen battle, a big, glorious redheaded kid who wanted to teach boys, who hoped one day to find God.

In 2006 I asked Jim Brananman out in Port Ludlow, Washington, what the combat situation had been in the spring of '51 when he and Bradlee and Wild Hoss Callan arrived in Korea as replacement officers. "Just before we got there the Chinese had launched a massive attack on the 7th ROK Division on our left flank and then after five or six days, as usually happened for logistical reasons, they ran out of steam. When we arrived, the 1st Marine Division then started attacking north. Everything was in a state of flux. They [Doug and Callan] went to a rifle company and I was assigned to Recon. I knew Doug was in the field as a platoon leader but that's all I knew. We were supposed to be amphibious Recon but all our Recon gear, rubber boats and all that stuff, was in storage way down south, so there we were, doing reconnaissance in jeeps. We were just like George Patton."

Much classier than poor but honest foot soldiers, I remarked, although Brananman wasn't having any.

"Yeah, but you sat in a jeep with no armor and they were shooting at you. Fortunately, over open sights from a thousand yards. There was a lot going on in Korea right then, and all I know about Doug that June is that all the rifle companies were on the attack pushing north against the Chinese."

The Chinese killed Bradlee when he was twenty-three.

That same week in that same fighting, Wild Hoss Callan, the

rancher's son, went down. So maybe his daddy would lose the ranch after all. Long after the war the giant forest ranger Bob Bjornsen from his log cabin retirement home, with its towering flagpole and scarlet and gold Marine flag, set in the high mountains along the California-Nevada border, postulated his theory about their deaths. Bob was a thoughtful type who'd been promoted out of active forest ranging by the National Forest Service and loaned out to third world countries to help them reforest raped timber country and turned out to be not only an expert at the craft, but an instinctive diplomat on alien turf. Of course, the fact he was six-five and could still don spiked climbing boots and scale a redwood certainly helped make an impression on the locals. Bjornsen had been one of us in Quantico and went over in the same replacement draft with, among others, Bradlee and Callan.

"They were killed and I wasn't," he said. "We were in the same push against the Chinese. I've thought about it ever since. I'd been a mustang who came up through the ranks, and was maybe more savvy, a bit cuter at avoiding unpleasant consequences. Was that what kept me alive? Doug and Wild Hoss maybe were more innocent. And they died." But that was theory, Bjornsen's theory. Could a man's innocence kill him or was that simplistic? Was "innocence" just a polite synonym for "ignorant," not wishing to speak ill of the dead? And was life or death in battle that easy to puzzle out or might it be just a rattling good roll of the cosmic dice?

I was at Quantico in the Basic School when I got the news in a Western Union wire from his father, Malcolm Bradlee. "Word received Doug's death in action 3 June. No further details."

That was all. People later told me Mr. Bradlee was never really the same after that. That he never got over it. Nor did all those boys out in Colorado get the education Doug might have provided them. Nor would some bright, pretty girl in Cambridge or on the Cape or along Boston's North Shore in the lobster and fishing villages ever find a big, redheaded husband who played football for Harvard and coached boys at a little prep school in the Rockies and would almost surely have made a wonderful father, and been good with kids.

Whenever I hear politicians bravely speechifying about the glories of war, I remember Doug. I think of that.

41

*Stacking the rifles, one last time,
and sounding "Recall"*

IN THE SPRING OF 2000, THE FIFTIETH ANNIVERSARY OF THE START
of the Korean War, I got a call in Manhattan from the White House.
One of Mr. Clinton's speechwriters. He'd read two books of mine on
the fighting in Korea and asked if I could help him write a speech for
the president to deliver June 25 to the nation at the Korean War memorial in Washington. I was a Democrat who'd voted twice for the
man but said I'd have to think about it overnight, and I called back in
the morning. I said I was honored to be asked but that "my differences
with the president are so deep and so varied, I would feel a hypocrite
to write a speech for him on any subject." I wished the gentleman well
with his assignment and thanked him for his courtesy.

My book publisher raised hell with me (all that potential public-
ity!) but I've been forgiven. Then on a sunny Tuesday morning in 2001
the World Trade Center was attacked and suddenly we were once
again at war, starting with Afghanistan. And I was writing columns
about people I knew who were dead, civilians, including a boy simply
having breakfast in one of the Towers, columns about Americans being mobilized, Marines again saddling up. We chased Osama up into

the great mountains on the Pakistan border and then we lost interest. And started a silly war with Iraq. Where a new generation of Americans, Marines and others, began to die. The president was very patriotic about it, of course, though with a mind closed to books and spared any history of the region and its tribal hatreds. Cheney was enthusiastic and Rummy was arrogant, and all those bright fellows in Washington who had never heard the bullets' song, were running around with American flags in every lapel and Vietnam draft deferments in every pocket, issuing startling declarations that if you weren't all for the Iraq adventure you were at the very least marginally "treasonous."

As I write, we are still at war. Which calls up memory of a time when I was young and a Marine.

I never caught up to Doug and Wild Hoss. They were dead. But I eventually got to Korea and the division myself. I was twenty-three years old and learned to fight as one of Captain Chafee's three rifle platoon leaders up in the snow and cold of the Taebaek Mountains of North Korea the fall and winter of '51–'52, got promoted, ended up fighting the Chinese that spring and summer over in the sandstone hills north of Seoul. By now I knew what I was doing and was in that Memorial Day fight against the Chinese on the hill we called Yoke, a fight Jack Rowe told about.

Unknown to me at the time I'd been written up for a Silver Star on Yoke, but nothing ever happened with the recommendation. The usual Marine Corps distaste for paperwork and erratic record keeping, I suppose, until years later Colonel Stew McCarty, who as a first lieutenant had commanded on Yoke following Rowe, took it on himself to run a trace and revive my recommendation years later, successfully getting me a more modest, and probably more appropriate, Bronze Star.

I had gone to war frightened and unsure, a boy not so much fearing death as afraid I might fail the others, get other Marines killed by my own weaknesses and failings. Which is why the Star and its citation meant something to me as an old man, knowing what I'd done as a youth.

My earliest concerns in Korea weren't death or wounds but of failing my men, of letting down the side. It was that, more than anything, which motivated me on Yoke, kept me going earlier in the Simonis "rescue," and meant that I hadn't failed anyone, least of all myself, fearful and lacking in confidence as I had been. So for me it was the men, the Marines on either side of me, who got me through the bad times, who made me a Marine, a Marine who fought.

There was still plenty of bad fighting after that, mostly in the foothills on the far bank of the Imjin River, bloody brawls between Chinese regulars and our 1st Marine Division and the Brits and several U.S. Army divisions. The North Koreans by this time were pretty much wasted and the Chinese carried the battle. The armistice talks at Panmunjong ground endlessly on in the little old schoolhouse. One day, of course, there was the very real danger that peace might break out and the fighting stop. Even the Hundred Years War eventually came to a close. Foreseeing an eventual truce, Mao spake from on high, Joe Stalin behind him. He ordered his armies to keep up the pressure, go on the offensive, capture as much ground as they could, especially (being a guerrilla fighter Mao understood such things) the high ground, before a truce deal shut them down. The more Americans who died, the more eager we might be to settle on Mao's terms.

It was on these attacking orders from Chairman Mao that half-assed little hills like Yoke, which in peacetime a man could climb in fifteen minutes, took on a strategic worth. They were outposts in no-man's land, between the lines, and therefore of value, much more to the shrewd bargaining Chinese with their obsession with face than to us. But in a fight, when one side pushes forward, every instinct cries out for the other side to push back. So the Chinese took those little outpost hills by night, overrunning our positions. And by day we tried to take them back, repair the wire, dig in and wait for another night to fall, another Chinese attack. As spring of 1952 became summer, there was some of the worst fighting and heaviest casualties of the entire war. And that would go on into the next year, '53, when the damned thing would finally end in July. That last year of the war was the bloodiest of all, stupid, stubborn stuff, wasteful and useless. Which didn't mean the dead were any less dead.

So the war went on, but I didn't go to it anymore. There was shelling, of course, and the odd sniper, and as always the mines, damn them. But they didn't send me out on any more patrols. For which we are duly grateful, Lord. Then to the battalion in June, a new S-2 came aboard, a tall, distinguished gent with a dapper mustache, a regular and a captain, and he not only outranked me but actually knew something about intelligence. So he took over my scouts and my job. "Hang around," Colonel Gregory told me. "We'll find something for you to do." Old Gregory sure hated to let go of a good rifle platoon leader. Or maybe it was my winning charm. Why didn't they ever ship me to motor transport or PX management a life away in the rear? I didn't say that aloud, of course, embarrassed to do so.

Late that month word came down that I was being rotated home. I'd heard yarns, about how once a man knew he was heading stateside, he got careful. And you don't want to be around "careful" Marines; they're so occupied with "being careful" and staying safe they get other people killed. There was one fellow people remembered who, on being notified his time was up, refused to get out of his sleeping bag. When it was chow time or a run to the head, this guy just hopped, a six-footer, like Harvey the invisible rabbit, standing erect in the zippered down sleeping bag, hopping around the company area until he got where he was going and did what he did. Chowing down or taking a piss. An exasperated first sergeant wanted to run him up on charges. But the company commander said, "The hell with it." He was a good man once and would soon be out of there.

Mack Allen's name was on the list of those going home, but Mack, still the battalion adjutant, went to the colonel and asked if there was a chance he could get a company, become a company commander? I tried to argue Mack out of it. We'd done our tours, we were still whole, our turn had come. Neither of us had ever gone on a five-day R&R to Japan. The opportunities came along and we'd passed. We'd never become rear-echelon pogues. But he was stubborn, Mack was. I went back up to the MLR to argue with him, maybe to say goodbye. He was already back in harness and dug in.

"Ever since I was commissioned, maybe since VMI, I wanted to command a Marine rifle company in battle. Gregory says if an opening comes along, I'll get it. In the meantime, I'll have a rifle platoon again."

"You're crazy." I wouldn't have gone back to running a platoon and pulling all those patrols for anything. How many lives does a rifle platoon leader have? But Mack re-upped for another three months. That's the kind of Marine he was. A better man than I was, I'll admit that straight out.

July came along and, on the third I think it was, we were trucked south, away from the main line of resistance, away from the Chinese and the fighting, boarded onto freight cars, and dumped at a big base camp called Ascom City. Because of numbers I was named a company commander, so even if it was just a rotation company, I got there ahead of Mack. I had about a dozen officers under me and as many senior NCOs, top sergeants and gunnies, and about four hundred men, so there wasn't a hell of a lot for me to do, just leave it to the exec and the sergeants.

The camp commander seemed like a jerk, issuing mimeographed, nearly illegible sheets of paper with complicated, useless rules and bureaucratic regulations, all a lot of crap, so to avoid trouble with him I made one speech, standing on the roof of a six-by truck so the guys could see and hear me. I told them we were all going home and let's make it easy for all of us, and just do what the sergeants tell you. I added just this one thing, told them my name, and said I'd been there since November with a rifle outfit the whole time, so let's not have any shit. Since about half of these guys were riflemen from up on the line and could say the same thing, and the other half, the supply depot guys and motor transport people, the rear echelon pogues, didn't count, we had no misunderstandings and all got along fine and that jerk of a transit camp CO gave me no trouble.

July 6 we were trucked down to Inchon to board lighters to go out across the tidal mudflats to the troopship, the *General Meigs,* which I think had been an old President Liner, and when a small Japanese freighter carrying ammo caught fire at the wharf where a thousand of us waited, there was some excitement, bazooka shells shooting off into the air this way and that, other munitions blowing, with chunks of metal rattling against other boats and storage sheds along the quay, shrapnel falling on top of us, with some Jap sailors courageously fighting the fire and others, the smart ones I guess, diving into the Yellow Sea, but beyond that, no sweat. We all put our helmets back on and waited it out. It said something about how a man felt after being at war for a while. You shrugged off shrapnel in disdain, almost contempt. Let it fall, you didn't care.

It was near midnight and raining by the time we boarded the *Meigs*, the July rain warm and almost gentle, and I was berthed in a big stateroom with eight or ten other officers, most of whom I didn't know, and who cared, anyway? One first lieutenant, fat and sleek with the look of a job in supply, had smuggled aboard some liquor. One of the rifle company men, a hard customer, took two bottles away from him without asking too politely, and passed them around. The hell with supply. Nothing ever went down easier than a Johnny Walker Black out of a crummy aluminum canteen cup at midnight aboard a ship at sea. We all took a slug, unbuckling gun belts, shedding wet uniforms, kicking off mud-crusted old boots. Someone even started a bridge game.

There were three-decker bunks, and we sorted them out without argument or dispute—no one cared, because we were alive—and I had a top bunk, and as I lay there waiting for sleep to come, I felt the easy lovely movement of a big ship getting under way on the tide. I stared at the shiny, white-painted, riveted overhead a few feet above my face and realized how long it had been since I was inside an actual structure and not under canvas or sandbags and logs or sleeping out under the stars. And I guess I never felt happier leaving anyplace ever in my life.

I was twenty-three years old and had fought a war and now I was going home. Like so many other Marines in so many other wars, I'd campaigned in foreign climes, I'd responded to orders, had gone to duty beyond the seas, had faced the enemy, fought the best fight I could, and now was heading stateside. Going home. If only Mack and so many others weren't still there, some of them forever . . .

Behind us, as the ship got under way and moved seaward, unseen in the dark and the rain, Korea fell away, Korea and the war, damn it. The only war I would ever attend.